ORNAMENTAL TURNING.

ORNAMENTAL TURNING:

A WORK OF PRACTICAL INSTRUCTION IN
THE ABOVE ART.

BY

J. H. EVANS.

———

WITH NUMEROUS ENGRAVINGS AND AUTOTYPE PLATES.

———

ASTRAGAL PRESS
Mendham, New Jersey

Library of Congress Catalog Card Number: 92-84020
International Standard Book Number: 1-879335-35-2

Published by
THE ASTRAGAL PRESS
5 Cold Hill Road
Mendham, New Jersey 07945-0239

Manufactured in the United States of America

PREFACE.

—:o:—

IN submitting this volume on the art of ornamental turning to his subscribers and the general public, the author desires to first tender his sincere thanks to those gentlemen, who by their courteous encouragement prompted him to undertake the task.

The work is introduced with a view to assist amateurs who are interested in the development of the resources connected with this most interesting and scientific amusement, and it is hoped, that the large amount of detail displayed will facilitate the manipulation of the various instruments and apparatus described.

So many works have been published descriptive of plain hand-turning that it is the author's intention to proceed at once with the necessary details of all that appertains to that branch of the art from which this book derives its name. In order that the tyro may participate in the reproduction of the various specimens illustrated, the descriptions of each will be rendered as concise as the amount of minutiæ required will admit; and if the book proves to be of interest to the large number of influential patrons who desire to honour it with perusal, the author will feel amply repaid for the many hours of labour expended in its compilation.

INTRODUCTION.

———:o:———

THE art of decorative turning necessarily embodies many distinct classes of work, which may be applied to either the surface, cylinder, or the shaping of compound solid forms, polygonal figures, and a variety of other and distinct shapes; the different instruments being applied in combination with almost equal facility for all and any of the same.

The decoration of the surface, by various groupings of fine lines, and the intersection of circles together with other curves, has been liberally treated in different works for some years past, and practically leaves little to be said; it has therefore been considered advisable to pass over this particular section, and at once enter upon the descriptive analysis of the tools and apparatus used for the production of the numerous specimens illustrated.

Although the group above referred to as not necessary of repetition has received the advantage of description by so many experienced authors, it is only within the last two years that the art of decorating compound solid forms has been treated to any extent.

The details connected with the manufacture of the instruments are published at the express wish of many scientific amateurs, who delight more in making tools than applying them to their several uses.

It is obvious that to do full justice to many of the specimens is a difficult task, and as the autotype process was found some years ago fairly successful in connection with a publication entitled "The Turner's Manual," in which the author was interested, he has adopted the same, failing to find a better substitute. In nearly every case the specimens have been turned by himself, but he has much pleasure in expressing his due appreciation of the kindness of many gentlemen who offered to lend any of their work for the purpose of illustration, and to the Earl of Sefton, Captain R. P. Dawson, and the Rev. C. C. Ellison, his best thanks are due for the loan of the specimens illustrated by their kind permission.

As this book is devoted to the description and illustration of the modern ornamental turning lathe and apparatus, reference will not be made to such tools and appliances as were available only in the very early period of the lathe's history, and which although interesting from a literary point of view, are not likely to add to the experience of amateur turners of the present generation; in conclusion it is scarcely to be anticipated that so large an amount of detail will be absolutely free from slight errors of some kind, and should such be discovered the author will feel grateful for information, in order that it may be corrected in the reprint.

TABLE OF CONTENTS.

—:o:—

CHAPTER I.

The Ornamental Turning Lathe.

CHAPTER II.

Mode of Chucking and Adjustment of Work.

CHAPTER VII.

Materials appropriate for Ornamental Turning.

CHAPTER VIII.

Polishing of Ivory and Wood.

CHAPTER IX.

Overhead Motion.

CHAPTER XLIII.

Circular Miniature Frame.

CHAPTER XLIV.

Electrotyping.

FULL-PAGE AUTOTYPE PLATES.

——:o:——

[In order to facilitate the entry of any notes that the amateur may wish to make in connection with his progress in reproducing the various designs contained in this work, as well as for their retention, blank pages have been placed to precede the various plates. It is hoped that this provision will prove of considerable service.]

——:o:——

1. Examples of work executed by the Eccentric Cutter
2. Simple examples of work done with the Vertical Cutter
3. Patterns descriptive of the use of the Horizontal Cutter
4. Ivory Vase decorated, or reeded, with the Universal Cutter
5. Ivory Tazza, and other specimens of Drill work
6. Vase and examples of the use of the Curvilinear Apparatus
7. Examples of Decorated Cylinders, executed with the Eccentric Chuck
8. Elliptic Miniature Frame in Ivory, equally divided by the Segment Apparatus
9. Specimen of work produced by the Rectilinear Chuck, turned by the Earl of Sefton
9A. Examples of work decorated with the Dome or Spherical Chuck
10. Specimens of work produced with the Spiral Apparatus
11. Specimen of Compound Spiral Turning, executed by Capt. R. Pudsey Dawson
12. Examples of Surface Spiral Decoration, produced by the Reciprocator
13. Ivory Candelabra for seven candles
14. Specimen Vase, turned by the Rev. C. C. Ellison, employing the Rose Engine, Ellipse Chuck, and Spherical Slide-rest
15. Vase with deep base, turned and ornamented with the Spherical Slide-rest
16. Ivory Elliptic Casket, turned with the Spherical Slide-rest and Ellipse Chuck
17. Large Ivory Miniature Frame, highly decorated by various instruments

———

The whole of the Engravings contained in this book were carried out by Messrs. WATSON AND SCOTT, *of Imperial Buildings, Ludgate Circus.*

ORNAMENTAL TURNING.

——:o:——

CHAPTER I.

THE ORNAMENTAL TURNING LATHE.

THE illustration represented by Fig. 1 is a lathe of the most modern description, and the author deems it expedient to give the details of such in the opening chapter, so that amateurs of little or no experience may be able to obtain an idea of the lathe most suitable for their purpose. As the details of the various adjuncts will be fully described in future chapters, the engraving is simply of a lathe of the particular type most suited to the art of ornamental turning.

It is a 5-in. centre lathe with traversing mandrel, which is bored throughout its entire length; and, as all lathes of high-class manufacture should do, runs in hardened steel collars; the mandrel is also perfectly hard. The latter being bored through adds considerably to the convenience of the lathe for many purposes; long rods of steel or other materials, for instance, may be passed up the aperture while the end projecting from the chuck is turned; and in the case of a large number of small articles being required, each one may be cut off, and the material withdrawn and again fixed.

On the rear end of the mandrel steel screw-guides are fitted, of different pitches, six being the usual and sufficient number. These are employed to reproduce the screw on the work, and are actuated by an eccentric, fixed to the headstock immediately under the mandrel. The eccentric carries a metal plate having six arcs, in each of which a thread is cut to match the steel guide; and when required to be used, the arc is placed in gear with the

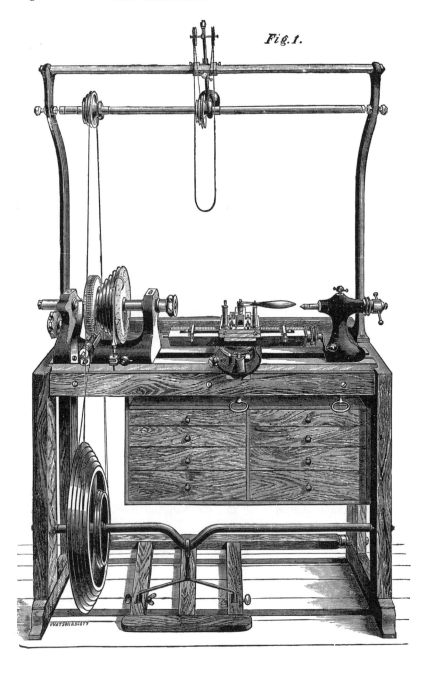

Fig. 1.

guide by turning the eccentric round with a lever until sufficient pressure is obtained to allow the mandrel to move backwards and forwards with the necessary freedom, but without shake, while the thread on the guide is reproduced on the work.

The screw may be cut in the first instance with a double angle point tool (Fig. 26), placed in the slide-rest, or begun and finished with the chasers (Figs. 55 and 56), which are for internal and external threads; but when the turner is sufficiently experienced, the slide-rest may be dispensed with and the chaser used by hand, fixed in the socket handle (Fig. 60). In adopting the latter course, the tool is held to the work, and the lathe receives a backward and forward motion by the foot on the treadle so that the pulley rotates the number of turns necessary to the length of screw required; the tool is released from cut while the lathe turns the reverse way, but again applied directly the return journey commences; this may be easily acquired by practice. When the screw is partly cut, the guide may be removed, and the steel sleeve replaced so that it may be finished by continual revolutions of the lathe while the chaser is under the guidance of the hand. Left-hand screw-guides are equally applicable, but, being seldom required, are not made unless specially ordered.

The driving pulley is made of gun-metal from preference, and is put together in the following way in two parts: the body is turned all over inside and out, the former being necessary to the freedom of surperfluous weight at any part; the front is then recessed about $\frac{3}{16}$ in. deep, and undercut to about 4°; the face is then turned over on both sides, and a corresponding angle turned on the periphery, but the diameter left about $\frac{1}{16}$ in. larger than the recess in the pulley; a hole is turned out in the centre of the plate to pass over the socket which fits over the mandrel. The body is then placed on a hot plate until it expands sufficiently to allow the face to drop in, and when cold the two are firm and immovable. The two angles agreeing, no joint is visible, and this is undoubtedly the proper mode to adopt. Some advocate soldering the faces in, but this is not to be recommended, and should not be used for high-class work.

On the face of the pulley eight circles of division are drilled—namely, 360, 192, 144, 120, 112, 84, 96, and 12. The zero or starting-point of each circle is drilled on an arc described from the point of the index-peg when in its place, and set about midway on the screw at the lower extremity where the adjustment takes place; by this the index can be raised or depressed. If the zeros are drilled on a radial line, it is not possible to move from one circle to another without a re-adjustment, but, when placed on the arc, any of the series are available without this. The complete index is seen in its place. (*Vide* Fig. 1.)

There are various ways of fixing the ball that receives the pin of the index, either as seen in the engraving, or it may be fixed at the back, which some prefer; another, and very excellent way, is to have a strong steel pillar fixed at the back, with a hole at the top, into which the pin of the index fits, causing the blade to lay across the top with the peg towards the front of the pulley. This is more convenient in many ways, and, when fitted in this manner, the arc upon which the starting-points are drilled is described by the index when in its place. In this position, also, it is more elevated, and a better light is available.

The popit-head, or back-centre, is fitted with a steel cylinder and a leading screw of ten threads to the inch, with a drop lever, by which the screw is actuated. The screw is retained in its place by a metal cap, which screws on to the body of the head, and the front of the steel boss through which the lever passes is divided into one hundred equal parts, by which the movement of the cylinder may be read to thousandths. The front of the cylinder is bored out to a taper hole to receive the different centres, and the front of the leading screw is made long enough to eject them when the cylinder is wound in. The advantage of this needs no argument in its favour, when compared with the obsolete plan of being compelled to force the centres out when the screw is not made to operate upon them.

The hand-rest is made in the usual way, and is fitted with tee-rests of different lengths and forms. The boring collar is also a most useful addition, and this also carries a guide for slender turning, which is fixed to the head by a bolt in the same way as the circular cone-plate.

The slide-rest that should accompany such a lathe may be either of those represented by Figs. 13, 14, and 17.

It will be observed that the heads are mounted on cast-iron bearers, which are 3 ft. 6 in. long, and these are fitted to a massive double frame of mahogany, the front of the bed being covered with the same material. The crank is made of wrought-iron, and the hook, which has two arms, is made of the same. This particular style of fitting up the lower part is an improvement by the author, and it will be at once obvious that, the treadle being supported at both sides, is far superior to the original way of a single hook attached to the centre-rail only. The foot can be placed on any part of the treadle without fear of springing it, and the action altogether is much better. The fly-wheel is of cast-iron (massive), and turned with seven speeds, suitable for quick or slow motion; underneath the bed is a nest of drawers, in which all the apparatus is fitted, one lock operating on them all.

The overhead motion forms a very important part of the apparatus employed in the art of ornamental turning, and that attached to the lathe (Fig. 1), also illustrated by Fig. 11, whereby it is fully described, is without question the most useful and convenient at present designed, and is now well-known as Evans's Improved. It consists of two standards bolted to the frame and connected at the top by a triangular bar, fixed at each end by a nut and washer. Beneath this a steel spindle runs between centre-screws, and carries a pulley and drum, or two grooved pulleys; the top bar carries a frame which can be moved laterally, and this also holds another frame that works upon centres, and through which a tension-bar slides, having guide-pulleys at the front, and a counterbalance weight at the other extremity.

A band passes from the fly-wheel to the pulley on the spindle, which has grooves of different diameters, to alter the speed; a second band passes from either the drum or second pulley over the guide-pulleys on the tension-rod, thence to the pulley on the instrument in the slide-rest.

The great advantage in this design of overhead is found in the second band not requiring to be altered, and it is obvious that this is a great boon. In applying it, all that is necessary is to pull down the band until it passes over the pulley of the cutter-frame. The tension required for work of different kinds is altered by moving the counterbalance-weight nearer to or farther from the centre-frame in which the tension-bar slides, the bar itself being also moved in the frame when required. It has been urged against this form of overhead that, in consequence of the guide-pulleys attached to the tension-bar, there is an undue amount of friction; but this exists in theory only, and such a statement is perfectly erroneous: also, that the oil from the guide-pulleys, from the fact of being overhead, is likely to be dispersed over the turner's head; this is also a delusion. If properly lubricated, there is not the least occasion for such a result, as practical experience has clearly proved.

The best evidence the author can put forth in support of these remarks is that he has now fitted this form of overhead to the lathes of many well-known amateurs—notably, the Earl of Crawford and Balcarres, the Rev. C. C. Ellison, L. V. Lloyd, Esq., T. Hutchinson, Esq., the Hon. Wilfred Brougham, Sir George Pechell, Bart., and very many other distinguished amateur turners —who, one and all, express the greatest satisfaction, and testify to its actual superiority.

CHAPTER II.

MODE OF CHUCKING AND ADJUSTMENT OF WORK.

THE means of holding the material for further operations, commonly known as chucking, is perhaps one of the most difficult branches connected with the art of turning, and one in which more failures occur than in any other, thus disheartening the turner. There are various ways of preparing the rough material previous to chucking it: take, for instance, a piece of boxwood in the rough, about 6 in. long; a small hole should be drilled in the centre to admit the point of the prong-chuck; the wood is then driven on the prong until sufficiently indented to prevent its turning upon the centre; the opposite end is then supported by the popit-head. The next process will be to select a cup-chuck of the most suitable size; the end of the wood should be turned perfectly true both on the face and diameter, and slightly taper; if the face is not true, it will cause the wood, when driven into the chuck, to be considerably out of truth. The material should never, unless for special purposes which will be referred to later on, touch the bottom or be driven against a shoulder; it should be held entirely by the circular grip of the chuck. It is not at all necessary to make a deep fitting: about a quarter of an inch is ample for large and heavy work; but it is certain that unless the material is correctly fitted it will never hold in its place while the necessary work is executed upon it, while, if accurately fitted, a much less depth of fitting will answer all the purpose. When fitted, the wood is held in the left hand while the end is struck with a hammer; the chuck should not be placed upon a surface. The author recommends great care in the practice of chucking the work, even in this minor form, as the time so spent will be well repaid in the end. There is nothing more annoying than to find the work moving in the chuck.

The Universal Chuck, with self-centering jaws moved by a right and left-hand screw simultaneously, is a most useful tool to employ. In the case of materials of large diameters and short lengths, it does away with the necessity for using the popit-head, and at the same time will allow a good deal of work to be done on the face in consequence of the absence of the back-centre. This chuck may also be employed to hold other than circular work; flat substances and uneven materials are held in it while reduced to a state of concentricity. The extreme diameter of the plate, however, renders it inconvenient for the purposes of ornamental turning, and, where it can be dispensed with for one of less bulk, it is better to do so, and regard it as simply a means of preparing the work for smaller chucks which are more convenient.

The American scroll-chucks, although decried by some, are a very useful addition to a lathe; up to a certain size, and for the purpose for which they are intended, they answer very well indeed.

The old-fashioned die-chuck, with two screws moving independently of each other, may now also be regarded as entirely obsolete. The die-chuck invented by a Mr. Bennett, from whom it takes its name, is a most valuable tool and supersedes many others in existence. It is illustrated in Fig. 1 on the mandrel-nose.

By the aid of this chuck, articles of different sizes, from less than $\frac{1}{16}$ in. to 1 in. in diameter, can be held not only concentrically but eccentrically. The principle of the chuck is this: it is always true one way, while that part which carries the die is made to slide past each side of the centre by tapping it at either end; and when the work is thus centered, the screw is tightened on to it and firmly held. For holding drills or metal between the sizes above mentioned, there is nothing to supersede this chuck.

Boxwood spring-chucks with metal rings are also most useful chucks to employ. These are made from thoroughly seasoned

boxwood about 3 in. long, divided into sections of different numbers according to the size, and turned taper, so that when the ring is
pressed on, the sections all collapse and hold the work tightly in
the chuck. A further improvement in this kind of chuck is found
in a metal spring-chuck with steel rings. These do not shrink and
become untrue like the wooden ones, and are most useful for many
purposes, such as holding a number of articles all the same size,
or presumably so; which means practically that there is some slight
difference. As an example, take a set of draughtsmen. The best
way to proceed with such a job is to turn the material, whatever
it may be, to a long cylinder, first selecting the spring-chuck that
will best suit it for size in diameter; the pieces should then be all
parted off with a narrow parting tool, all being made as near as
possible the same width. This done, the spring-chuck is placed
upon the mandrel-nose, and each piece can then be placed in
it as required, and, the ring being gently forced on to the
chuck, the work is securely held without further trouble.
Before beginning to ornament such a number of pieces as are
contained in a full set of draughtsmen, it is a good plan to
turn the faces over on each side, and, by setting the depth
of cut with the stop-screw on the top slide, this is easily done,
rendering them all alike in thickness. Having decided the depth,
the tool need not be moved until all are faced, which saves a deal
of time and trouble in measuring, the result being in every way
satisfactory.

Cement composed of beeswax and shellac forms a very excellent
means of chucking many objects which, from their uneven shape,
are difficult to hold in any other way. In some instances the
cement is held against the chuck while it revolves, and heat
enough obtained by the friction. The material is then simply
pressed to it. This, however, is not to be recommended, it being
most difficult to centre the work correctly before the cement cools
and is too hard.

There are very many objects that, from their limited thickness
and uneven edges, are very difficult to chuck or hold, and the
best way to overcome this is to apply the cement, but in a

different way; also, if three or more of any particular object are required to be the same thickness, it is a great assistance. To hold them securely, the following is the proper way: procure a well-seasoned wood chuck, preferably boxwood; face it over perfectly flat and true, then arrange the work upon it so that all the surfaces can be turned over. When so arranged, have the cement melted in a small ladle, and with an iron spoon pour it all round the edges of the work so that it be practically encased about an eighth of an inch deep or more; when cold, the entire number of pieces may be turned with great ease, and to remove them the chuck only requires a tap with a hammer. And here it may be mentioned, that in doing such work care must be exercised not to let the tool catch, as the jar from such sudden occurrence may possibly displace the work before the desired time.

The component parts of the cement are: three of rosin to one of beeswax, well melted together; other ingredients are at times mixed, but those mentioned are found to be quite sufficient.

Those readers who practise metal-turning will find the same principle exceedingly handy if carried out with solder in place of the cement, in which case a metal-face chuck should be kept for the purpose.

The face-plate affords a ready means of holding such work as may require operating upon in various positions eccentric to its axis; the surface of the work being placed upon the face of the chuck and secured tightly to it by bolts and clamps. These are only tightened just to hold the work from slipping round while the chuck is rotated to ascertain the correct position; which when obtained, the bolts are finally fixed.

Many of the objects illustrated in the following chapters have required to be fitted to boxwood plugs, and will be fully described as the subject is detailed. When necessary to resort to this means, the ivory, for such it will invariably be, must be accurately fitted and fixed with thin but good glue; and when it is to be removed, it is placed in warm water until the glue dissolves, and so releases the ivory. From the natural inclination of the wood to expand under such treatment, considerable care is necessary. The risk is far less when the fitting is slightly taper.

Work of large diameter, or ellipses of extra size, are more easily prepared and shaped under such treatment. As an example, suppose a ring is cut off the end of a tusk of ivory, there would be some difficulty in deciding the best mode to adopt. Such inconvenience may be readily disposed of: surface a boxwood chuck, and then with strong and rather thick glue the ivory is firmly held to it; the glue is required thicker for such a purpose than is necessary for holding ivory work to the wood plugs upon which they are ornamented. One great advantage in adopting this mode of chucking the work is, that the material may remain for a longer period unfinished without altering its position.

CHAPTER III.

ADJUSTMENT OF TOOLS, CHUCKS, &c.

ALL forms that have been previously brought to the desired shape by hand-turning, or under the influence of the slide-rest, &c., may be so shaped by the various chucks and revolving cutters that they may be decorated in almost endless ways—by perforations, flutes, beads, pearls, reeds, facets, &c.; and the various ornamentations are equi-distantly arranged by the employment of the index-peg and division-plate while the various cutters are presented to the work and driven from overhead. Other means of equalising the spaces laterally are provided by the main screw and micrometer of the slide-rest, arrested at intervals by the fluting-stops, or, for finer adjustments, by the number of turns or divisions that are made. The partial rotation of the mandrel, under the guidance of the worm-wheel and tangent-screw, also gives results equally necessary to the decoration of compound solid forms. The work is not in any way confined to circular shapes, but by the various instruments may be reduced to polygonal figures and many other forms. In the case of the original shape being retained, the work is simply held stationary by the index-point while the distinct cuts are made at the required intervals by the different cutters; or, for the alteration of the form, the work may be carried in a rectilinear direction, or partially rotated while the tool revolves. All the various movements in combination result in very curious and beautiful designs, enabling the perforations, &c., to be placed in various groups to suit the design of the object.

CHAPTER IV.

Division Plate and Index.

In the summary of the ornamental turning lathe, reference is made to the compensating index, but further notice of it is necessary in a full explanation of the manner in which it is constructed, and the advantages obtained by its employment.

The index as made in a plain form, without power of adjustment, is simply a straight flat blade in the form of a spring, with a pin at the lower extremity to fit into the ball at the base of the lathe head, and a point at its upper extremity, which fits into the holes drilled in the division plate, and by which the mandrel is arrested at the spaces contained in the circle, whichever be used. This form of index, for ordinary purposes, such as dividing polygonal figures, or drilling certain numbers of holes, as obtained from the plate itself, is generally found to be sufficient.

There are various forms or designs of compound and adjustable index-points; the latter, as seen in the illustration (Fig. 1), is that which is generally used, and, from its powers of elevating and depressing the point which holds the plate, it is a most necessary adjunct and the most appropriate for ornamental turning. It will be observed that the pin which fits into the ball at the bottom of the headstock has a projecting square boss on the end about $\frac{3}{4}$ in. square, through which the lower extremity of the index passes, the latter being screwed with a fine thread, on which two circular metal nuts are fitted, one working between a gap cut in the square, the other acting as a lock-nut to fix it when the necessary adjustment has been made. The nut which is embraced within the slot in the square, forms the means of moving the blade in either direction, the result being a partial rotation of the mandrel and pulley, and consequent alteration in the position of the starting-point, or the relative positions of the succeeding cuts to be commenced.

This power of adjustment is of very considerable importance, for although, when the work is in progress, the index remains at the same length, there are many instances in which the like result could not be obtained with an index devoid of the same means of adjustment. It sometimes happens that the first cut may be started without considering whether the number of holes taken for each successive cut will divide equally into the number of holes contained in the circle, and this affords an opportunity to illustrate the advantage of the starting-point of each circle being drilled on an arc instead of a radial line. If, for example, a pattern has been started at the 192 division, it is possible that, to suit the diameter of work, radius of the cutter, or other of the various points to be considered, the exact distance required cannot be obtained in that particular circle; the index can then be moved to another without the necessity for adjustment in any way; whereas, if the starting-points were drilled on a radial line, the point, moving on a centre and describing an arc, would consequently require adjusting each time a different division was employed upon any similar object.

Another example is found in the fact that it may be required to make perforations or other description of ornamentation at the half of any odd number of divisions that may have been taken—say 3 or 5; this, with the means at hand, is easily effected. The 96 circle divided by 3 will give 32 consecutive cuts; if from any cause it should be desired to cut between the spaces, the division is moved one hole forward, and by aid of the adjustment the mandrel is partially rotated until by trial the exact half or centre of the preceding cut is found to be correct. The movement of the dial-plate is then conducted in precisely the same way as before, by moving three holes each time, and thus in the end 64 cuts have been made.

To facilitate the movement of the pulley and replacing the index, the circle containing 360 is figured at every 10 with numerals, and has a dot to indicate every fifth hole. The 192 has numerals at every sixth hole with indicator at every third; 144 in the same way; the 120 has numerals only at every fifth hole, the

112 at every seventh hole, the 84 at every sixth hole, and the 96 at every sixth hole. Thus very many of the divisions are in full view and go a great way to prevent mistakes. The circle containing 12 holes only is added with a view to saving unnecessary wear to those of larger numbers, and is used for the smaller numbers, required for polygonal figures, or when a division of not more than the number contained in the circle is for any special purpose desired.

The use of the division plate and its accompanying index having thus far been explained as, perhaps, the most important factor in connection with the ornamental turning lathe, the author now takes the opportunity of bringing before his readers an Automatic Counting Apparatus, invented by T. J. Ashton, Esq., which forms a most valuable addition to a lathe. All who have been engaged in ornamental turning have experienced the very considerable attention that must be devoted to this part of the work, and not a few have found that, having nearly finished an elaborate piece of work, the whole has been spoiled by the point of the index being placed in the wrong hole, either through an interruption, failing light, defective sight, or some other cause; while valuable time and, not unlikely, temper, has also been lost.

The liability to error is general, and acknowledged by most amateurs; and various contrivances for counting automatically have been introduced from time to time, but they have all failed to accomplish the object with the same precision and ease as that now to be considered.

In the year 1882, Mr. Ashton so far solved the problem, and, at the conversazione of the Amateur Mechanical Society of that year, he exhibited the Automatic Counting Apparatus (Fig. 2), which the author has since been manufacturing with considerable success, and of which the following is a detailed description:—

A steel sleeve having a flange in its centre, fits over the end of the mandrel, in the same manner as the ordinary cap used to retain the mandrel between the collars in the headstock; a ring of steel having two arms of different length and definite angles to each other is fitted to the sleeve, and on the side of the flange nearest the lathe head, where it is retained in position by a nut and washer, at the same time rotating freely on the sleeve.

To the short arm is attached a circular cam, having two projections on its periphery. Through the one the pin connecting it with the arm passes, the centre corresponding with a continuance of the line of the circumference. A large aperture is cut in the cam, permitting the sleeve to pass freely through, at the same time allowing a perfectly free action to the cam.

Fig.2

To the long arm is attached a lever, and this, by means of a strap or link, is connected with the cam; a spring acts on the lever and retains the cam eccentrically. On the outside or left of the flange on the sleeve, the division wheels, of which there may be several, are fitted; but one of 192 and one of 120 will give most of the divisions generally used, or likely to be required.

The wheel is securely held to the sleeve against the flange by a steel nut and washer, so that it cannot move except with the rotation of the mandrel. The wheels are 7 in. in diameter, and are slotted, or cut with the necessary number of divisions, all being accurately placed equidistantly round its circumference.

Under each slot or tooth a small hole is drilled, and these are numbered as in the division-plate on the pulley. A steel pointer is arranged to stand perpendicularly, so that the numbers required to be indicated are always in full view. A pawl, as seen by the engraving (Fig. 3), is connected with the long arm, and falls into the slots cut in the edge of the wheel. A longitudinal bar is firmly attached to the bottom of the lathe-head, and carries a strong spring, to which a detent, constructed to fit accurately into the teeth or slots in the wheel, is fixed exactly at the centre of the axis of the mandrel. An arm extends inwards from the spring to about an eighth of an inch beyond an imaginary line, which would be indicated when the circular cam before mentioned is concentric with the mandrel.

A semi-circular plate, seen in Fig. 2, is fixed to the back face of the mandrel frame or headstock, having a curved ·slot cut in it, which carries an adjusting stop with a regulating screw, a second stop being permanently fixed to the plate, the object of the stops being to determine and regulate the movement of the arm to which the pawl is attached.

The action of the apparatus is very simple. Suppose that a wheel of 120 teeth is fixed on to the sleeve, and that it is desired to divide the work into twenty-four equal parts or divisions, the wheel is rotated till the pointer indicates zero, or 120; the detent will then fall into the thirtieth slot, or a fourth of the whole number. The long lever rests on the lower or fixed stop, and the pawl is made to drop freely into the slot by means of the regulating screw. The lever is then raised to suit the number of divisions required, and retained in that position till the movable stop is brought in contact with it; hence, it follows that each time the lever is raised the pawl will fall into every fifth slot or division in the wheel.

c

All being now adjusted, the first cut in the work is made, the arm is then raised by the left hand as indicated by Fig. 3, following the dotted line, and, the lever being pressed on, the circular cam is brought concentric to the axis of the mandrel, and at the same time impinges against the arm connected with the spring,

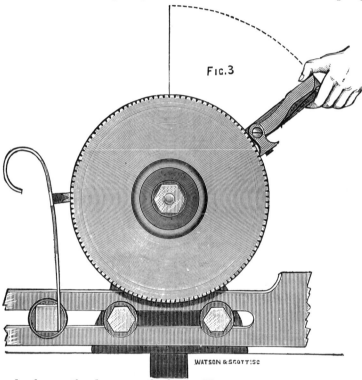

Fig.3

WATSON & SCOTT:SC

and releases the detent at the back. The arm is then lowered until arrested by the stop, and on the lever being released the deten falls into the thirty-fifth slot and immovably fixes the mandrel.

One of the most tedious patterns in ornamental turning is that known as basket-work, and is cut with the universal cutter (Fig. 122), or with the vertical cutter (Figs. 94 and 95). The variations in patterns obtained by the different movements of the division-plate in combination with it are very great. With the apparatus we are now considering, they are effected with much greater facility, and consequent rapidity. Thus, having cut first at, say,

the same division every five, the tool is moved by the main-screw
of the slide-rest exactly its own width, denoted by the micrometer;
the detent moved, say, one slot or division, and the same number
five taken all round again.   This will leave the cuts all the same
width and length, but one division away from the starting point.
This particular style of work is fully illustrated and explained in a
future chapter devoted entirely to it.

Before concluding the remarks with reference to the division-
plate and index, the following table of the number of parts into
which each circle may be divided will be found of considerable
service, as it shows clearly which row may be used for any number of
cuts that are required. Various divisions not contained in the table
may be obtained by adjusting the micrometer of the adjusting index-
peg a certain amount for each consecutive cut, but this will be found
a tedious proceeding, and practically it is seldom, if ever, required.
The adjusting index, however, for compensating and obtaining an
equal space between any of the different holes, is indispensable.

TABLE OF DIVISIONS OF THE CIRCLES CONTAINED IN THE FACE
OF THE PULLEY.

360 will divide by :
2, 3, 5, 6, 8, 9, 10, 12, 15, 18, 20, 24, 30, 36, 40, 45,
60, 72, 90, 120, 180.

192 will divide by :
2, 4, 6, 8, 12, 16, 24, 48, 64, 96.

144 will divide by :
2, 3, 4, 6, 8, 9, 12, 16, 18, 36, 48, 72.

120 will divide by :
2, 3, 4, 5, 6, 8, 10, 12, 15, 20, 24, 30, 40, 60.

112 will divide by :
2, 4, 7, 14, 16, 28, 56.

96 will divide by :
2, 3, 4, 6, 8, 12, 16, 24, 32, 48.

84 will divine by :
3, 6, 7, 21, 28, 42.

12 will divide by :
2, 3, 4, 6.

CHAPTER V

THIS is a very important point to consider, and although con stantly referred to in the details of the various subjects illustrated, a brief summary of the general adjustment will be of service. Although the centering of the tool, when so required, to the precise height of the axis of the mandrel is the most important, there are many styles of decoration that require the tool set either above or below the axis of the lathe. The variation, or the result obtained by the three distinct arrangements, is at once seen by Figs. 4, 5, and 6, Plate 1.

To accurately adjust the tool to the axis of the lathe, the elevating ring on the pedestal of the slide-rest (Figs. 13 and 14) is the means to employ, but the testing of the precision is a matter which requires much care, and there are several ways of arriving at a satisfactory result. One of the most general is to turn a flat surface, and by adjusting the slide-rest until the fixed tool will turn off the whole surface without leaving the least semblance of a point or projection at the centre. In this there is no difficulty, but in many instances the tool is required to be re-centered when it is not possible to use this test.

To overcome this, a metal pillar having a broad base with a projection to fit the interval in the lathe-bed is employed. At the upper extremity a very fine ring is marked round the diameter to exactly correspond with the centre of the lathe ; by this it will be possible to adjust the tool to the correct height, irrespective of the relative position of the slide-rest on the lathe-bed.

Another description of centering standard is one that extends on one side of the centre, and in some instances this is of considerable service, as it is not always expedient to move the tool laterally, although from some cause the height may require further adjustment.

A more certain test is to set the slide-rest transversely across the lathe-bed and turn a flat surface, set the revolving cutter or whatever tool may be in use, fix the dial-plate by the index at zero, mark a fine line on one side of the centre, then turn the mandrel round to the half of the division employed, and carry the slide across the surface so that the tool will pass over the same line, which, if the height is absolutely correct, it will do; if not, the correction must be made by the adjustment of the elevating ring.

When elevation or depression of the height of centre is required, it is obtained also by the ring, and when the exact position of it is decided, the ring is fixed by a small metal screw fitted between the lever holes, the object of this being to prevent the ring moving when the slide-rest is moved from surface to cylinder, which from the weight of the slide it is likely to do. When cutting crescents on face-work, the slide-rest may be tilted over in whichever direction the deeper cut is required.

When the fixed tool has been correctly centered, all the revolving instruments should, when replacing it, present the cutters to precisely the same centre; but for many reasons the accuracy should be inspected previously to any cut being made, as the least interference with the under surface of the square stem will materially alter the precision; this may arise from shavings or even dust getting in the tool-box. These, however, are points that must to a certain extent be left to the operator, and may be simply regarded as hints necessary to the exact adjustment of this all-important point.

CHAPTER VI.

GRINDING AND SETTING TOOLS.

GRINDING the necessary tools required for ornamental turning and keeping them in proper cutting condition is one of the most troublesome and difficult operations that the amateur turner has to contend with, and, in his endeavours to help those readers who are not experienced in this branch, the author deems it necessary to set it forth in the following chapter, and as carefully as possible to explain the various instruments, their construction, and the correct way to employ them.

With all tools having straight and angular-cutting edges, it is most necessary that they should be retained in the same form and the edges as sharp as possible; to effect this the goneostat (Fig. 4) is absolutely essential. There are various forms of instruments used for the same purpose, but as the one illustrated is the most modern and perfect, no reference need be made to those of a less effective character, and which to a certain extent are now obsolete.

It will be seen by the engraving (Fig. 4) that the instrument is composed of two plates hinged together by a knuckle-joint and two steel screws, the top of the front plate having a mortise slot through which the steel arc fixed to the lower one passes, the arc being graduated from 0 to 70° for the purpose of setting the instrument to the necessary vertical angle, when it is fixed by the thumb-screw at the top, under which a steel grip fitting the arc is placed; two steel pillars are fitted in the lower plate, which act as feet, and when in use they rest on a surface while the edge of the tool moves on a stone or plate; at the lower extremity of the front plate a steel tool-box is fitted, the pivot passing through the plate and being held by a screw countersunk in the back. A semicircular slot is then cut out in the front of the plate to allow the fixing-screw for the tool-box to pass freely along; the front of the face is then graduated from 0° to 65° each side of the centre.

The two plates being hinged to work at right angles, one to

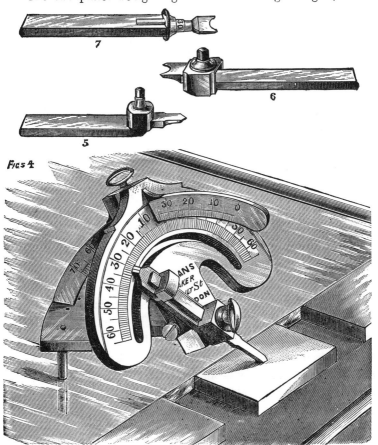

the other, the 0 on the steel arc forms the zero when the plate is precisely vertical, the graduations proceeding from thence round the arc to 70°; thus, it will be seen that, the two angular adjustments being employed at the same time, the tools are not only ground to the angles required, but can at any time be

re-ground or set with exactly the same result. All the tools that
have cutting angles are marked at the lower end of the shaft by
figures, which denote their facial angles, while those which differ
in shape, such as the square and bead tools, have figures which
represent their widths in hundredths.

It is usual to have a box with three drawers, each having a
separate slab of oilstone, brass, and cast-iron, upon which the
tools are ground; but the author has found it much more convenient to have the three slabs all fitted to the same plate, as seen
in the engraving. These are all fitted to be on the same level
with a sheet of plate glass, upon which the feet of the goneostat
move; the different slabs can then be used one after the other
without the necessity for withdrawing and replacing a drawer each
time. The plate glass is also a vast improvement upon the wood
surface as previously used.

When about to employ the instrument to grind up a single or
double-angle tool, it is set to the angle required, both vertically
and horizontally. The vertical angle for tools that are to be employed for ivory or hard woods should be 35°. The tool is placed in
the tool-box, leaving the cutting edge projecting so that the lower
plate, or base of the instrument, will lay parallel to the glass tablet
upon which the feet move. As the tools are now usually made of
one uniform length in preference to those gradually diminishing
with the size of the blade, a line can be marked on each one
requiring the use of the goneostat, which will save any further
trouble in adjusting the necessary amount of projection in order
that the lower-plate may assume the required position. When thus
arranged, the tool is rubbed with gentle pressure upon either of
the plates, the movement being a series of circles within the
capacity of the plate; the instrument being held in the right
hand, the pressure is created towards the point of the tool, but
care must be exercised not to tilt the instrument forward. The
feet in the base must always remain in contact with the glass plate
upon which they work.

The substitution of the plate-glass for the wooden surface has
many advantages: the feet of the instrument do not wear it into

an uneven surface, it does not collect the grit, which cut the feet away, and it always remains a true surface level with the plates. In the case of any considerable fracture occurring to the tool, the oilstone is the first to use, followed by the brass plate charged with oilstone powder and oil. This powder is usually kept in a small tin can; it is, however, always likely to collect other and coarser grit, and the safest way to procure the powder is to keep a piece of oilstone and chip off a small piece, which can be reduced to the finest cutting powder in a few moments; it is then sure to be free from any other substance. The tool having been ground up so far on the brass plate to the angles required, the vertical angle should be diminished by 3° and the tool carefully applied to the brass plate; this produces a second facet of less acuteness, which enables the tool to longer retain the excellence of its cutting edge. Having ground both angles thus, the oilstone powder is removed from it, and the second or obtuse facet finished upon the cast-iron plate charged with very fine crocus powder and oil, and with this it is not only finished grinding, but, the crocus having little or no cutting power, it is brilliantly polished, which adds greatly to the beauty of the work cut with it. When the facets have been thus finished, there will possibly be a very slight burr on the face, the extent of which, however, will depend much upon the hardness of the tool; this is removed by placing the face of the tool on the iron plate and gently rubbing until it is removed It may be possible that recourse to the brass plate will be necessary; in any case the burr only must be removed without altering the face of the tool, as that denotes the exact height of centre.

The eccentric cutters having angular-cutting edges are operated upon in precisely the same way, and are held in the small socket (Fig. 5); the vertical cutters assuming the same position in the socket (Fig. 6). The socket (Fig. 7) is applied in the same way to hold the drills, the astragal and angular facets of which are treated in a like manner.

The sharpening of curved edges, both concave and convex, has been the subject of considerable thought for some time. The

instrument (Fig. 8) designed by the author overcomes the difficulty with regard to the round nose or convex edges. It will be
seen that it is made to carry the tools and different sockets in the
same way as the goneostat, and has a steel rod passing through the
centre at an angle. On the end of the rod a small ball is fitted, and,
the instrument being moved round on this as a centre, causes the

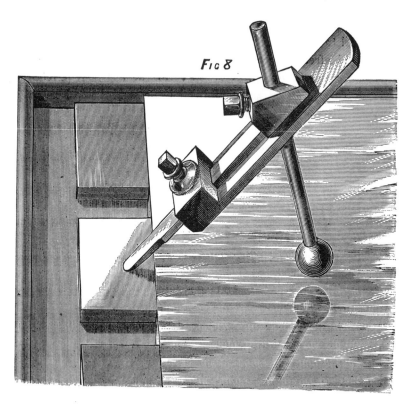

Fig 8

tool to follow its curve on the oilstone or brass plate with the cutting
powder upon it. The vertical angle or cutting bevel is altered by
moving the ball nearer to or farther from the centre. It has
been found to fully perform all the necessary actions required of
it, and is largely used by the leading amateurs.

We next come to the sharpening of bead and moulding drills.
For this purpose a series of cones are required, and these are made

to revolve in a small lathe-head fixed in the hand-rest and driven from the overhead motion, or by a pulley on the nose of the mandrel, with a short band from thence to the instrument. The cones are revolved at high speed, charged with the different powders, the same that are used on the flat plates. When thus revolving, the bead is passed up the cone until it fits the diameter, when it is held there, the cutting substance being held to it on the finger.

For the various moulding tools and drills, a series of slips of Arkansas stone and brass of various sizes are necessary, the latter being charged with the cutting powders as before mentioned. The shape of the moulding tool will admit of the different slips of numerous shapes being applied, when they are gently rubbed over the forms at the precise angle or bevel at which they are made; this is an important feature in such tools, as a rounded edge is not capable of cutting cleanly.

The various fillets and curves are thus sharpened independently of each other, and the goneostat always employed for the transverse astragal or terminal edge.

There are various kinds of grinding machines fitted to mahogany frames, similar to a lathe; first, the vertical grinding machine having five different spindles, each of which requires to be changed when another is used. The spindles are fitted with two stones, one brush, one buff, one metallic lap; it has a drop-can and water-trough also fitted over the stone.

The horizontal grinding machine is fitted to a double frame, and carries separate plates of iron, brass, and lead. This is used for setting tools in the goneostat, and for grinding a variety of other tools; it is also used for cutting and faceting stones and other substances.

Fig. 9 illustrates a newly-designed combination grinding-machine by the author, which embodies all the necessary appliances on one stand. By reference to the engraving it will be observed that the machine consists of a short double frame of mahogany, with fly-wheel, crank, and treadle. One side of the frame is carried upwards, and receives the centre-screw; at the opposite side an iron standard is fixed, through which the end of the spindle passes, forming a mandrel; on the spindle are fitted a stone, buff, and metallic lap, a driving pulley being also attached to it over the fly-wheel.

In the front of the mandrel are fitted the various cones for sharpening the bead-drills, and this forms a great feature in the

Fig 9

machine; it does away with the necessity for the small lathe and cones previously alluded to, and, not only is this a consideration, but it is sometimes important that a drill should be sharpened when the work is in hand, in which case the small lathe cannot be used unless a second complete lathe is in readiness, whereas, with the machine under notice, it is always accessible. The mandrel may also carry drills and the various polishing buffs, &c.; in fact, it forms really the second lathe, the want of which is so often felt.

To the right of the mandrel a horizontal grinding-machine is fitted, the frame passing through the bed. In this a steel collar is fitted, and a steel mandrel similar to a traversing one, the object of this being to raise and depress the height of the plates by the centre-screw at the lower extremity; the nose of the mandrel is screwed to receive the plates, which are fitted in the same way as ordinary chucks. On the top of the frame a cast-iron table is fitted and can be removed at will. The centre of this is turned out to fit over the periphery of the plates or chucks. A pair of guide-pulleys, fitted one to each side of the frame, conducts the band from the fly-wheel to the pulley on the mandrel, which revolves between the frame and the table. By the centre-screw the plates are adjusted to a level with the table, and, when using the goneostat, this is of considerable importance. At the back, on the top-board, is fitted a piece of mahogany having the oilstone, brass, and iron plates, also the sheet of plate glass upon which the feet of the goneostat move; this is exactly like that seen in Fig. 4 upon which the instrument stands. The different plates are screwed on plugs to the side of the frame for convenience, and a cover fits over the flat slabs to keep them free from dirt, &c. In the water-trough a small tap is fitted to draw off the water, as in no case should the stone be allowed to remain immersed, or it will become soft at that part, and useless.

This machine has quite taken the place of those made separately, and is admitted to be the most useful of its kind that has yet been introduced. The author feels great pleasure in stating that the dispensing with the separate spindles and the introduction of the plate-glass table were instituted at the suggestion of Arthur Warre, Esq., who from experience proved them to be the best form.

CHAPTER VII.

Materials Appropriate for Ornamental Turning.

Of hard wood there are many varieties, but few that are really good for ornamental turning; African black being the finest to be procured for specimens to be highly decorated. This wood is obtained in logs of various sizes, but the result of cutting up one of large dimensions is often very unsatisfactory : the larger logs, or what should be termed the trunk of such a tree, is always faulty in the centre, and perhaps from a diameter of 15 in. to 24 in. nothing sound exceeding 3 in. to 4 in. will be obtained. Even when a satisfactory-looking piece is further operated upon, fresh blemish or worm-holes may appear; yet, although the waste incurred in cutting up any quantity is at times serious, the excellent quality of that which is really sound amply repays for the time and loss.

African black may certainly be said to rank next to ivory in every respect; sometimes it is marked with a few varying colours, but these die out in time and the whole is quite black. One of the real difficulties with regard to it is the limited size in diameter to be obtained. If it is cut from a large log, plankways, the necessary diameter can be procured, but although it is the only one of the hard woods that can be used in this form with anything like satisfactory result, it is better avoided if possible.

Cut up in the usual manner and turned the endway of the grain, it is as close and uniform almost as ivory itself, and for face patterns is quite equal to it, while in some kinds of work the pattern is even more effective. It acquires a beautiful polish, which can only be achieved in such material with a keen cutting tool.

Cocus is the next in quality suitable for ornamental turning, and, when exceptionally good, is almost as close in texture as the black wood. It varies considerably in colour; the lighter shades, however, get gradually darker by exposure. This wood, again, is not, as a rule, to be obtained in very large diameters, although at times it is possible to procure a piece from 7 in. to 8 in., but with a faulty centre; this can be plugged or covered with some other material as a centre.

For those subjects which are left in the form resulting from plain hand-turning, king, zebra, coromandel, and cam woods answer fairly well. Boxwood forms, perhaps, one of the most useful adjuncts to the amateur workshop : it is abundantly used for chucks; it affords a means of practising economy and saving time by making trials, both of form and decoration, previous to operating upon the more valuable materials, and should be regarded as indispensable to the practice of the art.

It is not the intention of the author to give a long detailed account of all the different woods to be turned, but only to say a few words upon those that he considers applicable for service in ornamental turning.

Ivory is, without exception, the finest material for the various purposes connected with the art we are now considering.

There are two descriptions that are generally used for turning purposes, the Indian and African ivory. The former is close and regular in texture, and somewhat white in colour, especially when first turned, but, if exposed to the air, it loses a deal of its freshness, and ultimately becomes yellow. It will take, however, some length of time to make a material change, and, if kept under glass and air-tight, little difference will be detected for years.

The African ivory is considered, and is, from its general tendency to retain its colour, more suitable for many subjects, and that which is termed green or transparent ivory, from its containing more natural moisture or sap, gradually dries to a very beautiful pearly white, which is very much more appreciated than the dead opaque white of the Indian ivory.

In preparing the green ivory, its natural state has to be considered, inasmuch as it should not be worked up immediately after it is cut from the tusk, as the contraction or expansion inherent with all materials used in a similar state will tend to destroy the fittings or joints, either screwed or plain. Such ivory should be cut into suitable blocks, then carefully turned up, glued or gummed over at the ends, and left for a long time—some months, if possible; in fact, the longer the better.

This short outline of the qualities of the two distinct classes of ivory will be sufficient to show that, in selecting such material for any specimen of ornamental turning, it is necessary it should be all of the same kind, either one or the other. Many handsome articles have been spoiled by a mixture of the two, one part being opaque, while the other is of pearly whiteness, the contrast being detrimental to its elegance.

There are, however, two drawbacks to the use of ivory; first the difficulty of obtaining it of large dimensions, and secondly the somewhat extravagant price which has to be paid for it. The largest size is naturally always at the hollow end, and in most cases this has a large aperture. When of this character, it is used for such objects as miniature frames, bases for pedestals, &c. The solid ivory does not commence till some distance up the tusk, where it becomes gradually smaller. The nerve, however, runs entirely through the whole length of the tusk; therefore wherever it is cut this will be seen, and sometimes it will be found wide of the centre, necessitating a recess of large diameter being turned out in order that it may be hidden by a solid piece, which should be as near the same texture as possible.

In building up subjects requiring many pieces of different diameters, it is almost impossible, without considerable waste, to cut it all from the same tusk, but this is not so important if the pieces are carefully selected. Small pillars or handles should be cut from corresponding tusks, commonly termed "scrivelloes;" but at times the diminished size required will not admit of this without great loss; therefore such pieces may be cut from the sides of a large hollow. Ivory is at times cut plankways, but when so used requires considerable care in the penetration of the tool and its excellence of cutting edge, in consequence of the different direction the grain takes.

CHAPTER VIII.

POLISHING OF IVORY AND WOOD.

ALL work in ivory that has been decorated with the various instruments, revolving cutters, &c., should not require any other polishing than that which is left from the tool, and the excellence of this is entirely dependent upon the condition the tool is brought to before being used. For work of shallow depth, the tool, when properly sharpened, will last to the completion of the pattern, but, for very deeply-cut work, the same will require to be sharpened perhaps more than once, and should always be reset for the final cut. There are no means to be employed to polish work of this kind except a soft brush, with whiting and water about the consistency of thick paste, with which it is well brushed and then washed with yellow soap and water, rinsed in clean cold water, and then dried in boxwood sawdust, the latter soaking all the water out of the excavations; when dry, a soft and perfectly clean brush should be used to remove any remaining portions of sawdust and finally polish it. It will then be as bright and clean as possible, provided it has been cleanly cut and the facets left bright from the tool; if roughly cut, all the brushing it may receive will not improve it.

All plain forms in ivory, portions of which are not to be in any way ornamented, should always be polished before any cutting is commenced, and it has been found advisable to polish carefully even that portion which is to be cut, as it may transpire that from some cause, or alteration of idea, the pattern to be placed on a certain part will be considerably improved by not being cut up sharp ; and, if this should be the case, the beauty of the facets left between the successive cuts will be greatly marred by being left unpolished. To polish the plain form, it should be got up perfectly free from marks, scratches, &c., then whiting and water applied with a soft rag, and well rubbed while the work revolves at speed. A still better result may be obtained when the work is so far polished by placing a soft circular lambswool pad in a chuck on the mandrel of the grinding machine (Fig. 9), and, while revolved at a quick speed, the work held against it; hand-buffs of the same material are also very useful for similar purposes. Oil of any kind whatever should be carefully kept from the surfaces.

Some description of ornamental patterns will bear finally polishing in the same way. The pedestal of the candelabra (Plate 13) was thus finished without in the least destroying the beauty of the sharp edges. All reeded columns the edges of which are not required sharp are also polished in the same way.

To create a better effect on black-wood subjects, a short soft brush with a very little beeswax may be employed, but this is hardly to be recommended, as the work, especially face patterns, should be left bright from the tool, and not require further treatment.

The question has been asked more than once as to whether the colourless hardwood lacquer, or varnish, will not aid the amateur in finishing the work. In one sense it will, as the work will never look well after it has been applied, no matter how carefully it is done, and it is strongly advised that all work should be left entirely free from any such treatment.

CHAPTER IX.

OVERHEAD MOTION.

FIG. 10 illustrates an overhead motion, which is so far superseded by the one previously alluded to, and fully described in the
following chapter, that its demerits will be at once obvious. The
spindle carries a pulley for the long band from the fly-wheel, and
a sliding drum (sufficiently long to suit the length of the slide-rest),
which may be fixed at any position along it. The frame in which

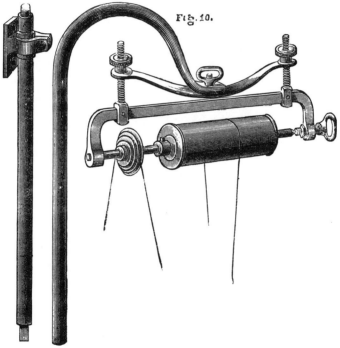

Fig. 10.

the spindle runs between centres is supported by two regulating
screws, which pass through nuts with curved ends that move in a
corresponding curve at each end of a strong steel spring. This is
held at its centre by a screw and bow-handle beneath the bent
arm of a single standard, the latter carried to the foot of the
standard of the lathe, where it fits into a metal washer, placed in the
frame to receive it; it is more convenient if the standard is put

together in two pieces. The regulating screws and milled-heads
are used for adjusting the tensions of the band.

The band passes from the fly-wheel to the pulley on the spindle,
and a second band from the drum to the pulley of the revolving
cutters, and this is a point of failure in this particular style of
overhead. A separate band is required for every instrument
having a pulley of increased size, or, in the instance of the
universal cutter, where the band has to pass over guide-pulleys ;
the alteration of the tension is troublesome, the vibration excessive
for want of support, and, although a useful apparatus, it is now
superseded by that illustrated by Fig. 11.

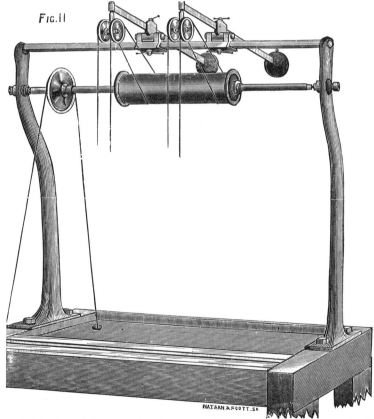

FIG. 11

This, it will be seen by the engraving, consists of two standards
firmly bolted to the lathe-frame, and connected at the top by a

triangular bar secured by a nut at each end; beneath this is a steel spindle running on hardened centres and carrying a pulley and drum. On the triangular bar is a frame that can be moved laterally; this carries a second frame working on centres, through which also a tension bar slides; at one end of the latter two guide-pulleys are fixed, and at the other end a counterbalance weight.

A band passes from the driving-wheel to the pulley on the spindle, which has various-sized grooves for alteration of speed, and gives motion to the spindle and drum. A second band passes from the drum over the guide-pulleys on the tension-bar, and thence to the pulley of the cutter-frame carrying the cutter.

This second band need never be removed, and it is obvious that in applying it all that is required is to pull it down till it passes over the pulley of the instrument in the tool-box of the slide-rest. As previously stated, it has been urged against this form of overhead that, in consequence of the pulleys above, which are attached to the tension-bar, there is an undue amount of friction; but this exists solely in theory, and the statement is quite erroneous : also, that the guide-pulleys being overhead, the oil is likely to be dispersed over the operator; this is also entirely a delusion. If properly oiled, there is not the least fear of such a result. Since the engraving was completed, the author has decided that a second pulley (as seen in Fig. 1) is preferable in place of the drum ; also a third pulley when the overhead is fitted with a second carriage and tension-bar, which is necessary for the complete working of the automatic slide-rest (Fig. 17).

The advantages possessed in this form of overhead motion are : its rigidity, its freedom from vibration, the ability to make use of it at any point throughout the length of the bed, the ease with which the tension is adjusted, which is done by simply moving the counter-balance weight to or from the centre, and, above all, the fact that no second band is required for the various instruments, the same that will drive the eccentric cutter or drill-spindle being equally effective with the epicycloidal, or rose-cutters. The different scientific amateurs who now use it, and whose names are alluded to in a previous chapter, are sufficient to certify its superiority.

CHAPTER X.

THE ORNAMENTAL TURNING SLIDE-REST.

THE general accuracy of the work produced by the aid of this tool, together with the comparative ease with which it is employed for plain as well as ornamental turning, renders it an indispensable addition to the lathe; and to those of only small experience it will be anything but a difficult tool to manipulate.

To show more clearly the advance that has been made in the general construction of the slide-rest, one of incomplete design, although not to be considered the primary instrument, is illustrated by Fig. 12. The tee-slide, which is 12 in. long, is fitted to a

Fig.12.

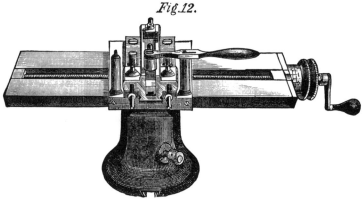

pedestal of cast iron; this is securely fixed to the bed in the requisite position by a dove-tailed slide, with a bow handle and washer at the lower extremity. The tee-slide is of proportionate width on the surface, and planed to an angle on each side. To this a metal plate is fitted, having on one side a bevel cast in the solid, while that on the opposite side is formed by a loose strip of the same angle, attached to the plate by two screws; two set-screws in the side of the plate, with their heads extending partly over the edge of the strip, are employed to set up the slide during its process of manufacture, and to be used for the same purpose in case of ultimate wear.

Two double-chamfered steel bars are now fixed across the plate at right angles to the tee-slide, and secured by two screws in each, the holes on one side being elongated so that set-screws in the side of the bar set the slide up to its bearing. The metal tool box is planed all over, the receptacle being made the standard size to receive the stems of the different instruments, which are $\frac{9}{16}$ in. square.

On the sides of the tool-box two projections are cast, and through each is fitted a screw of ten threads to the inch. These are termed the "guide" and "stop-screw;" both are squared at the ends to receive a key or winch-handle. At each side of the lower-plate a steel pillar is fixed, the top of which receives the body of the lever, the latter moving in a radial slot, the front of it being fitted to one of the clamps that hold the tools securely in the receptacle; the end of the lever terminating in a curve to suit the hand.

The tee-slide is accurately drilled at each end, and countersunk on the right side to receive the collar of the main screw, which is also ten threads to the inch; a metal plate is then attached to the end of the slide to retain the screw in its place. On the end projecting a metal micrometer is fitted, and divided into ten equal parts, and these are read from a line across the top of the end-plate.

When using a slide-rest of this limited construction, it is necessary to employ a set-square and set-bevel in its adjustment, and by these it is set parallel with, and at right angles to, the lathe-bed, the former position being required to turn a cylinder, while in the latter it is used to operate upon the surface. In order to facilitate the use of these instruments, it is necessary to turn a perfect cylinder and a true flat surface, and, when setting the rest to either position, the set-square is placed in the tool-box, and held with the blade in contact with the test while it is bolted to the lathe-bed. This plan is not to be recommended for many reasons, as it is likely to shift during the process of binding it to the bed. The set-bevel is used for setting the slide to angles, and is applied in the same way.

Fig. 13, although of a similar character, and to be used for the same class of work, is of a more complete construction. The tee-slide in this case is 14 in. long, but in other respects the metal slides are similar; the guide-screw on the left side of the tool-box has fitted to its end a steel collar divided into ten equal parts, and figured 0, 2, 4, 6, 8; in front of this a steel bridle is fitted, and fixed to the steel side-bar, so that the collar rotates between it and the pillar against which the point of the screw bears. By this addition the top slide is placed under complete control independently of the lever, leaving one hand always at liberty and free for other purposes. This is obviously a very great

Fig.13

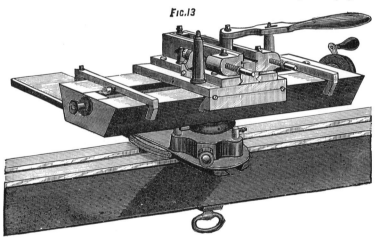

advantage, and, although some turners, from long custom, are still in favour of the lever, there can be no doubt that the ability to dispense with it is of considerable importance. The steel bridle is made open at the end, so that it passes over the screw, and, in removing it, all that is required is to take out the screw that binds it to the steel bar. A screw with a flat end passes through the pillar opposite the centre of the guide-screw, for the purpose of taking up any wear that may occur between the two faces of the collar, and so prevent any movement of the screw without a corresponding traverse of the slide, which, in other words, would be backlash or loss of time. It has been found a great advantage to have all micrometers as large as possible, as the readings are more accurate.

To the tee-slide are fitted, to operate one on each side of the traversing slide, a pair of fluting stops, one angle being in the solid and one loose, the latter attached by a steady pin and screw, and, by tightening it, the stop is securely fixed to the slide. These are used to determine the lateral traverse of the slide in either direction, and are indispensable for work requiring a series of flutes or excavations of corresponding length; they are provided with adjusting screws through the centre, by which a finer degree of movement is obtained.

The pedestal of the slide-rest (Fig. 13) is planed square on each side throughout its entire length to a depth of $\frac{4}{8}$ in., and fitted to a metal cradle; this addition is of the utmost importance, as will be seen. The cradle has a substantial tenon on the under side, planed to fit the interval of the lathe-bed; two adjusting screws are then fitted to set it accurately in case of wear. It is then carefully planed on the upper side at right angles to fit the pedestal of the rest, one side having a loose strip with set-screws for final adjustment. The clamping or holding-down bolt passes through the tenon.

By this arrangement the pedestal can be moved at right angles to the lathe-bed, and refixed without fear of inaccuracy. On the top of the pedestal two steel pillars are fixed, and have through each an adjusting stop-screw, which has contact with a steel pillar fixed to the under side of the tee-slide; and by this means the main slide is set to operate on the surface or cylinder, and may be moved and reset with the greatest ease, without reference to set-squares of any kind. A metal ring is also fitted to the pedestal, for the purpose of elevating and depressing the point of the tool to the correct height of centre, also placing the same above or below the axis of the mandrel.

By this improvement it will be seen that the set-square and set-bevel as required to operate with Fig. 12 are practically superseded, and for such purposes may now be regarded as obsolete. The end of the main screw of Fig. 13 is carried through on the left side, and provided with a socket, to which the wheels of the spiral apparatus can be attached.

Fig. 14 illustrates a slide-rest of the latest design and most complete construction, being provided with every action that can be required. In many respects it is similar to Fig. 13, but the various extra movements attached to it are one and all of great service, and it may be regarded as a most perfect tool.

The pedestal is made 4 in. longer than Fig. 13, to admit of extended movement from the axis of the lathe transversely. The metal cradle is in every way a facsimile of Fig. 13, and the tee-slide is 18 in. long and proportionally substantial. The slide-rest last described is provided with the means of setting it accurately, either parallel or at right angles to the lathe-bed, and consequently any angle between these two points can be obtained and the slide fixed by the binding-screw; but it will be noticed that in Fig. 13 there is no means provided of ascertaining the precise angle the slide may assume, while in Fig. 14 it is decided in the following way :—

A metal arc is attached to the pedestal below the elevating ring, concentric to the cylinder fitting of the stem of the slide ; it is fixed between the pillars that denote the two positions of the rest and held by a screw passing through the base, the hole being elongated for the convenience of accurate adjustment ; the vertical face of the arc is divided from 0° to 90°, and a steel-pointed index fixed in the under side of the slide indicates the precise angle at which it is set. Therefore, when the rest is set to turn a cylinder, the index will read at 0°, and, when turned to the surface, it will point at 90°. This, however, is provided for by the stop-screw, and the object of the divided arc is to ascertain and repeat any angle that may be required between the parallel and right angle. 45° is an angle that is very often necessary, and is employed when cutting hemispheres with the eccentric cutter, also for a variety of other purposes.

On the tee or main slide of this rest a metal plate is fitted in some respects similar to that in Fig. 13, but extended on the front side with an arc at the front. This forms the base of the

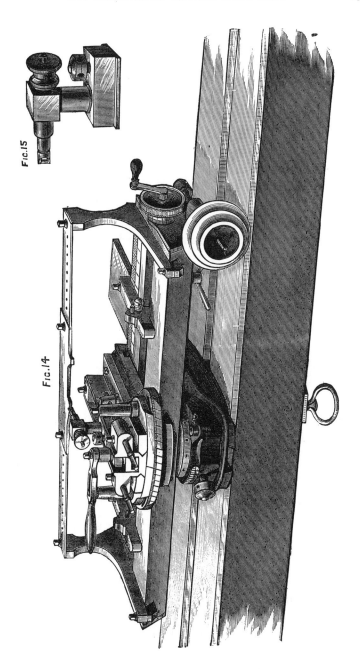

Fic.15

Fic.14

traversing slide, and to this a second plate is fitted to move upon a centre in the opposite side ; in the arc a semi-circular slot is cut out, through which a screw passes into the top slide to fix it to the lower plate. On the top of the second plate the tool-box is fitted to the steel double-chamfered bars in the like manner to Fig. 13, the clamps, &c., being fitted in the same way. The projection through which the depth and stop-screw pass have metal plugs let in, and the screws pass through a portion of them, so that, when the screws at the top are tightened, the main screws are fixed, or, when released, they are free.

The advantages of the slide which carries the tool-box turning on a centre and thus presenting the tool at different angles to the work are obviously very great indeed. Undercutting or dovetailed grooves may be produced, the shapes of the mouldings may be varied, pearls may be cut in relief, and in many instances the tool may be placed in contact with the work in such a way as without it would not be possible. The fluting stops, it will be seen, are fitted in a different way. In consequence of the arc projecting over the surface of the main slide, they cannot be fitted entirely across the bed of the slide, as in that previously alluded to ; they are there· fore shortened on the front side, and their holding power vested in one side of the interval in the slide and the opposite angle. They are fitted with improved spring readers to the adjusting screws, which cause the lines—that is, those on the screw-head and that on the indicator—to be always in close proximity, thus rendering a degree of accuracy not to be obtained by the screw simply passing through the centre. The stops fitted in this way are found to effect every purpose.

The left side of the screw is also provided with a socket to carry the spiral wheels.

On the right side of the slide is fitted an arrangement with worm-wheel and tangent screw, the micrometer on the screw being cut on its periphery to 75 teeth, a metal frame working underneath with a steel tangent-screw. This is thrown in and out of gear instantly by an ingenious lever-action, which was suggested by T. J. Ashton, Esq., and carried out by the author. For grailing or self-acting cuts it is a valuable addition, and can be applied to either the cylinder or surface. Grailing may be effected by the move-ment of the micrometer to a certain division, denoted by the reading line on the plate, and a double-angle tool inserted to a very slight depth at each movement; but this is a tedious and long job, requiring the greatest care. The effect of grailing work is so advantageous to all patterns cut upon the surface that it cannot be too strongly recommended, and it is produced with this action so much more quickly and correctly that the apparatus is justly considered a great acquisition. The result is actually a very fine screw, but this in no way deters or mars the beauty of the work. The lines may be made finer or coarser by altering the relative speeds at which the screw and the work rotate, but the lines, or rather the line (it being one continuous scroll), gives absolutely equidistant spaces. It is upon this that the beauty of such work depends, and when it is done in conse-cutive cuts by the movement of the main screw for each individual cut, it is, as before stated, a tedious, long, and somewhat uncertain matter. The cutting edge of the tool should receive special attention, as much depends upon it. With the self-acting motion, the tool cannot remain an undue length of time in any one part, which, in taking the consecutive cuts, it is likely to do, the result of which has a tendency to destroy the edge of the tool and create a slight difference in the appearance of the cut.

In the preparation of long cylinders or broad surfaces it has a great advantage, as, the tool being once set to the depth, it passes entirely over the work without further attention. For fluting also it is a most useful addition, and the divided scale on the surface of the main slide is a great assistance for this purpose. The exact contact of the slide with the fluting stop is not so accurately decided, but the index which points to the line on the slide will enable the lever to be moved out of gear at precisely the same division for each successive cut, and by reference to Fig. 16, which is an enlarged engraving of the action, it will be more readily understood. The worm-wheel is attached to the screw of the slide-rest; the end-plate which retains it in its place is extended at the underside, so that the frame which carries the tangent-screw can be pivoted through at one side; a right-angle lever is then fixed to the bottom of the main slide; the short arm which lies under the slide passes through a long mortise-slot in

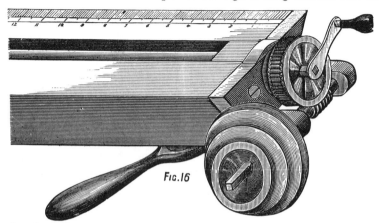

Fig. 16

the plate, the end of which is turned to a short cylinder, and works in a curved slot sunk in the frame that holds the screw, and, by moving the lever to the right or left, the screw is thrown in and out of gear instantly. The band may be crossed for the return cut, or the tool moved back to the starting point by the winch-handle, which is in some respects preferable. The scale on the main slide is divided in tenths, or at every turn of the screw, and figured at every inch.

The action of the tangent-screw gives such a regular traverse to the slide that it is vastly superior in this respect to that obtained by the winch-handle, although the latter is at times more appropriate. The slide-rest (Fig. 14), it will be seen, is fitted with the curvilinear apparatus attached to the slide in an improved fashion introduced by the author. This is fully explained in a future chapter devoted to the apparatus and its results.

CHAPTER XI.

AUTOMATIC STOPS.

A FURTHER development of the compound slide-rest and automatic stop is found in the illustration (Fig. 17 and 17A). The rest is provided with a second, or rather third, slide, and, as it slides also in a metal cradle, it is available as a fourth. The cradle is planed to fit the interval between the lathe-bed, and, again, at right angles to it; the lower slide is then planed to fit it, having a single bevel of about 30° on one side, the opposite being square, a set-screw passing through the side of the cradle to keep it always so. The under side has a dove-tail groove planed in it for the holding-down bolt. On this slide a substantial plate is fitted, with one angle cast in the solid and one loose strip adjusted by set-screws. This slide is actuated by a screw of ten threads to the inch, with a micrometer attached to it. In the centre of the plate a large metal socket is fitted, held by a steel washer of corresponding size on the under side, and this is fixed by a semicircular clip and screw, which passes through a short steel post in front of it. The centre of the metal socket is then bored out to fit the stem of the main slide, and, on the base of the socket, the pillars and stop screws, for setting the slide to surface or cylinder, are arranged; on the space between the same is a divided scale in degrees from 0 to 90, thus forming the means of obtaining the necessary angles between the two specified points, the slide being fixed by a screw passing through the lower rim of the socket.

The main slide and tool-box are both fitted with automatic actions, also the invention of T. J. Ashton, Esq., and form a most important improvement. The main slide is provided with fluting stops, which work automatically, and are fitted in the following

manner:—A metal frame carrying the tangent-screw is hinged on a
spindle; to one end of it is attached a driving-pulley having various

Fig.17.

Fig.17ª

speeds, and to the other end a toothed wheel gearing into an intermediate one; from thence to a third wheel, the latter being fixed

to the end of the shaft of the tangent-screw, the whole being fitted up on a metal block, which is attached to the bottom of the tee-slide, so that the tangent-screw will, by its own weight, fall out of gear with the worm-wheel. The mode of gearing is clearly shown by Fig. 17A.

The frame is retained in position by a catch, connected with a double lever, and runs the whole length of the main slide, being connected with the lever at one end. On the rod at each side of the traversing slide, which carries the tool-box, is fitted an adjust-able stop which can be fixed at any required point by a set-screw.

The action may be thus briefly described: A band from the overhead motion passes to the pulley, and by means of the wheel-gear (Fig. 17A) communicates the motion to the tangent-screw, and through the worm-wheel to the main screw, thus giving traverse to the tool-box.

The stops having been fixed on the rod at the required length of the flute, will, when pressed on by the advancing slide, so act on the lever of the catch that the tangent-screw immediately drops out of gear, and although the lathe is not stopped, the tool is at perfect rest. To make the next cut, the band may be crossed on the pulley, when a reverse traverse is the result; but as it is necessary that all finishing cuts should be made in the same direction, it is better to run the slide back by the winch-handle to the starting point, and place the frame in gear by raising it with the finger, when the succeeding cut is made.

The advantages effected by this arrangement are very great, and have been highly appreciated by many amateurs, who have used the self-acting rest.

The leading screw being driven from the overhead motion, both hands of the operator are perfectly free. In turning a cylinder, the relative speed of the lathe mandrel and the traverse of the slide is always the same, whether the fly-wheel be driven slowly or quickly; and the same remarks applies to the use of drills, or any of the cutters used in the different instruments, and thus all cuts, flutes, and mouldings, are produced with an exactitude, and freedom from the close attention otherwise required.

E

We pass now to the improvement in the upper slide, which carries the various tools and revolving cutters, affording greater facility in its use, and producing a mathematical precision in depth of cut, and consequent beauty of finish to the work.

The receptacle which holds the tool is constructed in the same manner as the ordinary rest, with the exception that the stop-screw and pillar, also the projection through which the screw passes on the right side, are done away with entirely, and only one screw is necessary. By reference to the outline engraving, Fig. 17* and letters thereon, the following details clearly indicate the advantages claimed by the improved action.

The screw, M, as will be seen, is of increased length, and works through the projection on the left side of the tool-box, its end passing through a frame, A, and cast in the solid, with the slide also marked A. On the end of the screw a micrometer $2\frac{5}{8}$ in. in

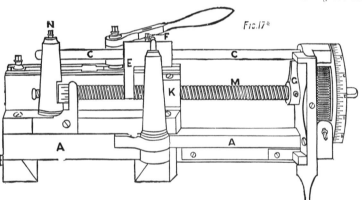

Fig. 17*

diameter is fitted, divided into hundredths of an inch, each division being again sub-divided by ten, so that each sub-division on the micrometer indicates one thousandth.

The front end of the screw has a collar fitted to it, bearing against the pillar, which is filed away to a flat surface to better accommodate it. A steel bridle the same as in the other rests, is fitted to retain it in its place, but can be easily detached when not required. A steel rod, c c, $\frac{3}{16}$ in. in diameter passes from the pillar to the frame, A, at which end a collar $\frac{7}{16}$ in. in diameter, is countersunk into the frame, and retained there by a small spiral spring.

A gun metal clamp, E, is fitted to slide on the rod, c c, and is fixed at any desired point by a set screw. The clamp is made semi-circular at the bottom, and is made to pass freely over the external diameter of the main screw.

A small steel arm, G, is fitted on the plain part of the screw, close to the face of the frame, A, and is fixed by a set screw when finally adjusted for work.

The adjustment and action of the apparatus thus made is as follows: The cut having been made to the required depth in the work by the gradual advance of the tool by means of the screw, M, the rod, c c, is pushed forward till the collar protrudes from the frame about $\frac{1}{20}$ in., and is held by the set screw, N, through the top of the pillar; the clamp, E, is then placed in close contact with the projection on the tool-box, and fixed to the rod, c c, by its set screw. The steel arm, G, is then turned round on the plain part of the screw till arrested by the collar projecting from the frame; the set screw, N, is then released, when the tool can be withdrawn to any extent; and on again advancing it, the rotation of the screw is arrested at precisely the same division of the micrometer at which it stood when the first cut was made, and the reason why such accuracy is obtained is manifested by the simplicity of its action.

Thus, the clamp, E, being fixed, the rotation of the screw, M, causes the wing of the tool-box to come in contact with it, drawing out the collar from the frame until further movement of the screw is prevented by the steel arm, G, which is fixed to it. The advantage in this arrangement is, that the propelling power and the stop both act in the same line, consequently there is no diagonal strain; and further, one hand only is required in its use. When worked in combination with the automatic fluting stops on the main slide, the work is executed with great accuracy in much less time than when done without their aid.

In concluding the remarks upon the slide-rest, it will be necessary to refer to that class of rest illustrated by Fig. 18, which is for the purpose of metal turning, and is also a most useful tool in the preparation of large and rough pieces of material, such as African blackwood, ivory, or in fact anything that may be considered beyond the capacity of the lighter slide-rests previously described. A stout gun-metal cradle is first fitted to the bed of the lathe, one side being planed to an angle, the opposite being square, with a steel strip between it and the cast-iron base, a screw passing through the side of the cradle to retain the rest always at a right angle to the bed. In the face of the lower slide a tee-groove is turned out, and in the centre of the plate a projection is left on which the main slide fits and revolves; two steel bolts with tee-heads are fitted to the groove and pass through two round holes in the base of the top slide, being tightened by hexagonal nuts with washers. This way of fitting up such a slide-rest is vastly superior to the original method, which consists of quadrant slots only, that simply admit of the rest

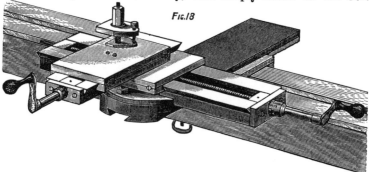

Fig. 18

being turned to a limited angle ; and if required for surface work the two bolts must be removed and replaced in different holes, or the cut must be taken over the surface with the top slide when moved to the extreme end of the lower slide. With the improved action which the author now adds to this particular slide-rest, by slackening the two nuts it can at once be moved to any desired angle, from its position of parallel to the lathe-bearers, to a right angle, or transversely across the bed to turn a surface; all of which are denoted by a divided scale.

The main slide is made longer than usual, which is found to be of considerable service, and is fitted with a screw of ten threads to the inch carried through at the end in order that the spiral apparatus may be adapted at any time. On the top of the main slide another one is fitted to work at right angles to it; for the purpose of setting in the depth of cut, and this is fitted with Professor Willis's tool-holder, provided with extra long centre-pin so that vertical slides or other useful adjuncts may be employed. The main screws are both covered, although not shown; this is to prevent the shavings and dirt getting to them, and prevents a deal of wear. The handles are fitted to the screws on a slightly taper fitting with a transverse mortise, and are divided close to the end into ten equal parts, and a line marked on the plate; this is a most useful addition for many purposes, especially screw-cutting.

Both for this latter purpose and also in ornamental turning, it is most desirable that the starting-point for all work requiring lateral traverse should commence at the zero on the micrometer, and in most cases it happens that the work and cutters are adjusted without reference to this, and not noticed until the tool is required to be moved in that direction, and to re-adjust it the micrometer can be set to zero and the slide-rest moved bodily along the bed until the point of the tool at its starting-point agrees with it. The necessity for this movement is avoided by having the micrometer fitted with an adjustable index which may be turned round until the 0 agrees with the reading line, no matter in what position the slide-rest is fixed.

It is made in the following manner: The end of the screw is turned down leaving a projection slightly beyond the metal plate; a ring of metal about $\frac{3}{8}$ in. wide is carefully fitted; the micrometer is then fitted to the same shaft, and beyond this a fine thread is cut and a milled head-nut to fit it, so that when any alteration in the position of the figures is required the nut is loosened and the index turned to the desired line, when the nut is again fixed. The winch-handle is fitted in the ordinary way, and does not interfere with the arrangement in the least. This power of adjustment is most valuable, and is now fitted to many of the best slide-rests.

The loss of time, or back-lash, inherent with most screws, especially those with square threads, is a feature which causes

great annoyance to turners; and much, if not all, is to be avoided
by the nut through which the screw passes being provided with
properly-fitted adjusting screws. The wear to such a screw will
in time admit of the nut being moved laterally upon the screw
without rotating the winch-handle; therefore, when the screw is
turned it moves a certain distance without carrying the slide.
This is of more serious consequence when the rest is connected to
the spiral apparatus, as, in such an instance, the work also
partially rotates without the corresponding lateral movement of
the slide. This will receive due reference in the chapter devoted
to spiral turning.

To avoid such loss of time, the nut should be severed about
$\frac{1}{2}$ in. from one end, before doing which two holes, one each side of
the screw, should be drilled, and that in the deepest portion of
the nut tapped to receive the set screws; the front is then countersunk to receive the heads. It will be seen by this, that by setting
up these screws the nut is tightened between the thread and space,
in consequence of which no end-play can occur, and, if carefully
adjusted, no loss of time in the screw need remain. It has been
found to answer in every way, and no slide-rest is allowed to leave
the works without being thus fitted.

CHAPTER XII.

SLIDE-REST TOOLS AND CUTTER-BARS.

THE ordinary tools made from square steel and forged at the end to the shape required are now seldom used except for special purposes, the cutter bars of various descriptions, having superseded them, and these, especially for amateurs, are a very considerable advantage, as they have short exchangeable cutters which are more easily ground, and do not require forging. The first of this class which bears special reference to the requirements of those who practise the art of plain and ornamental turning is the gouge cutter bar (Fig. 19). The stem is made to fit the tool box of the slide-rest, the front is bent to a suitable angle, so that the gouge when placed in contact with the semi-circular front fitting, the hollow of it will be presented to the work at the correct angle for cutting soft woods ; a steel strap passes over the frame and round the exterior of the blade, and a screw through the top fixes the tool firmly ; by releasing the screw the gouge can be adjusted to the height of centre. This has proved to be a most valuable adjunct, and for roughing over large material may be considered indispensable. A corresponding bar is made to hold flat chisels, but this is limited in its use, and has a decided propensity for intruding its corners, greatly to the detriment of the work. It is therefore of little service and not to be recommended, and the gouge previously alluded to if keenly sharpened will produce a surface as smooth as it is possible to require it.

Fig. 20 illustrates a cutter-bar necessary to the turning or boring of deep cylinders or internal work, and it has many advantages. The stem in this case is made to fit the tool box, and is forked at the end, so that a cylinder bar may pass through it a right angles to the stem. At the end of the rod a cutter is fitted, at such an angle that its cutting point is just beyond the end of the screw which fixes it in the centre, and is identical with the axis of the lathe; this at the same time is adjustable by

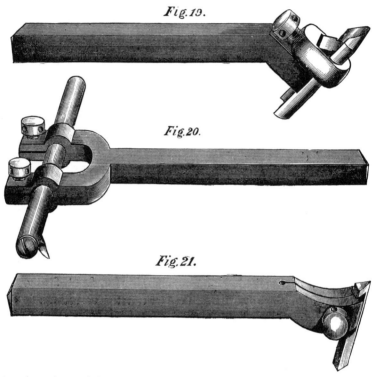

Fig. 19.

Fig. 20.

Fig. 21.

turning the rod in whichever direction is necessary, and fixing it by two screws as seen in the engraving.

When using this tool, deep internal work may be performed without turning the slide-rest round to the surface, and the full depth of the cut taken by one continuous movement of the main screw of the slide-rest; thus, supposing a deep box is desired, the exterior is turned with an ordinary tool or cutter-bar, as may be considered best. It is then required to turn out the inside and by placing the cutter-bar (Fig. 20) in the rest; it is done with considerable facility by one continuous cut. To effect the same object without its aid, the slide-rest must be placed transversely across the lathe, and the tool inserted by the depth and stop-screws, the capacities of which are, in many cases, insufficient for the depth of work. It will be seen that the rod which holds the tool may be increased in length, or reduced if less extension is necessary. For such work it is a most important addition, and is now largely used. It was invented and introduced by the author.

Fig. 21 is a cutter-bar designed for metal turning. The stem is fitted in the same way ; in the front a triangular hole is filed at the necessary angle ; the cutters are easily made, and may be adjusted

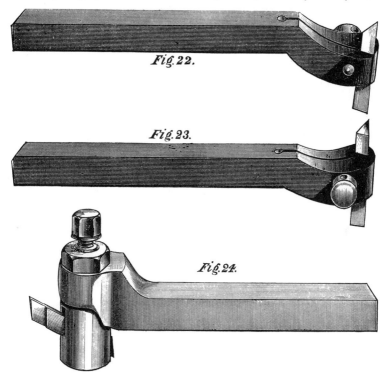

Fig. 22.

Fig. 23.

Fig. 24.

to height of centre. The edge may be sharp, round, or flat, to suit the material to be operated upon, and by grinding the top face, a more or less acute cutting angle is obtained. This tool, although appropriated to metal turning as a rule, may be applied to roughing-over ivory of uneven surface, which is more easily done with a sharp pointed tool.

Figs. 22 and 23 are tools for the same purpose, but bent in opposite directions, so that the cutting edge is presented to the right or left side of the work, and for such work as require their services they are most useful tools. The engravings show clearly what they are intended for; they therefore need no further explanation.

Fig. 24 is a very ingenious universal cutter-bar, invented by Mr. Garvin Jones, and supplies the three in one. It will be observed that at the front of the stem a socket is fitted, which carries the tool at the correct angle; on the top a nut with a left-hand thread is fitted, and when this is released the tool may be set to the front to turn a cylinder, or to either side for face work, when it is fixed by a screw at the top with a right-hand thread. This is a very useful tool, and is largely used in factories. It is also employed with excellent results in the planing machine. They are made as large as 2 in. in the stem for very heavy work. There are very many descriptions of cutter-bars, but further reference is unnecessary as those already detailed will be sufficient to establish the excellence of such forms over the original fixed tool.

CHAPTER XIII.

Tools Appropriate to the Ornamental Slide-rest.

The general advance in the improvements connected with the ornamental turning slide-rest gave rise to an equally valuable re-arrangement of the necessary tools to be employed in it. The slide-rest in the early period of its history, having screws of indefinite value, bore no reference to the tool beyond moving it a certain distance laterally.

The introduction of a screw of aliquot value renders the slide-rest more easy to manipulate, combined with the great advantage of as near absolute accuracy as possible, and the various tools now to be described are all made of definite widths in hundredths, so that the lateral traverse of the slide will carry them precisely their own width; as an instance, a tool $\frac{10}{100}$ in. wide will, by one turn of the screw be moved through the space of its cutting surface, while one half-turn of the screw effects the same on a tool $\frac{5}{100}$ in. wide. This has been referred to with respect to the details of the slide-rest in previous chapters, and will from time to time during the descriptions of the various specimens receive further notice.

Before using the small slide-rest tool as illustrated, the material should be reduced to approximate form by stronger tools, such as the gouge-cutter bar (Fig 19), either in the ornamental slide-rest, or, if the work is of very large diameter and proportionate unevenness, it is preferable to employ the metal-turning slide-rest (Fig. 18), as the lighter one, from its construction, is likely to be somewhat disorganised by being subjected to work beyond its capacity.

Fig. 25, the first of this class of tool, is a round-nosed tool, and s used for turning concave curves and hollows of different shapes.

It may be mentioned that all the tools to be described are made in sizes from $\frac{5}{100}$ to $\frac{30}{100}$ or $\frac{35}{100}$ in, wide, and at times of even greater width, and are now made of one uniform length of 3 in, in. preference to the original plan of decreasing the length in proportion to the blade.

Fig. 26, a double angle or point tool. This is largely used for cutting or tracing the very fine surface patterns, produced by the

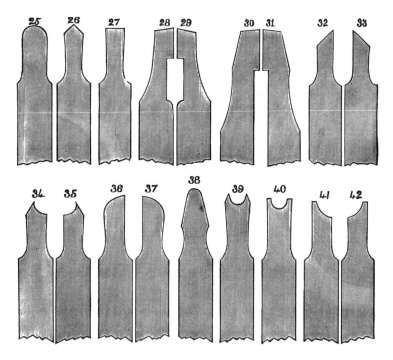

ornamental chucks in combination. It is also employed for grailing the surface of the work previous to its being ornamented, and for cutting deep V or angular grooves ; it has also many other purposes.

Fig. 27 is a square end, otherwise a chisel, also applicable to a variety of work. For cutting steps or recesses it is found very handy; it is made to cut on both sides, and may be used to finish the interior of a box-lid, and by withdrawing the cut carefully the fitting may also be finished at the same time.

Figs. 28 and 29 are right and left-hand side tools, they are used principally for excavating boxes or similar articles; the ends are ground to a slight angle to leave the point prominent so that the cut may be carried quite into a corner and made square with the surface at its base; for instance, the surface having been turned, when the tool arrives at the internal diameter the tool is withdrawn leaving the work perfectly clean and sharp.

Figs. 30 and 31 are tools of a similar description, but made on an improved plan introduced by the author, and the advantage of being thus constructed consists in the cutting edge projecting at the side, so that the depth to which they can be inserted is not limited as in Figs. 28 and 29, which it will be seen have the cutting edges level with the shaft of the tool. In this form they can be ground away until the projection is nearly gone, and still penetrate as deeply as before. They are now made in this way and found to supersede the original shape.

Figs. 32 and 33 are right and left single angle tools, made to a variety of angles to suit the various works, these are also employed for surface patterns and cutting angular recesses, and for many purposes connected with plain turning.

Figs. 34 and 35, represent quarter hollows, right and left with pointed terminals, and are necessary to the production of corresponding quarter rounds, and are much used to obtain the form of the work previous to its being operated upon by a drill or other cutter for seriated mouldings.

Figs. 36 and 37 are the reverse of these, being quarter round, right and left; therefore their employment results in the production of quarter hollows. These are also most useful for turning portions of mouldings, which may afterwards receive further decorations by the corresponding tools of shorter length, revolving in any of the several cutter-frames.

Fig. 38 illustrates one of the most useful of this series of tools, and is called a roughing or routing tool. It is employed for a number of different purposes, notably for turning down long cylinders or shaping up work with curved ends; it is also a tool particularly essential to the spherical slide rest, as it cuts more cleanly during its descent round the sphere, consequent upon its cutting edge extending round the sides. It is necessary also when using the curvilinear apparatus, as the continued curve of the front enables the tool to be more easily traversed over the undulations of the template.

Figs. 39 and 40 comprise two important factors —namely, bead-tools, Fig. 39 being pointed at the end, while Fig. 40 is astragal, or square. They are used in the production of beads of various sizes, either in close proximity or distant one from the other. The result of the two kinds is very distinct

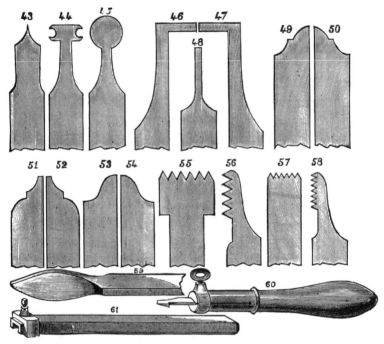

Figs. 41 and 42 are similar to Figs. 34 and 35, the only difference being that they are astragal at the end instead of pointed.

Fig. 43. In this tool, which is a double quarter hollow, especial use is found when employed in conjunction with the dome-chuck, for cutting reeds in close proximity, that is of course when a fixed tool is preferred. But as will be pointed out in future chapters,

the same result is better obtained with a revolving cutter of the
same description.   When placed in the socket-handle (Fig. 60), it
may also be used as a hand tool for a large variety of purposes.

Fig. 44 brings before our notice a tool which is necessary to
the turning of rings, and is therefore termed a ring-tool.   It will
be observed that it has two semicircular cutting edges, one on
each side of the shaft, and these identical in form.   To turn a
number of rings that may be required all alike the material is
bored to a tube, the size of the inside diameters.   The tool is
then inserted while the slide-rest is at right angles to the bed, the
depth being decided by the stop-screw of the top slide ; it is then
penetrated laterally into the material by the screw of the slide-rest,
until the form of the bead is cut; it is then withdrawn and passed to
the outer diameter, the same depth being maintained.   The cut is
then carried back in the reverse way, and when the bead is cut on
that side, the ring will be detached and perfect in shape.   In this
way, employing a series of different sized tools, the chains forming
part of the candelabra (Plate 13) were made.

Fig. 45, a ball or spherical tool, is used principally for undercut or for shaping concave curves, and may be found of equal
service either in the slide-rest or as a hand tool.

Figs. 46 and 47 combine the right and left side parting tools,
and are devoted to the cutting out of rings, and, in the case of
ivory being worked, they are a means of saving a deal of valuable
material.   As an instance, assuming that a large and solid piece
of ivory is to be shaped, from which a deal of the interior is to be
removed, the same may be cut out in substantial rings, which are
always worth saving.   To effect this, the ivory is turned out at the
centre to admit the blade of the tool (Fig. 47), it is then inserted
by the guide-screw to the depth required, and by the lateral
traverse of the slide-rest the blade of the tool is carried into the
material its own depth, or less, according to circumstances.   The
tool is then removed, and with the front parting tool (Fig. 48)
it is cut through from the face opposite the end of the incision
made by Fig. 47, when the ring will be released.   In some instances
it is necessary to remove the substance from the margin of the

work, and not the centre. The same process is then performed with the opposite tool (Fig. 46). These tools are made of various widths and lengths. When of considerably less dimensions than those illustrated, and with rounded points, they are used to recess the back of an internal screw.

Fig. 48 is simply a parting, but when made of a short and appropriate length it is used as a fixed tool in the slide-rest for cutting the different patterns illustrated on Plate 7, executed by the eccentric chuck.

Figs. 49, 50, 51, 52, 53, and 54 are examples of figure or moulding tools. These require to be very carefully made, and render some very beautiful forms, which may be then cut with corresponding tools of less length, revolving in the several instruments, such as the horizontal, universal, or vertical cutters. In the first named, the tools may be applied in their full length. Those illustrated are only a very few of the different shapes that are made, but they will serve the purpose of explaining their employment.

Figs. 55, 56, 57, and 58 are illustrative of the screw-chasers, which are made to match the screw-guides of the traversing mandrel, and for cutting short screws are of valuable assistance. These, also, are largely employed as hand tools.

Fig. 59. In this we have a parting tool constructed to withstand considerably more pressure than Fig. 48 is capable of resisting. It was introduced by the author at the suggestion of an amateur turner, who fractured many of the original plan, and it has been found most satisfactory. By reference to the engraving it will be seen that the blade not only extends below the shaft or stem of the tool, but above in a similar way, thus creating a resistance against the pressure of the work as it revolves. The cutting edge is still maintained in a line with the surface of the tool, and no alteration is required with regard to the height of centre. As a proof of their excellence, it is found that though many are made but few are broken.

Having concluded the few remarks essential to the introduction of these tools, the socket-handle (Fig. 60), which forms the means of employing them as hand tools, is now to be explained. The metal socket which holds the tool has a mortise hole of the required size made in it; it is then cut through the centre into a hole drilled through the end near the handle; a steel ring with a fixing screw is then fitted to the end, so that when the tool is placed in the slot it is readily held by the screw. This handle is a very necessary adjunct, and by its aid the tools already described can be used for a double purpose.

Fig. 61 is made so that the same tools may be extended in length to a greater distance from the slide-rest, which at times it is necessary to do. A steel bar is made to fit the tool receptacle, and planed out at the end to receive the tools, the recess being deep enough to allow the face to draw up to the same centre as if placed in the tool box. To fix the tool a steel strap is fitted over the stem and will move to any part; a steel binding-screw passes through and holds the tool firmly in its place.

CHAPTER XIV.

The Eccentric Cutter.

WHEN the art of ornamental turning is commenced it is generally the eccentric cutter, the drilling instrument, and the vertical cutter that first claim attention, and form the primary study.

The intention of the author to pass by the group of fine line decorative patterns confined to the surface only, and upon which much has been written in works already published, has been referred to in the introduction. It remains therefore to proceed at once with the detailed description of the manufacture and

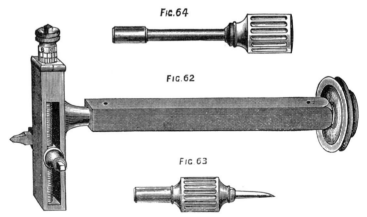

Fig.64

Fig.62

Fig.63

manipulation of the instruments that are to be employed for the more advanced work, comprised in the formation of elegant designs, compound solid forms, polygonal figures, caskets, &c., which are endless in variety, and afford a most interesting pursuit.

The eccentric cutter (Fig. 62) is constructed in the following way :—A square stem is fitted to the tool box of the slide-rest; it is then bored through, and turned out at each end to receive two steel-hardened collars. A steel spindle, to which is attached a right angle slide, is then accurately fitted to revolve in the stem. On the rear end a steel pulley is fitted, having in the front a collar with a cone to fit that contained in the collar in the stem. The pulley is held to the spindle by a flat on the end, and a screw in the spindle. The right angle slide is made to carry a small tool-box or receptacle to hold the various tools as required. This is actuated by a main screw of equal value, 10 threads to the inch, but from the fact of its being so small in diameter it is necessary to make it a multiple pitch; consequently it has four threads. To the opposite extremity of the tool-box a steel washer and clamping-screw are fitted. The main screw is retained in its place by a metal plate fitted to the slide, against which the collar on the screw bears. A metal micrometer is then fitted to the screw, and divided into 10 equal parts, which read to $\frac{1}{100}$ of an inch; it is again sub-divided with intermediate short lines to read to $\frac{1}{200}$ of an inch. By these divisions it will be seen that the tool may be moved along the slide in equal ratio with the slides of the eccentric and other chucks, &c. The centre of the instrument is coincident with the axis of the spindle, the face of the right angle slide being filed to the exact half, and when the tool is fixed in the centre, which for testing purposes should be a double angle, it will cut a minute dot upon touching the work. The zero line on the micrometer must then correspond with the index line on the end plate of the slide.

The value of the screw being 10 to the inch, it will be noticed that each complete turn will move the tool $\frac{1}{10}$ of an inch from the centre, three turns $\frac{3}{10}$, and so on; the tool cutting a circle double the size of the radius to which it is extended: for example, if the tool is advanced three turns of the main screw, the circle cut would be $\frac{6}{10}$ of an inch in diameter, if moved ten whole turns the circle will be two inches; the proportion being of course the same if the movement is divided by the intermediate lines on the micrometer.

When setting out the radius of the eccentric cutter for any particular pattern, it must not be forgotten that it refers to the tool at its centre line. For instance, a moulding tool similar to any of those from Figs. 82 to 93, set out $\frac{5}{10}$, would cut a circle 1 in.

F 2

in diameter at its centre, therefore the extra width of the tool must be considered when adjusting the radius; that is, if the extreme diameter is required to be one inch.

The eccentric cutter is also largely used when decorating black wood with ivory, as it is capable of cutting out larger circles than can be effected by a drill.

A further development of its resources is found in its application to the shaping of square, hexagonal, and polygonal figures, both on the surface or in the form of pillars, &c. Plate 1 illustrates a few examples of this class of work. Fig. 1, in the first place, is reduced to a cylinder $1\frac{1}{4}$ in. in diameter, and turned down at each end to $\frac{7}{8}$ in. in diameter, or just below the sides of the square; when thus turned the eccentric cutter is placed in the slide-rest, having a round-nosed cutter (Fig. 70) in the tool-box; the eccentricity is set out by the main screw of the instrument to cut a circle sufficiently large in diameter to bring up the corners of the square. When so far adjusted, the cut should be inserted by the depth screw of the top slide, and then traversed the entire length of the material by the main screw. It will be obvious that, by rotating the pulley a fourth of its diameter, and repeating the process each time, a square is produced; should the corners not be quite sharp, the eccentricity must be slightly extended and the cut carried deeper. So far we shall have produced a plain square, but, by reference to Fig. 1, it will be seen to have a series of cuts, each deeper and less in length than the first. To effect this, the eccentricity must be reduced to cut a circle the size of the recess required; the fluting stops are then employed to arrest the cut at each end, by which it will be observed the end of each is left circular, the diameter of the circle depending upon the radius the tool is cutting. To cut the second step the eccentricity is again reduced, and the tool advanced to the necessary depth. When cutting out the recesses the round-nosed tool is replaced by one with a square end; and the process repeated four times.

Fig. 2 represents a different pattern. It was in the first place cut to a plain square, then recessed in the same way as Fig. 1; it was afterwards cut in the following manner: the eccentricity of the cutter

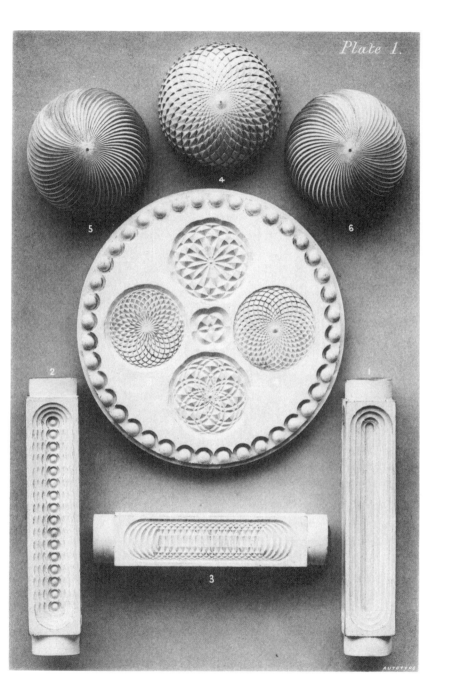

Plate 1.

slightly extended and the tool inserted to the depth of the first step; the first cut, therefore will be when the tool is arrested by the fluting stop, in which case the micrometer on the slide-rest screw should stand at zero, or the number at which it does point be noted; the tool is then withdrawn and moved laterally by the main screw of the slide rest two whole turns, $\frac{2}{10}$, and the second cut made; this is repeated along the whole length of each step. When the four are thus cut, the eccentric cutter is removed, and the drill spindle substituted having a bead-drill $\frac{12}{100}$ wide. The drill is returned to the centre of the first cut, being arrested by the fluting stop; it is then penetrated to the depth required to bring up the bead, and is inserted at every second turn of the main screw. It will be seen at a glance the wide difference in effect obtained by this comparatively simple alteration in the manipulation of the instrument.

Fig. 3 is again varied, and although a very simple pattern to produce, is most effective. As in the two former cases it is first cut to a plain square, after which a double angle tool of 45° is used in place of the round-nosed tool, the diameter of the circle reduced to the required size, and the tool inserted to bring up the pattern sharp, the lateral movement of the screw being one turn, $\frac{1}{10}$. This kind of pattern may be extended to a large degree by various alterations in the movement of the main screw; for example, take the first cut and move the screw one turn, or $\frac{1}{10}$, withdraw the tool, and for the next cut move the screw $\frac{1}{20}$, or half a turn, and cut again; for the third cut move the slide $\frac{1}{10}$ and repeat the movements alternately. The intersection of the circles at varying distances is most effective, and very beautiful effects result from such combinations.

We have thus far considered the eccentric cutter, as applied to the shaping and decorating of square pillars, &c. It is desirable now to take a brief view of the same instrument when used for the ornamentation of the surface by deep cutting, and the four primary examples illustrated in the centre figure of Plate 1 will suffice to demonstrate the fact that a wide difference is produced by a very simple alteration in the adjustment of the settings. This particular subject affords an opportunity of explaining the manner in which the four examples are so placed by the aid of the eccentric chuck, which will receive further demonstration in a future chapter.

In the first place the work is mounted on the eccentric chuck, carefully surfaced with a sharp tool, and polished. The slide of the chuck is then moved out $1\frac{1}{10}$—11 turns of the main screw— to enable the four separate patterns to be placed as seen in the illustration. Having set out the slide of the chuck, the tool is moved towards the operator $7\frac{1}{2}$ turns, which will cause it to cut a circle $1\frac{1}{2}$ in. in diameter. This is repeated at each quarter of the dividing wheel, 96, 24, 48, 72. The fixed tool is then replaced by the eccentric cutter, and a double angle tool of 40° employed. The first of the four (Fig. 1) is an extremely simple example, and is generally known as the barley-corn. There are twelve consecutive cuts, the division of 96 on the dial-plate being used, arrested at every 8th hole, the tool being allowed to penetrate $\frac{3}{20}$ deep, which will bring the points of the pattern to the shape required.

Fig. 2, it will be observed, is different in its appearance through a simple alteration in the adjustment of the division. It is cut with precisely the same tool and the same amount of penetration, but first cut at every twelfth hole of the same circle; the dial plate is then moved forward two holes, and the tool again inserted at every twelfth hole from that point, thus rendering the pattern as seen.

Fig. 3, it will be noticed, differs widely again, a left side tool of 55° (Fig. 67) being employed, while every fourth division is used, by which twenty-four cuts result, the angle on the outer diameter being caused by the figure of the tool being presented in that direction.

Fig. 4, it will be seen, presents all the points in exactly the reverse direction, which is caused by simply replacing the left side tool by a right side of the same angle (Fig. 68), the latter being on the reverse side to that which cut Fig. 3, the outer diameter is carried in square. These four patterns, simple and comparatively insignificant as they are, will be all that are required to illustrate the action of the instrument for such work, and it is almost needless to say the variety may be extended to any degree. The circle of large beads round the edge of the box lid were executed with a bead tool, also used in the eccentric cutter, being set, of course, to the centre of the instrument, in which case it answers the purpose of a drill and effects a similar result. The same may be cut with a drill if preferred, but these examples were cut entirely with the eccentric cutter to illustrate its capabilities.

Following the various uses that this instrument may be devoted to, we arrive at its application to the dome or hemisphere, and on such forms very beautiful work is produced. In this class of work the tool may be used to shape up the work to a very great extent in the first instance.

Fig. 4, Plate 1, may be styled the primary example of this description of ornamentation. To proceed with work of this character, the material should be first roughly shaped by hand-turning to the form required; presuming that a hemisphere is desired, after the form is roughed out, the eccentric cutter with a round nose tool is placed in the slide rest, the eccentricity extended to cut the diameter of the dome, and the slide-rest turned to an angle of 45°. The tool is then advanced to remove as much material as is necessary, and revolved at a high speed while the work is slowly rotated by hand, or preferably by the worm-wheel and tangent screw of the segment apparatus : by this operation it will be found that the bare form is accurately shaped. The eccentricity is then reduced and a double angle tool of 55° substituted for the round nose one. To cut such a pattern, the slide-rest must be set to bring the tool very accurately to the centre of the lathe-axis, in order that all the points may radiate to the centre.

Fig. 5, it will be observed, is of a totally distinct character, prepared in the first instance in exactly the same way, the slide-rest being set to the same angle ; which is necessary in all cases where a hemisphere is to be ornamented. The slide-rest for the pattern under notice is then elevated $\frac{1}{10}$ above the centre of the lathe-axis and a single angle tool, left side 55°, used in place of the double angle. The penetration must be only sufficient to bring the edge of the figure up sharp, or the true form of the hemisphere will be destroyed.

Fig. 6 will show most clearly that a very small and simple alteration in the arrangement of the tools will give a wide range of effect in the figure produced, and, as in the present case, it is only to depress the tool to $\frac{1}{10}$ below the centre instead of elevating it above, there is really no further explanation necessary with respect to these so far primary examples of the productions of the eccentric cutter. When adjusting the tool above or below the centre, it is necessary to do so in accordance with the depth of cut required. If the tool is allowed to penetrate deeper than the depression or elevation will admit, without touching the opposite side, the desired effect will be destroyed.

The eccentric cutter is also largely used, in conjunction with all the ornamental chucks, for the shaping and ornamenting of compound solid forms: this will be again referred to as the subjects are approached.

CHAPTER XV.

Eccentric Cutters.

These tools are illustrated by Figs. 65 to 81, and it will be seen in most instances they are precisely similar in form to those previously described as appertaining to the slide-rest. They differ, however, in size, being made to fit into the tool-box of the eccentric cutter. Although they will be recognised in form as similar to those already described, they have each a widely different part to perform when employed for the purposes for which they are intended. They vary in width, from $\frac{3}{100}$ to $\frac{25}{100}$, in some cases even wider, being extended beyond the stems, but this would only be required for a special purpose.

Fig. 65 is a double angle tool largely employed for surface patterns, either of a light and shallow character suitable for printing, &c., or for the deeply-cut barley-corn pattern illustrated by Figs. 1 and 2, in the centre of Plate 1. They are usually made about $\frac{15}{100}$ in. wide at the cutting portion, and ground to various angles from 10° to 60°, and are marked on the face to denote the angle or width, as seen in Figs. 65 to 79.

Fig. 66 is of the same character, but for some purposes is very much more useful from the fact of its being made to cut at the same angle its entire width. In cutting a very deep pattern, it has been found that the limit in the width of the blade is a distinct disadvantage, and that the pattern could not be brought up in consequence of the side of the tool penetrating the work and so destroying the figure required; therefore, in many instances, Fig. 66 may be employed with much better result, as the cutting edge has the angle carried through the whole width.

Figs. 67 and 68 are right and left single angle tools, and although in most instances applied in the same manner as Figs. 65 and 66, the result obtained is of a distinct character. This will also be seen by reference to the centre medallion in Plate 1; as already intimated, Fig. 3 was cut with the left side tool (Fig. 67), while Fig. 4 was executed with its companion (Fig. 68). Now the result of the two tools is, that the terminal points are directed in different ways, equally effective; but at the same time, the variation is so apparent that it shows the opposite character of the tools enables them to be used for distinct purposes.

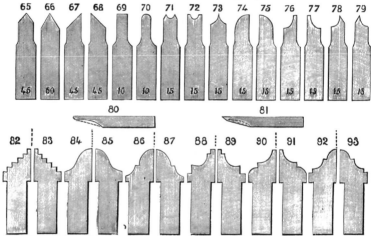

Fig. 69 is a chisel or square-end tool, and valuable for smoothing surfaces or recessing the fillets of moulding on square pedestals. These tools are also made from $\frac{3}{100}$ to $\frac{25}{100}$ in. wide, and should cut on the sides as well as on the ends, the cutting edges being well relieved. Such a tool would be used to recess the square pillar seen in Fig. 1, Plate 1, also Fig. 2 in the same plate, and is of equal service for such patterns as are illustrated by Plate 2, when it is placed in the small saddle (Fig. 96).

Fig. 70, being a round-nosed tool, is of great service for roughing out the bare form, whether it is a hemisphere, square, hexagon, or any other shape; and is much used in the vertical or other revolving instruments when shaping up mouldings, either of a continued, or seriated form.

Figs. 71 and 72 are tools that are continually in use when ornamental turning, and may be used in the various revolving instruments, but are more generally employed in the universal cutter when used in any of its obtainable positions. They are a most essential tool to this instrument when employed for reeding columns in connection with the spiral apparatus, or for straight reeds. Reference will be found with respect to these, as having also been used in the vertical cutter for the patterns illustrative of that instrument in Plate 2.

Fig. 73, a double-quarter hollow, is, perhaps, one of the most difficult tools to make in a perfect form. This is also used for reeding in various forms, especially where the reeds are required in close proximity, and it will be found that in cutting a taper shaft, or hemisphere, that the gradually varying diameter causes the shape of the reed to be different at the centre, or smaller than it is at the margin. This does not destroy the effect however, and is explained simply that it may not be regarded as an error. It is necessary to be very particular when spacing the work, in order that the full quadrant of the tool, and that only, may be employed; if only a portion of it is allowed to cut, the reed will be more of an elliptic shape and not semi-circular.

Figs. 74 and 75 represent quarter-round tools which are necessary for the production of various mouldings, and are used in the horizontal or universal cutter, they are available also for cutting long continuous mouldings, by the traverse of the slide-rest; or for seriated scollops; they are also used in the eccentric cutter, where the terminals are required of their shape.

Figs. 76, 77, 78, and 79 are the quarter-hollows, pointed and astragal, employed for a similar purpose to Figs. 74 and 75, but to produce the reverse forms, and are indispensable for many mouldings.

Figs. 80 and 81 represent the side views showing the manner in which the back of these tools are shaped. Fig. 80 it will be seen is hollowed at the back of the blade, this is to reduce the friction as much as possible, and is advantageous when only light work is required of it; but Fig. 81 shows an improved form, which is

simply filed at an angle, the dotted lines representing the curve
given to Fig. 80, shows clearly the amount of substance removed,
which is sufficient evidence that the tool must by this means be
much weakened, and the stronger tool (Fig. 80) is more substantial altogether, especially for deep cutting.

Figs. 82 to 93 represent moulding tools to be used in the
eccentric or any of the revolving cutters. These tools were introduced by the author some years ago, and are most valuable for
cutting deep and bold mouldings. When employed in the eccentric
cutter, they may be made to perform the part of a drill, by
adjusting the right side, or dotted line, to the centre of the instrument, and the power vested in the eccentric cutter from the
impetus gained by the revolution of the right angle slide, enables
most beautiful work to be done by it, and finished in one cut,
instead of having to use two or three tools to produce the same
result.

Figs. 83, 85, 87, 89, 91, 93, show the same tools made as
duplicates, and when these are used as drills the centre line is still
on the right side, but the figure being made on the reverse
side when used as a drill the result obtained is a pyramid, the
exact counterpart of the figure of the tool. These tools are also
largely used for cutting mouldings, either in the horizontal, vertical, or universal cutters, and when the figure is required on both
sides of any portion of the work, the tools being made in pairs, the
mouldings are produced exactly alike. Placed in the socket (Fig. 5),
used for holding the eccentric cutters in the goneostat, and held in
the socket handle (Fig. 60), they may be used as hand-tools, or in
the slide-rest as fixed tools, to produce their shapes on the work
prior to cutting the same with the revolving instruments. These
tools have been proved to be very valuable indeed for the purposes
for which they are intended.

It is scarcely necessary to state that the eccentric cutters are
available for the various instruments, such as the eccentric cutter,
the rose cutter, the epicycloidal cutter, the elliptical cutter, and
by using the small saddle, Fig. 96, are held in the instruments
which have mortise holes of the larger size.

CHAPTER XVI.

The Vertical Cutter.

THERE are several instruments by which vertical cutting may be effected, either the universal cutter, the horizontal cutter, or that now under notice, there are two or three ostensibly for the purpose, and as the frame, from its size, is more convenient, Fig. 94 is generally used for such work. The engraving is illustrative of

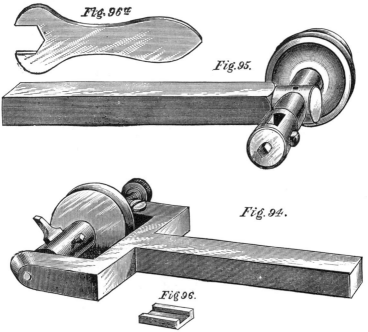

Fig. 96ª

Fig. 95.

Fig. 94.

Fig 96.

the instrument; the spindle revolves between two centres, one of which is fixed in the left side of the rectangular frame, while on the opposite side of the frame a centre-screw is arranged. The latter is adjustable, and fixed with a screw, the side of the frame being split so that it closes tightly round it. The left side, that in which the dead centre is fixed, is chamfered to an acute angle, so that the frame may be placed in closer contact with the work. It may here be mentioned that the inability to present this cutter-frame in close proximity to work upon which deep shoulders are attached, is one of its drawbacks. It has pulleys of different diameters, so that the tool may be set at various radii. The saddle (Fig. 96) is for the purpose of employing the eccentric cutters, and (96a) the spanner for removing the pulley. Fig. 95 represents another style of vertical cutter, which was invented by Dr. Stodart. This is a more convenient instrument in many ways, its chief advantage consisting in its ability to approach the flange or shoulder of the work. The spindle, it will be seen, revolves in a steel collar, which is fixed in the end of the stem at a right angle to it. The mortise in which the tool is held is made near the end of the spindle, and the driving-pulley fixed to the opposite extremity; by this means the cutter can be carried close to a shoulder with every facility. The tools illustrated by Figs. 109 to 117 are made to project over the extreme end of the spindle, and so the cutting edge has nothing to prevent its approach to the work.

It has been suggested that, made in this way, the spindle is likely to wear to a slight angle from the continuous pressure of the band, and ultimately to occasionally stick fast. This has been proved to be quite an erroneous idea if the instrument is correctly made, and it is considered by well-known amateurs to be the most convenient design of vertical cutter. In adjusting the instrument for use, there are two points to be considered—first, the radius at which the tool is extended from the centre of the spindle, secondly, the width of the tool to be employed, which should be of a definite size, so that the movement laterally may be more conveniently determined by a corresponding traverse of the main screw of the slide-rest in equal ratio, or as may be otherwise required, and denoted by the divisions on the micrometer. The penetration is governed entirely by the guide and stop-screw of the top slide, the bridle being always on, so that the slide is moved independently of the lever, which is now seldom used.

Mouldings of various patterns may be cut with a series of tools, or to a certain extent with one tool in which the whole figure is contained; but in most cases the separate tools are preferred. Those objects which are curved or conical may be orna-mented with satisfactory result, without the aid of the curvilinear apparatus, but the greatest care must be exercised with regard to the depth of each series of cuts, taking care that the original outline is maintained throughout. Should the turner, however, be possessed of the curvilinear apparatus, much trouble will be saved and greater accuracy attained.

The cuts may be arranged in a number of different ways upon cylindrical or taper forms, some in contact, while in others an interval is left between each; there is in fact no end to the varia-tions to be produced.

The following simple examples suitable for serviette holders, will suffice to illustrate a few of the minor patterns to be cut, and at the same time explain the manipulation of the instrument for the production of this kind of work.

In the first place the rings are all turned out to the same size inside, in order that one chuck may do for all, thus saving a deal of time: for this purpose a piece of well seasoned boxwood is driven into a metal chuck, preferably of less diameter than the material. Chucking work of all kinds should always claim great attention from the amateur turner, as efficiency in this branch of turning renders the work very much more easy and enjoyable, for there is nothing more annoying, as previously intimated, than to find the work has been gradually shifting on or in the chuck, during its progress, or to discover that it is split through being driven too hard on to the chuck.

To hold rings similar to those under notice the following few hints may be serviceable: The chuck should be turned very slightly taper and the ring fitted to it, then gently tapped on with the handle of a tool or a light mallet, and set quite true, which if correctly fitted will not be found a difficult matter. There are, as will be seen, several distinct applications of the cutter to the work, the continual rotating of the winch handle causing the removal of uninterrupted segments of circles, the length of each being determined by the fluting stops.

Fig. 1, Plate 2, is a perfectly simple application of the instrument, and may be considered a primary example. The slide-rest is placed parallel to the lathe bearers; the vertical cutter is then placed in the tool-box and adjusted to the exact height of the lathe-axis, and the tool extended to a radius $\frac{7}{10}$, a round-nosed tool being employed. The fluting stops are then set, one on each side, to arrest the traverse of the slide at the desired length. The necessary depth is ascertained by trial, and, so adjusted, that the terminal cut will bring up the pattern without reducing the diameter of the work. In this way the first and second cuts are made, and if a small space is left between them the tool must be advanced to cut deeper, and when once set, the stop-screw is fixed. The 96 circle was the division used, advancing six holes for each cut. The tool is moved slowly by the winch handle laterally, while it is revolved at a quick speed, and by this means a highly polished surface is obtained. All such work can only be left from the tool, and it is necessary to pay the greatest attention to its cutting edge, or no good work will result.

Fig. 2 having been chucked in the same manner, is then cut, as seen by the illustration, with a series of consecutive cuts, the slide-rest still parallel to the lathe-bed; a square end tool, $\frac{1}{10}$ in. wide, replaces the round-nosed one previously employed, the 96 division being again used.

The tool is adjusted for the first cut by moving it laterally to the position required, and the figure at which the micrometer reads noted. The depth of cut is then ascertained by two trial cuts as before; the winch handle is then removed from the screw in case its position should by any means be altered. The first series is then cut round at every sixth hole, the tool is then moved laterally exactly its own width, which being $\frac{10}{100}$ in. will require one turn of the main screw, the division-plate is moved forward three holes, and the second circle cut at every six. By reference to Fig. 2 it will be seen that the termination of the second row of cuts is precisely in the centre of the first; for the third, return the index to zero, and again

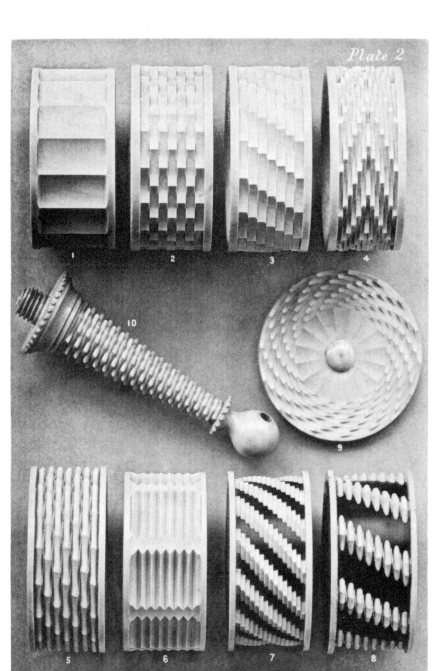

cut round at every six holes, each time moving the tool its own width, the same movements being repeated throughout the length required.

Fig. 3 it will be seen differs again in effect, although cut with the same tool and division, also equal penetration, the only alteration required being in the movement of the dial-plate, which instead of moving three holes forward and returned to zero, is moved only one hole, and then cut at every six as before, for example, the first circle cut at 96—6, 12, 18, 24, 30, 36, 42, and so on to the end. The second series begins at 7, 13, 19, 25 and 31. For the third, the starting point will be 8, 14, 20, 26, 32, and thus the pattern is carried out its entire length, the tool being moved its own width for each circle; and it is in this way that the spiral effect is obtained. The twist or pitch of the same may be easily altered by varying the division.

Fig. 4 represents a further development of the manipulation of the instrument, showing that the pattern may be reversed, rendering a very considerable difference and elegance to the work. The settings for this figure differ from those already alluded to, in the following way :—The radius of the tool is reduced $\frac{2}{10}$ in., a tool of just half the width—namely, $\frac{5}{100}$ in., is used in place of that of $\frac{10}{100}$, and each series of cuts carried round at every eighth hole of the 96 division, advancing two holes for each series, instead of one, as in Fig. 3. The tool is moved laterally its own width, and having repeated this seven times, the index is moved two holes in the reverse direction, and the first cut made of the return journey, the tool again moved half a turn for each cut, the division moved eight holes, and then proceed as in the first instance, with the exception that it is done the reverse way. This is also a very effective pattern for the interval between the lids and bottoms of boxes, and very many other subjects.

Fig. 5 is cut in the same manner as Fig. 3, a bead-tool being substituted for that with a square end. The 96 division is still used, arrested at every sixth hole, the tool moved its own width, $\frac{10}{100}$ in., and the division advanced two holes instead of

G

one; it will be seen that a considerable difference is derived from the cuts being rendered the shape of the tool employed.

Fig. 6 is cut in still a different way. The tool (a round-nosed one) is set out to a radius of $\frac{9}{10}$, but having only eight consecutive segments cut, every twelfth hole of the 96 division was employed, each cut having a space intervening. The tool now has the radius reduced $\frac{2}{10}$, and the division moved forward six holes, which brings the centre of the space between the previous cuts into position. These are then cut up sharp, the depth ascertained by trial as before.

The round-nosed tool is now replaced by a double angle one of 45°, the slide-rest is then set so that by seven revolutions of the main screw, a like number of consecutive cuts are produced. The cut is set in deep enough to bring the angle up sharp, the depth being again ascertained by two trial cuts. Having made the first cut on each segment, the tool is moved $\frac{1}{10}$ in., by one turn of the screw for the second, and then inserted all round again. This is repeated through the length required, in each of the eight segments, with the result seen in Fig. 6.

The majority of these examples are termed basket-work, and the variety is endless. Fig. 7 is another description of the same class, and it will be seen that the material is cut through, and afterwards filled in with black wood or other material. This is one of the most decorative of its kind, and the following is the correct way to proceed with it :—The inside of the work should be turned out perfectly true and smooth, and then accurately fitted to a boxwood plug or chuck, and fixed with very thin glue; it must be so fitted that the ivory touches the wood all over, if not, when the tool passes through that part not adhering, the material will be likely to break and splinter, and spoil many hours' work; in other respects the work is performed in precisely the same manner as when the figure is not cut through. The settings for Fig. 7 are, every sixth hole of the 96 division for the first sixteen cuts : move the tool laterally its own width, $\frac{5}{100}$ in., or one half turn of the main screw, move the division one hole and cut round again at every sixth hole, these movements being carried out the entire length of the work.

Fig. 8 it will be observed bears a very different appearance, although cut in a similar way, the alterations being the substitution of a bead tool $\frac{12}{100}$ in. wide in place of the square-ended one, and instead of sixteen cuts, only eight are made, leaving a wider interval between each; the radius of the tool is extended $\frac{2}{10}$ further from the centre. Such work can be lined with ivory and stained various colours, and by doing so very effective work is produced.

Fig. 9 brings us to the employment of the same instrument for face work, and for this it is very necessary to be able to reduce the radius of the tool as much as possible, but, from the construction of the vertical cutter (Fig. 94), it is not possible to obtain sufficient reduction for many patterns, from the fact of the driving-pulley projecting beyond the diameter of the spindle that holds the tool.

The universal cutter (Fig. 122), which is the most useful of all, may be employed, and the small screw in the end of the spindle, used for keeping the tool always in the same position as to centre, may be the means of holding it alone, and the screw passing through the side of the spindle removed; thus, with a short tool, a very small radius is obtained, and the beauty of the work when cut is greatly increased.

To cut a similar figure to that now being considered, there are one or two points, the explanation of which will be of value. The work is first turned smooth and true, the slide-rest of course set transversely across the bed, the universal cutter (Fig. 122) placed in the tool-box; a square-end tool (very short) is then fixed by the screw in the end, and that usually employed removed; a tool, $\frac{6}{100}$ in. wide, is adjusted to a radius of $\frac{4}{10}$, the index set at 96, the slide-rest arranged so that the micrometer stands at zero, the tool made to penetrate deep enough to bring the points up, and cut round at every six. The tool is now moved laterally by turning the slide-rest screw exactly one half-turn, which is equal to $\frac{1}{20}$ in. or $\frac{1}{100}$ less than the width of the tool, the division-plate moved two holes, and the cut repeated at every six. This is, so far, precisely similar to the movements required for the same process on the cylinder as seen by Figs. 3, 4, and 5. It will be observed that

G 2

the tool used for the figure under notice is $\frac{6}{100}$ in. wide, although the lateral movement is only $\frac{5}{100}$. The reason of this is, that the cutter revolves in a true vertical plane, and, when the work is moved round by the two divisions for each succeeding cut, the terminal points produced are really at angle one to the other, and if the width of the tool is identical with the movement of the slide-rest, a very small portion is left adhering to each point, which is a decided objection, and the removal of it is not practicable without considerable risk of damage to the work. This process is repeated eight consecutive times, with the result that the pattern formed is of a semi-spiral character, as seen by the illustration.

Having made the eight cuts, the remaining portion is taken out to the centre by the traverse of the slide-rest, the fluting-stop being fixed on the left side, so that no damage can occur to the last series of the basket-work; the centre is then filled with a small plain semi-circular piece of ivory. These patterns like all others may be increased to any extent, and cut in both ways, or otherwise varied to suit the taste of the operator.

Fig. 10 shows the same pattern, cut on a taper pillar, the tool being exchanged for a narrow pointed bead-tool; the plain form is first turned, the slide-rest being set to the necessary angle, the vertical cutter is then adjusted to a short radius, six cuts are first made at the large end, the tool then moved exactly its own width, the dial-plate moved half the number of divisions, and the cut repeated. The pattern is then carried the entire length of the shaft, the first at 96 moving 16 holes, for the second series, the index moved 8 holes, and cut round at every 16 from that point. For the third return to 96, and so on alternately, the starting points will be 96 and 8, by which the ends of each succeeding cut terminate in the centre of the segment preceding it. This is a most effective style of work, and may be carried out in a spiral form by employing the combined movements in the same way as for Fig. 3.

By reference to Figs. 97 to 106, it will be seen that the tools required for these instruments are identical in form to those already described as used in connection with the slide-rest and eccentric cutter, but from the size of the stem, which is the same as the slide-rest tools, the cutting edge of each may be greatly

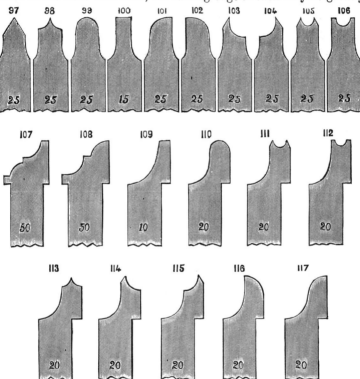

increased; in the instance of moulding tools of which Fig. 107 and 108 are merely examples, the figure may be extended beyond the width of the stem.

Figs. 109 to 117 represent vertical cutters, which do not appear to have been described in other works, but which are at the same time a most valuable addition, and for some work indispensable. It will be seen that their cutting edges are extended to one side of the stem, so that when used in the universal cutter, Fig. 122, there is nothing whatever between the shoulder of the work, and the cutting edge of the tool; therefore the pattern may be cut in close proximity to any projecting flange, and by such tools many subjects may be completed, from a decorative point of view, that would otherwise have been left plain from inability to approach that part.

It is necessary to have a few of the ordinary vertical cutters of of intermediate lengths, about $1\frac{1}{2}$ in. These, however, are used generally in the universal or horizontal cutters, which will accommodate their length, and they are most essential to shaping work requiring large curves. The shapes of the various tools in this group being facsimiles of those previously referred to, it will not be necessary to repeat the details; they vary in length from $\frac{7}{8}$ to $1\frac{1}{2}$ in.

CHAPTER XVII.

The Horizontal and Universal Cutters.

The horizontal cutter (Fig. 118) is made after the same manner as the vertical cutter, the rectangular frame being considerably larger, the centres are both adjustable for the purpose of setting the tool more accurately to the precise height of the axis of the mandrel, which is an important point with this, as in all other instruments.

The revolving spindle in this case stands in a vertical position while the tool revolves horizontally. To conduct the driving-band

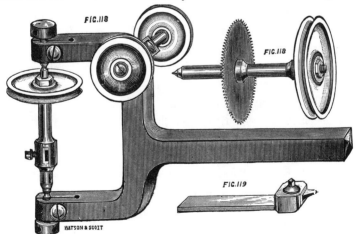

FIG.118

FIG.118

FIG.119

WATSON & SCOTT

from the overhead motion to the pulley of the spindle, two guide-pulleys are fitted to a transverse spindle on the top of the frame, which has sufficient length on each side to admit of their self-adjustment to the diameter of the pulley used. The revolving spindle has an oblong mortise, the same size as the vertical cutter, and this is made in such a position that the tool is held precisely opposite the centre of the stem, which is the height of the axis of the mandrel. The tool is fixed by a square-headed screw. This is found to be easier to manipulate than the screwdriver, as made in some instances, and is less dangerous; a slip with a screwdriver, while operating on a spindle running between centres, is very likely to occur, and will cause considerable damage to both fingers and work. The square head should be made to occupy as little space as possible, and will be found more convenient in every way. The instrument being made for work of a larger character, the screw-head will not come in contact with the work.

There is a second spindle fitted to hold circular cutters, which are used more generally for metal work, but are at times employed for purposes connected with ornamental turning. A thin circular saw, fitted to a spindle, and figured also 118, is a most useful tool for dividing work into halves or segments. The saw is adjusted to the exact height of centre, and when revolving at a high speed may be passed along a cylinder, which it will divide accurately into as many parts as may be required. It may also be used to operate on the surface by shifting the slide-rest, and it was found extremely useful in dividing the rings which form the branches of the ivory candelabra, Plate 13. There are many other purposes to which it can be applied.

The centre screws, having some length of adjustment, are used at times to set the tool above or below the centre, as may be required. This does away with the necessity for altering the height of the slide-rest, and answers the same purpose, unless for any special reason a greater elevation or depression is required than the centre screws will allow. The various spindles each receive three different sized driving-pulleys, the largest just passing the back of the frame, and is only used when considerable power is required, necessitated by using one of the slide-rest tools for a long sweeping curve, the smallest being used when it is necessary to approach nearer to the work.

Fig. 119 is a socket which holds both the vertical and eccentric cutters, which are very often used in this instrument.

From experience, the author finds that few amateurs know really the extent to which this as well as many other instruments may be applied. The work may be approximately roughed into shape by hand, but unless a deal of time is spent, the exact curve that would be cut by the tool when extended to a certain radius, is not arrived at; but if the tool is first adjusted, and then placed into cut by the slide-rest screw, it can be revolved at a high speed, while the work is slowly rotated by hand. For such work it is not necessary to use the segment apparatus; shaped in this way, it will be clearly seen that the desired curve is at once cut.

It is always better to use the main screw of the slide-rest for inserting the cut, when it is set parallel with the bed, although in some instances it is perhaps more convenient to turn the slide-rest round to face the work, and decide the depth by the guide and stop-screw of the top slide. When the slide-rest is set parallel to the lathe-bed, the left side fluting-stop is fixed, to arrest the tool at the correct depth for each successive cut, and with the slide-rest set in this way the work is more conveniently executed.

A few specimens of the work thus executed are illustrated on Plate 3. Fig. 1 shows a piece taken from the end of a column; it was cut with a pointed bead tool (Fig. 105), set precisely to the centre of the lathe axis. This is a point which must claim the utmost attention, as a defect in this adjustment entirely alters the character of the work. There are twelve distinct cuts, the projection between the reeds being left by the angle on the point of the tool; it is cut at every eighth hole of the 96 division. When the tool has received sufficient penetration, it is traversed throughout the length required, by the main screw, and if desirable can be arrested at any point by the application of the fluting-stop. Having made the twelve cuts, the index is moved four holes, this will bring the projection left between the reeds to the centre; the bead tool is now changed and replaced by one with a square end $\frac{10}{100}$ wide, set just deep enough to remove the sharp point, and reduce the top below the diameter of the reed.

Fig. 2 illustrates another variety of forms to which a cylinder may be reduced, the section (Fig. 2) cut from the column shows the distinct shape of the figure; this was cut from the cylinder $\frac{12}{10}$ in. diameter, the deep concave recess being cut with a round-nosed tool $\frac{16}{100}$ in. wide, and traversed by the main screw as before, the six cuts being made, the tool is removed and replaced by a bead or reeding tool (Fig. 106), having a square, or astragal end in place of the pointed one used for Fig. 1. This is a figure in which attention must be given to the depth of each cut, in order that due proportion is attained. Here again any length may be cut, and the tool arrested at intermediate portions of it. In cutting columns of this particular character, the radius of the tool should be as short as possible, although any reduction or extension of the same does not in any way alter the shape of the figure, unless the cut is arrested at any point within the cylinder.

Fig. 3 introduces an entirely different application of the instrument, it will be seen that the pattern is carried entirely over the shape first turned. In producing this, the material is first roughly shaped by hand. The cutter is then placed in the slide-rest, which is set parallel to the lathe-bed, the tool (a round-nosed one) being adjusted to a radius that will cut the curve as nearly as possible to the shape turned, is then set in and the work slowly rotated by the hand on the pulley. By this proceeding the exact shape is again produced; the round-nosed tool is now removed, and a double angle one of 50° substituted, the following being the safest way of setting it to the same radius as the one previously used :—The slide should be left in contact with the fluting stop; the tool may then be removed from the spindle, and the one next to be used placed in it, and extended to touch the surface of the work and then fixed by the binding screw. The fluting stop is then released, and the depth of cut ascertained by two trial cuts being made sufficiently deep to bring the angles up sharp. This decided, the fluting stop is again clamped tightly to the slide and the succeeding cuts made. The top slide once set to the depth, is not moved, the cut being made from right to left by the traverse of the main slide until arrested by the fluting stop, which will render all the cuts exactly alike. The slide is traversed the reverse way to withdraw the tool out of cut while the dial plate

Plate 3.

is altered. It may be removed from contact with the work by the top slide, but it is preferable to release it by the main screw. There are 32 cuts, and when all have been thus made upon the curve, the slide-rest is moved towards the margin of the work in order that the edge of it may be cut. To effect this the tool must be re-set to the correct depth of penetration by trial cuts, and is then passed over the width of the edge, the same division of course being employed. Should the tool require to be sharpened, it must be remembered that the greatest accuracy is required when replacing it in its original position, and the readiest way is to place the tool to the extreme depth of cut, leaving the slide in contact with the fluting stop, and then remove it from the spindle; it may then be sharpened and returned to the original depth, and again tightened in the spindle, by which the depth and radius are both maintained.

Fig. 4, it will be observed, is cut with a round-nosed tool in place of the double angle one, the outer edge being also curved instead of square; the cuts being narrower as they near the centre in consequence of the diminishing diameter, gives great and varied effect to the work. Again, there are 32 consecutive cuts; the bare form being cut in the first place in the same way as Fig. 1; in fact, all corresponding figures require the same treatment. The slide-rest is then brought forward, and the radius of the tool reduced and adjusted to cut the second curve, as seen in the illustration.

Fig. 5 demonstrates the variation of effect to be obtained by raising the tool above the centre, which, in this case, was elevated to $\frac{2}{10}$ in. above the axis of the mandrel, and it will be seen that a double angle tool was employed, and the simple changing of the tool, employing more or less elevation and increased depth of cut, all tend to alter the result obtained. Very elegant designs emanate from first cutting with the tool elevated, say, $\frac{2}{10}$ in. above the centre, and again with it depressed below the axis to the same amount.

Fig. 6, although a simple example, is illustrative of the accuracy required, and the means employed to obtain the precise height of centre, which is so important in all figures.

To obtain the precision necessary, the slide-rest is set transversely across the lathe-bearer, and a very delicate cut made on one side of the centre, the division plate then moved one half-turn, and the tool carried across to the other side; if the point of the tool does not agree accurately with the line, the height of the centre must be altered till it does.

It will be seen that the face of the pattern is flat, although it is cut with the tool revolving at a radius of $\frac{6}{10}$, but the fact of passing the tool entirely across the face of the work, and exactly at the centre, leaves the points accurately placed in that direction. This particular pattern is one that fully establishes the necessity of extreme accuracy in the adjustment of the tool in this particular respect. These few examples will suffice to show how the horizontal cutter is employed for work of this class.

CHAPTER XVIII.

The Universal Cutter.

This instrument is similar to the vertical and horizontal cutter in many respects, but from its being made to set to any angle midway between its horizontal and vertical positions, its powers are greatly increased.

Fig. 121 represents one of modern style to a certain extent, but like many other tools it has its defects. The spindle, which is forged in the solid with the frame, passes through the square stem and has fitted on the end a gun-metal arc, which is graduated on

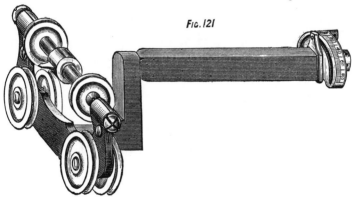

FIG. 121

both sides of the zero from 0° to 90°, and fixed by a screw against a steel plate on which the reading line is marked.

The spindle that holds the tool revolves between two centre-screws, which serve also for the finer adjustment of the height of centre when the tool is cutting in the horizontal position. On each end of the spindle a driving-pulley is fixed, and when used in an angular or horizontal position the driving-band is conducted to it by a pair of guide-pulleys attached to each end of the frame.

The spindle has a mortise hole in its centre like all other instruments, more or less, of this character.

Although a useful instrument for its various purposes, it is limited somewhat by the small amount of radius to which the tool can be extended without coming in contact with the frame, and from the size of the latter coupled with guide-pulleys on each side, it is prevented from being placed in sufficiently close contact with many kinds of work; it has also been found wanting in power for deep cutting.

Fig. 122 is a new description of universal cutter, designed by the author, and its advantages are obvious. First, it has greatly

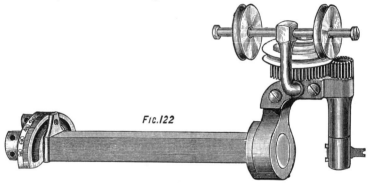

Fig.122

ncreased power from the speed obtained ; the tool can be placed close to the work in every direction, the driving-pulley is entirely out of the way of the work in all cases, in fact, it affords many facilities not to be obtained by Fig. 121 without being encumbered by extra guide-pulleys, and is more convenient and effective in every way.

The spindle is forged in the solid with the arms, and is fitted through a square stem in the same way as Fig. 121. On the front of the square stem there is a round collar, $1\frac{3}{8}$ in. in diameter, for the face of the arm to bear against to prevent any vibration. In the arm a steel collar is fitted, into which the spindle that revolves and holds the tool is fitted; this is also coned in the front. On the top of the spindle a pinion of nineteen teeth is fixed, having also a steel collar in it; this is held on firmly by a steel screw in the end of the spindle; behind this a steel stud with a cone at the base is fixed, on which a wheel of forty teeth is fitted to revolve and gear accurately with the pinion on the spindle in front, and is retained in its place by a steel screw in the stud.

It will be seen that the driving-pulley, which is fixed to the wheel, is entirely out of the way, leaving the front of the frame and the spindle free to be presented close to the work, and, by using a short tool, vertical cutting of a distinct and unique character may be executed. On the right side of the frame a curved arm is fixed, which has a transverse bar, on which a pair of guide-pulleys revolve similar to those on Fig. 118, also with power of self-adjustment. The pulley has two speeds, and the wheel-gearing being in the proportion of two to one, a quick speed is obtained. As in the case of the old-fashioned vertical cutter, it has been argued that this style of instrument is likely to wear to an angle by the pressure of the band, also that the wheel-gearing is likely to leave its mark upon the work, but this is entirely a mistake if the instrument is correctly made. This particular design of instrument has met with great favour with many leading amateurs, and has given every proof of its efficiency.

A second spindle is sometimes made to carry circular cutters, or a thin circular saw like the horizontal cutter. Another advantage it has is, that a long tool, such as the slide-rest tools, can be used at a radius of $1\frac{1}{2}$ in., describing a circle of 3 in. in diameter. This is a great convenience in cutting large patterns when it is found necessary to set the tool to an angle. The tool when fixed with the spindle in a vertical position points to the axis of the shaft, which passes through the square stem, and, when set for work to be cut at the centre, is identical with the axis of the lathe mandrel. The divided arc at the back is in every respect the same as that in Fig. 121.

A very great advantage is manifested by the instrument being set to various angles between the vertical and horizontal positions. Fig. 7, Plate 3, shows the effect of it employed upon a cylinder to form a column, which may be cut in any number of different ways. It was first turned to a cylinder $\frac{7}{8}$ in. in diameter, the slide-rest set parallel with the lathe bearer, the universal cutter (Fig. 122) placed in the tool box, and set over to an angle of 60°. The first cut is then made with the index at zero, 96 being again used. The tool is made to penetrate, so that the actual cuts are below the original diameter of the cylinder. Having carried the cuts round at every six, the tool is moved laterally $\frac{1}{10}$, by one turn of the main screw, which will bring it to the desired position for the succeeding cuts. Although in appearance it is somewhat similar to the basket-work, it is totally different, and it does not necessitate any further movement of the index beyond a repetition of the movement to every sixth hole, therefore it is only to continue this, and for each series, move the tool forward one turn. Here again many variations may be made, and useful decorative results produced.

The advantages obtained from the ability to set this instrument to any angle between the vertical and horizontal position is not confined to work executed upon the cylinder. It is equally effective when devoted to work ornamented upon the surface. Fig. 8, Plate 3, represents an example of the effect produced by the cutter being set to an angle. It is an extremely simple pattern, but will show clearly what a wide range is possible in such work.

The face of the work is first turned perfectly true and flat, the tool then extended to a radius of $\frac{8}{10}$, and cut round at every six of the 96 divisions, the instrument being set over to an angle of 55°. Having cut round thus, the instrument is reversed to the same angle on the opposite side and the pattern cut over again.

The ivory paper-box or sugar-sifter represented in Plate 4 is a useful and ornamental subject. It may be produced with either the universal or horizontal cutter. The former was employed for the subject now illustrated. It is composed of six separate pieces, which, for many reasons, is more advantageous, economy of material being not the least important, the facilities for chucking and the ready means of ornamenting being a great consideration.

When reproducing this or any similar object, it should be first turned and put together in the plain form to determine the necessary proportions. In the present instance the foot had a plain

Plate 4.

recess about ¼ in. deep and 1 in. in diameter turned in the base, by which it was chucked on a boxwood plug, the hemispherical body was then turned out inside and screwed to receive the top, and by this screw it was again chucked, and the opposite extremity screwed to fit a corresponding thread on the foot. The base of the first concave curve which forms the top was then screwed to fit the body, and attached also to a wood plug. The second concave portion is then treated in a like manner.

These parts being thus attached to separate chucks, can be put together to prove the proportion, the foot being left on the chuck to which it is fitted. The contour of the figure being satisfactory, the different parts may now be ornamented, the foot or base being the first to be done.

The slide-rest is set parallel with the lathe-bearer, and the universal cutter placed in the tool-box with a round-nosed tool, the instrument being set so that the tool revolves horizontally. When the radius of the tool is adjusted, it is revolved at a high speed and the work slowly rotated by hand. Having by this means obtained the necessary curve, the round-nosed tool is replaced by a double quarter-hollow, Fig. 73, the index set to zero of the 96 division and the tool penetrated at every fourth hole, the fluting-stop on the left side being set to arrest the cut at the desired depth.

When cutting reeds on a curve of this character, it will be noticed that they differ in shape at the diminished diameter. This is caused by only a very small portion of the tool taking effect at that part, while at the larger diameter its full figure is employed.

The base being so far finished, a small ring having fourteen beads cut with a drill, is next fitted; the body is then mounted on the dome or spherical chuck (Fig. 168), the universal cutter is turned to 90° on the right side, which will bring it to the reverse position to cut vertically; and having been carefully sharpened, the same tool, Fig. 73, is used. The work is then set by the screw of the dome-chuck, so that when rotated, or rather partially so, the tool will follow the curve. It is then made to penetrate to the depth required, which is ascertained by trial cuts, and the

H

segment-stop used to arrest it at the centre. The wheel of the dome-chuck is then moved round by three turns of the tangent-screw for each successive cut, which will produce thirty-two consecutive incisions. This operation will be again referred to in the details of the dome or spherical chuck.

The upper part is then place on the lathe, and the row of beads, forty in number, cut with a bead drill $\frac{12}{100}$ in. wide, the universal cutter is again placed in the slide-rest and turned to zero, to cut horizontally; the same double quarter-hollow tool being used, set to the desired radius, and a similar pattern to that on the foot repeated. A third row of beads, a size smaller and twenty-four in number, are then cut; and the second concave curve cut in the same way as the first; the fourth row of beads is then cut, the convex top with a series of holes, and the plain curve, forming the final.

This particular specimen, although not elaborate, serves in every way to illustrate the use of the instrument employed, which may lead to very interesting results indeed.

CHAPTER XIX.

The Drilling Instrument.

This instrument affords such a very large field for variety of application that it is one of the most important of the series used in connection with the art of ornamental turning. Its employment extends to the decoration of pillars, surfaces, cones, curves, and numerous compound solid forms, and it operates more or less in conjunction with all the ornamental chucks and different apparatus. It will be constantly referred to as the various specimens illustrated in the autotype plates are approached, from which a general idea of its manipulation will be gathered.

When used for the purpose of fluting a column, reeding the body of a box, or similar object, the length of each flute is determined by the fluting-stops, which are fixed at the desired point on the slide-rest, thus arresting the progress of the drill. When used for the purpose of beading or piercing, the instrument once placed in position, will not require lateral traverse of the main slide, the penetration being decided by the depth and stop-screw of the top slide.

Fig. 123 illustrates a drilling instrument of the most modern form; the spindle is made to pass through a square steel stem of the standard size, having in each end a hardened steel collar, coned at the mouth; the corresponding cone on the spindle being made to fit it accurately. On the rear end of the spindle a steel driving-pulley is attached; in this also a hardened collar with a similar cone to that in the stem is fixed. The object of the double cone is to admit of the accurate fitting of the spindle being maintained, and when any play between the two arises from the constant wear of continued revolution, by tightening the screw at

the back of the pulley the spindle may be again adjusted to a
perfect fit. This is a most essential point, as undue freedom in
this respect prevents the work being cut as smooth as it should be.

The front is bored out to a taper hole, to receive the shank of
the drills and has a mortise filed across the end of the hole at
a right angle to its axis; the shank of the drill is fitted accurately
to the taper-hole, and the end filed down to the centre, to fit on to

Fig. 123.

Fig. 125.

Fig. 124.

the flat of the mortise, one side of which is filed accurately to the
diametrical line; the object of this particular style of fitting is to
prevent the drill from turning in the hole, which from any extreme
pressure it is likely to do; the aperture also affords a means of
extracting the drills by inserting a small lever or wedge and
forcing it forward, which is necessary in its removal, as the drill
must fit firmly in the hole. It is, however, the taper hole which

is relied upon for the truth of the drill, the fitting at the end being the means, as before stated, of preventing its turning round.

Fig. 124 shows the same kind of instrument with the pulley fitted to the front instead of the back. This has many advantages, especially when used in the spherical slide-rest. Those readers who have had experience with this particular kind of slide-rest may have found that when cutting a series of flutes round a sphere, that the band from the angle at which it inclines is likely to run off the pulley of the instrument. This is not so much the case when the overhead motion (Fig. 11) is employed, at the same time it is likely to occur; the pulley being placed on the front of the instrument causes the band to run at a much less angle, because, when the circular movement of the rest is rotated, the band moves within a radius of very much less diameter than when the pulley is at the back, the difference consisting in the length of the stem of the instrument.

A few hints as to making the drills may be of service to many readers, and will assist them in replacing a fractured one without being compelled to forward the spindle to the maker, which is generally the case, as all such tools must be turned in their own spindle. The shank is first turned down to fit accurately into the tapered hole; it is then filed at the end on one side to fit the mortise; the spindle is then mounted on the slide-rest, preferably a metal turning one (Fig. 18), so that the hand-rest can be got to it. It is then driven from the overhead motion, and the drill turned true, and to the size required.

In some cases the figure of the drill, if a moulding-tool, may be turned approximately to shape; when so turned, a minute point should be left at the end perfectly true to its axis, this acts as a guide to file the surface, which must be reduced exactly to the half of the test point. It is necessary that great care is used in this respect, as the accuracy of the drill depends upon it; as an example, if the face is reduced below the centre, when used for piercing or beading, a dot will be left at the centre of the figure; f the surface is left above the centre it will not cut cleanly.

When making moulding-drills, which have their cutting edges to the left side of the stem, after the shank is fitted, the tool is made red-hot, then placed in a steel socket made to receive it, and the front, or blade, bent over to the left side; it is then replaced in the spindle, and a test-centre formed by turning a minute point. The face of it is then reduced to the diametrical line, and the right side filed at an angle until it is also reduced to the exact half of the test on that side of the centre; the cutting angle is then filed to about 35°, and the back of the drill reduced to the required substance. The next process will be to harden and temper it; and here difficulties may occur, from the tendency of the blade to depart from the actual truth; it is always preferable to heat the shank first, and let it run down gradually, having a vessel of water at hand to cool it immediately the proper heat is obtained, which, with fine steel, should be a very deep blood-heat; any excess in this operation will render the drill worthless.

The face should now be cleaned, and the drill tempered to a light straw colour; this may be done either by holding the shank in a small pair of red hot tongs, or by heating it with a blow-pipe. Upon replacing it in the spindle, it may be found to run out of truth, which is the result of the heat it has been subjected to in the process of hardening. This may be corrected with a small hammer, by the narrow end of which the hollow of the drill is struck, until its original position is regained; fresh disasters may again arise, as they very often break short off.

It often happens that in spacing out the work too great a distance will occur between the cuts, this may be altered by advancing a less number of holes in the division-plate, or by employing a drill a size larger, or if the beads are too close together, a drill of less dimension may be used. From this will be seen the necessity of making such drills of gradually increasing sizes; they are generally made to vary from $\frac{4}{100}$ to $\frac{35}{100}$ in.

By reference to the engravings, Figs. 126 to 131, it will be seen that these drills have their centres precisely true, both axially and diametrically. Fig. 126 is a plain drill for piercing holes. Fig. 127, a plain round-nosed fluting-drill, it can, however, be applied for many

other kinds of seriated or continuous figures. Fig. 128, a pointed
bead-drill, is perhaps one of the most important of the series. It
produces beads of different diameter, according to the size of the
tool; but such a drill cannot be moved laterally without destroying
the figure. Fig. 129 is a tool of the same character, but made with
a less amount of curve, which is at times desirable. Fig. 130, also
a beading-drill, but with astragal or square end in place of the
point, as in Fig. 128. Fig. 131 is a similar style of beading-drill,
having wider astragals, so that the beads may be left wider apart,

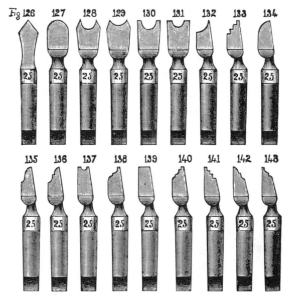

and thus prevent any possibility of the external diameter of the tool
interfering with, or distorting the bead previously cut. A square
end or chisel-drill is a most useful kind, either for piercing seriatim,
or for producing long flutes with a flat surface at the bottom and
square sides, in distinction to the shape left by the drill (Fig. 127).

Fig. 132 represents the first of what may be termed the second
series of drills, and it will be seen that it is of an entirely different
construction, inasmuch as its centre is reduced to the diametrical
line, and the cutting edge all on the left side of its axis, and
as illustrated, all the tools in this series are made in the same

way. Fig. 132 is a quarter-hollow reeding-drill, and will produce work similar to that seen on the body of the ivory pepper-box, Plate 4, when used in conjunction with the dome-chuck. Cylindrical or taper pillars may also be decorated in the same way. Fig. 133, a step-drill, is used to ornament work in a number of different ways, one of the most effective being long step flutes, either on cylinders or surfaces; and when applied in combination with the spiral apparatus to cut a long twist, very beautiful results are obtained. This is seen in Fig. 1 Plate 10, also the bottom of Fig. 2 in the same plate. Fig. 134, a quarter-round drill, is used principally to scallop out the interior, or the edges of various works requiring to be so excavated. Fig. 135, is an ogee moulding-tool, used for cutting flutes of the same shape, or for seriated mouldings. Figs. 136, 138, 140 are also for the same purpose, resulting in the figure of the tool, and the shapes may be multiplied in form and size to almost any extent. Fig. 137 is a tool which produces a small ring of the shape the tool is made, the centre of the bead being eccentric to the axis of the drill itself. These tools are made in many different forms, and are extremely useful in various ways, but from their construction it will be seen they cannot be traversed laterally. Fig. 139, is a routing drill, also a very useful tool for fluting or cutting out semi-circular recesses with the segment apparatus, or in combination with the ornamental chucks.

Figs. 141, 142, and 143 are examples of the moulding drills, which produce pyramids of their own form, in distinction to the previous series, which execute flutes of similar shapes. These have the figures made in the reverse way, so that it is reproduced in a pyramidal form, and for many styles of decoration are most essential. These like Figs. 128 to 131 cannot be traversed laterally, but are only used for producing their forms, as above mentioned. All the drills alluded to in this series are made in different sizes, varying from $\frac{4}{100}$ to $\frac{40}{100}$ in. wide, but when larger than $\frac{25}{100}$ wide are generally fitted to a spindle having a larger hole and a binding screw instead of the transverse mortise, as the power required to drive them for deep cutting is more than the smaller shank will bear without vibration, also the increased size of the cutting edge cannot be readily obtained from material used for the smaller drills.

Figs. 144 to 149 illustrate bent drills, and the shape of the cutting part is made similar to those already described. These are from preference fitted to the spindle with the large hole. The figures stand at a right angle to the stem and are employed mostly for internal work, after the same manner as the internal cutter (Fig. 125), but the depth of their operation is limited. A certain amount of basket-work can also be executed on the face by setting the slide-rest parallel with the lathe-bed, which it will be seen brings the

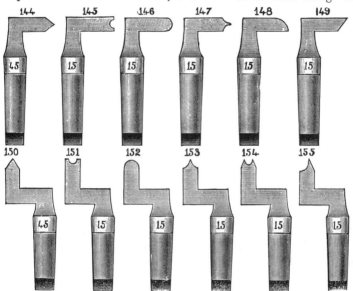

bent cutter to the same relative position as the vertical cutter would be in with the slide-rest adjusted in the reverse way. When these tools are made with a very small radius, they may be applied where it is impossible to get the internal cutter. Like their predecessors, they also require to be made in sets of different radii and widths, as there is no power of extending or reducing the same, except by changing the tool. They are made with the cutting edge to the right, as seen in the engravings.

Another form of drill, or rather cutter, is illustrated by Figs. 150 to 155. These to a very small extent supply the place of the eccentric cutter, and in a few instances are used with good effect, inasmuch as the absence of the right angle slide of the former will allow patterns to be cut which could not be done without them, especially when the work is placed upon either of the ornamental chucks, the projecting slide at times preventing the eccentric cutter being placed in contact with the work. These it will be seen are made precisely the same shape as those in the previous series.

Having given a brief outline of the various drills, it may be mentioned that they will be referred to in many instances connected with the description of the various specimens of turning. The examples on Plate 5 having been done entirely with drills, affords an opportunity of illustrating the way in which they were used for such work. Fig. 125 shows the internal cutter; it is made in the same way as the drilling instrument, with the exception that the spindle is much longer in front, and, instead of a hole bored to receive a drill, a transverse mortise is filed to fit the eccentric cutters; it is used for decorating deep interiors. It has been found a most useful addition to this instrument to have a few drills fitted to the end; it does not interfere with the mortise hole at all, and enables work to be done at the bottom of a deep cylinder, that could not otherwise be accomplished.

SPECIMENS OF DRILL WORK.

Following the details of the drill-spindles and the various drills, which may practically be multiplied to almost any extent, the specimens of work executed with the same, and illustrated in Plate 5, will now be considered, and as there are many different ways in which the drill has been employed, it is hoped it will be found a means of elucidating many of its applications for work of a similar class.

The tazza is made in four pieces, and in the first instance the parts are screwed together and the desired shape and proportions satisfactorily decided, the base, which in the first instance is semi-circular, is turned out inside, and then fitted to a corresponding form on a boxwood chuck and glued to it : the diameter of the base is barely 3 in. A plain flat end drill $\frac{25}{100}$ in. wide is first employed, and

Plate 5.

twelve holes bored $\frac{5}{20}$ in. from extreme base; the 96 circle of the dial-plate is used and moved to every eighth hole for the twelve consecutive cuts. The drill is then moved $\frac{3}{20}$ nearer the edge, the division moved four holes forward, and the drill penetrated again at every twelfth hole from that point. Upon completion of this, the dial-plate is moved to four holes on the opposite side of the zero, and the twelve cuts repeated. This, it will be seen, leaves only a portion of the curve cut by the drill on the work, the result being that the three holes represent a kind of semi-Gothic form.

The plain drill is now removed, and a moulding-drill substituted. The figure of the latter being a quarter-hollow, with a fillet and astragal end, the division-plate is moved four holes, so that the centres of the three following cuts will be in the centre of the space left from the three holes previously cut. Having cut round at every eighth hole, the dial-plate is moved four holes on one side of the starting-point, and the slide-rest moved $\frac{1}{10}$ laterally to the right and the cuts repeated all round, the dial-plate is moved four holes on the other side, and the same process repeated. The slide-rest, while these two series of cuts are being made, is set to an angle, about 15°.

The rest is now moved to an angle of 40°, and a large pointed bead-drill, $\frac{35}{100}$ in. wide, replaces the moulding-tool. The starting-point for this drill will be the same as that previously used for the moulding-tool, but, as there are eighteen beads, every third only will present itself to the centre of the spaces left. The eighteen beads are then cut, great care being necessary in letting forward the drill. As the 96 circle cannot be equally divided into 18, a fresh division must be employed, the 144 divided by 8, and being drilled on an arc as previously described, no difficulty will arise in changing from one division to the other; a small step-tool is then placed in the spindle, the division moved to half the number of holes, so that the point of the drill is placed between the beads, the slide rest moved $\frac{3}{20}$ to the left side, and the drill penetrated the necessary depth. A small round-nosed drill is then used for a imilar operation on the opposite side, the index is removed to the 112 circle, and the same drill inserted at every hole; the closely seriated pattern thus produced is a great relief to the larger and more prominent work.

The slide-rest is now turned to the surface, and the same patterns as produced by the moulding tool in the second group is again carried out on the face, the terminal points being cut with a plain flat-end tool $\frac{14}{100}$ in. wide. So far the base may be considered finished, and can be removed from the chuck by immersion in warm water.

The short cylindrical part extending from the base, having been carefully fitted to a boxwood plug and glued, is next drilled out, the slide-rest again set parallel with the lathe bed, a piercing drill $\frac{6}{100}$ in. wide is employed, and when commencing a piece of work requiring as this does a great number of holes, it is advisable to have two or three duplicate drills, in case of an accident. First drill the twenty-four holes nearest the base using the 96 circle, advancing four each time ; having drilled these, move the slide-rest laterally one half turn, and advance the dial-plate two holes; drill round at every fourth hole, move the dial-plate one hole, and the slide-rest another half turn of the screw to the right ; drill round and then move the division-plate to one hole on the opposite side of the zero, and drill round again, move the dial-plate back to the zero as used for the first hole, and the slide-rest another half turn further still to the right and again drill round, and the result is as seen in the illustration, which may be continued through any space required.

The dish, or tazza, may be next operated upon, the same drill being employed. The lower series of holes forming the fringe is drilled first; there are ninety-six, and the drill is adjusted to leave rather more than the semicircle, which gives it an elegant finish. Above these are seventy-two beads, to produce which a pointed bead-drill $\frac{8}{100}$ in. wide is used in place of the piercing-drill; they are spaced to approach as closely as possible without touching each other, the 144 circle, every alternate hole being used. Beyond these beads, forty-eight holes are drilled in the lower part, with the same drill as previously used. Having drilled these, the remaining part is executed in precisely the same way as that forming the first example of this style of decoration. Close above the intervening plain curve, 120 smaller beads are drilled with a pointed drill $\frac{6}{100}$ in. wide, also in close proximity one to another.

The single row of pierced work at the top has forty-eight holes, cut at four consecutive operations, resulting in the same figure as the lower part, which have been drilled in the same way. Having drilled this circle, a small step-drill is inserted above each hole, and the terminal pattern on the top cut with a small drill similar to Fig. 150. This can of course be cut with the eccentric cutter, but these specimens being entirely the result of employing the drill-spindle, that alone was used.

The stem is cut with a step-drill and the spiral apparatus, the wheels of the train being 144 on dividing chuck gearing to 18 on double arbor, 120 on the same, gearing to 15 on lower socket or slide-rest. To cut the reverse twist on the upper part, the intermediate arbor with wheel of thirty teeth is interposed between the 144 and 18. This example, in its entirety, is really more a matter of patience than anything else, one of the principal things being the chucking of the various parts.

Fig. 2 in the same plate is illustrative of the drill when employed to produce the beads in a more prominent form, and when so cut are termed pearls. This is by far the most effective style of ornament, and does not require at all a difficult manipulation of the instrument. There are two distinct ways of obtaining the same result, that is, the drill may be presented to the work at two or more different angles. The example under notice was cut in the following way: The part upon which the pearls are to be cut is first turned to the width and depth of the drill to be used, and as those on Fig. 2 stand at an angle to the surface, the slide-rest was adjusted to 45°, the drill then inserted to complete the bead at that point. The slide-rest was then set transversely across the bed and the drill carefully adjusted to remove the superfluous material on the front; the rest is then set parallel to the bed and the material cleared from the opposite side. By this it will be seen, that to produce the pearls in relief, as illustrated, three distinct settings are necessary, and all that is required to obtain a satisfactory result is, extreme care in the adjustments. The face and concave curve were cut seriatim with a large size round-nosed drill.

When beading work of this character, much depends upon the way in which that part of the work upon which they are to be cut is prepared, and the close proximity of the beads is at times a difficult matter, requiring a careful selection in the size of the drill and the division employed; it is sometimes an advantage to have a greater interval than can be cut with the astragal sides of the drill. In this case the beads can be placed as desired, and the interval afterwards removed by other means.

The perfection of the cutting edge of the tool must be carefully studied in every way, and after cutting a number of pearls in the rough, so to speak, the tool should be carefully sharpened for a finishing cut.

Spiral forms of many different degrees of twist may also be produced, either in recessed or projecting figures; as an example of this particular style of decoration, suppose a long pillar is required to be so treated, it will require the support of the popit-head; the first series of holes would be drilled at a certain division, for the second row the drill is moved laterally by the main screw of the slide-rest, the division moved forward two or more holes according to the twist desired, and the drill inserted again. These movements are repeated throughout the entire length of the shaft, unless the twist is to be made in the reverse way for the second half, in which case the division plate will require to be moved in the opposite direction.

The majority of the plain and moulding-drills may be employed for the purpose of fluting or recessing the various portions of work, either seriatim or continuously, and the perforations at times are so arranged that they cut into those preceding and following; they may be also spaced to leave an interval or plain part, which may afterwards receive some other description of ornament.

Star patterns and facial decorations also afford considerable scope for display of taste and design. Fig. 3 is a simple example of the former. It is in the first place held in a boxwood chuck, faced over perfectly flat and screwed in the centre; it is then fixed to another chuck equally flat, and screwed at the centre to fit the hole in the ivory; a little thin glue is then put on the face of the chuck and the ivory screwed up to it. (If allowed to get thoroughly dry, such work will receive safely almost any amount of perforation, and it will not splinter away when the drill passes through at the back, as it is in close contact with the face of the chuck.)

The external diameter is then turned to $1\frac{1}{2}$ in. diameter, and the face hollowed away gradually until the edge is $\frac{1}{20}$ in. thick. The plain form thus turned should be highly polished, which adds greatly to its ultimate appearance, and cannot be done after it is cut or pierced. A square-end bead-drill, $\frac{5}{10}$ in. in diameter (keenly sharpened), was used to cut out the largest curves on the edge, which are twelve in number, the 120 division arrested at every ten being employed. The large drill is then replaced by one $\frac{2}{10}$ in diameter, and moved towards the centre by the main screw of the slide-rest, so that it will cut partly into the hole made by the one first used. A small drill, $\frac{6}{100}$, is then arranged to cut the small hole nearer the centre and opposite the aperture.

The division-plate is then moved five holes, to bring the following series in the centre of the part left uncut from the previous perforation, the drill, one of $\frac{15}{100}$ in., is then moved laterally two whole turns of the main screw, and a hole pierced at every ten. A drill of $\frac{6}{100}$ in. is then employed to pierce the two sides, the centre of the drill being adjusted to cut a semi-circle only. The same drill is then set to pierce a hole in the centre of the points left from the primary cut, and another drill of $\frac{4}{100}$ in. was then traversed forward to the centre by one and a half turns of the screw. A drill of $\frac{3}{100}$ in. in diameter is then employed for the inner circle, to complete the star. The drilling instrument thus used will result in some very excellent and highly decorative ornaments.

Vandykes cut upon the lips or edges of vases or other subjects are also a most effective class of work to produce with the drill; and these may be arranged in many different ways, the perforation in some cases being in contact, while in others spaces may be left between each. The vandykes may be cut out either with a drill similar to that used for the star, or with a routing-drill (Fig. 139). Fig. 4, Plate 5, is a simple pattern of this character, and was cut with a series of different sized drills.

The work is first turned to the necessary diameter inside, then chucked on boxwood and glued. The outer diameter is then carefully turned and polished. A square end-drill, $\frac{5}{10}$ in., is then employed to cut out the largest curve, which, when cut all round at every four of the 96, leaves 24 points, a few only of which are seen in the illustration. The slide-rest for this operation is set parallel with the lathe-bed, and the drill penetrated clean through into the boxwood plug, by which all chance of splintering the ivory is prevented. The points being perfectly sharp and delicate, great care must be exercised, as the absence of one of them, caused by a fracture, entirely mars the beauty of the work. The drill is changed for one of $\frac{2}{10}$ in., and then moved by the slide-rest screw one turn and a half to the right, so that the hole pierced by it will cut into that previously drilled. A third drill, $\frac{1}{10}$ in., replaces the second, and the slide-rest again moved one turn and a half, or $\frac{3}{20}$ in., in the same direction. The index is then moved forward two holes, so that the drill that follows is presented to the centre of the form left from the previous perforation. The diameter of the drill is $\frac{16}{100}$ in., and the position laterally being the same, its centre is opposite the points left by the last drill used for the first series. A drill of $\frac{8}{100}$ in. is now substituted and moved laterally one turn and five divisions of the micrometer, so that about two-thirds of its entire diameter are left. The final drill used is one of $\frac{4}{100}$ in., moved laterally to pierce the centre of the diametrical line cut by that previously employed, and afterwards arranged to pierce the spaces resulting from the last cut of the first series and the first of the second. The top of this pattern is set off by a circle of small beads, cut with an astragal bead-drill, $\frac{5}{100}$ in. in diameter, using the 120 circle of division moved to every hole.

The proportion of the vandykes will depend upon the diameter of the material to receive them, the number required in a given space, and the diameter of each consecutive series of drills. The points may result from a series of perforations all executed with the same drill, and as before stated, there is practically no restriction to the variety of forms to be obtained from the above and similar proceedings.

A very effective result is obtained by using a round-nosed drill in the following manner, either on the diameter of a cylinder or the face of the work (a drill about $\frac{20}{100}$ is a very good one to employ) : cut all round at such a number that each succeeding cut will overlap or cut into the neighbouring one, then move the index exactly half the number; move the slide-rest laterally, so that the drill will cut as nearly as possible the same amount into the side of the circle, and cut again all round at the same number used for the first. The second circle being cut, the index is moved back to the zero, and the slide-rest moved the same distance, denoted by the micrometer; by these alternate movements, the pattern terminates similar to a honeycomb, and for some subjects is most appropriate. The drilling instrument will be again referred to as the different illustrations are approached.

CHAPTER XX.

THE CURVILINEAR APPARATUS.

WHILE offering a description of this apparatus, it will not be desirable to occupy time and space by reference to it as originally made, it being obvious that since its introduction, more than half a century ago, it has been very much improved and more fully developed. It will now, therefore, be considered only in its latest form with all the recent improvements.

By reference to the engraving of the complete slide-rest (Fig. 14), it will be seen that the apparatus is mounted upon the main slide, and from the manner in which it is now fixed, as introduced by the author, no alteration in the construction of the rest is necessary, not even to the extent of drilling and tapping holes in the slide to receive the two screws which fix the standards to it. These it will be seen are attached in the same way as the fluting-stops, one angle being cast in the solid with the standard, while the other is fixed with a screw and steady-pin, so that it can be clamped in any position, thus doing away with the holes in the face of the slide, which are, under any circumstances, a decided objection. On the top of the standards a steel bar is fixed, and is made about 1 in. shorter than the slide. A series of holes $\frac{1}{2}$ in. apart, are drilled throughout its length and tapped to receive the screws which fix the templates to it, the guides also have the holes elongated to admit of increased adjustment laterally; the two screws that hold the bar to the standards are simply screwed into the latter.

A variety of templates or shaper-plates may be made, a few of which are illustrated by Figs. 156, 157, 158, 159, 160, and 161. They are made of steel in order that their precise form may be more accurately retained. Should, however, any special shape

be required, which is often the case, sheet brass will answer
quite as well. Some are made in pairs, which are employed to turn
and decorate the bowls of tazzas or similar objects. Although,
of course, any number of templates may be made, a limited supply
will do a large variety of work, as, at times, a portion only of the
curve may be used, the traverse of the slide being arrested by the
fluting-stops when the exact distance is decided, that is, with
reference to that portion of the curve to be applied in relation to the
material to be operated upon. The way in which. the standards
are now fixed, and the bar being rather shorter than the main

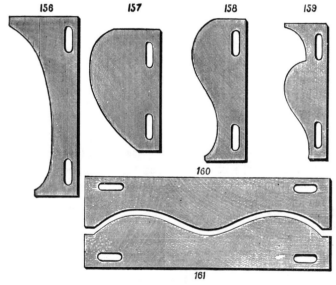

slide, an additional means of lateral adjustment is accessible, without altering the position of the template on the bar.

The rubber forms a very important feature of this apparatus,
and may be made in various ways; one form is in the shape of a
plain pillar, fitted at the base to the tool-box, having a small screw
with a capstan-head fitted to the front, for the purpose of letting
the tool forward for increased depth of cut. The top of the pillar
is filed to a taper vertical wedge with a narrow edge to bear against
the template. This form, however, has been greatly improved
upon by the introduction of that shown in Fig. 16, which is made

similar to a small popit-head, and has a leading screw with milled head, by which a more convenient means of adjusting the depth of cut is obtained. It is composed of gun-metal, fitted at the base to the tool-box, and is fixed in position by a capstan-head screw, which binds it to the tool or cutter placed in the tool-box. At the top is fitted a small steel cylinder, the end of which is bored out to receive different rubbers, that seen in the engraving being the most effective. It is in the shape of a small roller, which as it passes over the undulations of the curve, performs its operation more smoothly; but as at times a narrow edge is required, the roller can be replaced by one, and to remove it the cylinder is wound in until the end of the leading screw pushes it out, after the manner of the ordinary popit-head. This particular form of cylinder has been recently introduced, and is found to be a very considerable advantage. The height of the cylinder is so arranged that the centre of the rubber takes effect upon the edge of the template.

As may be conceived from its name, the apparatus is employed to turn and ornament curved forms, which may be produced either on the surface or the cylinder, that is, with the slide-rest set parallel to the lathe-bearer or transversely across it, and the necessary actions are supplied by the combined movements of the traverse of the main slide, and the oscillation of the tool-box, caused by the rubber being kept in close contact with the template by the lever, the bridle of the guide-screw being removed, and, as neither it nor the depth-screw are required, they should be screwed back out of the way. If either be left in contact with the pillars against which they generally abut, the true forms of the template will not be produced. Should a portion of the work be required of a cylindrical form, the stop-screw may be employed to prevent the rubber from reaching the curve.

When about to turn the form of any particular template, the material should be reduced in the first place to a plain cylinder the length required, and then as much as possible of the superfluous material removed by hand-turning, thus saving a considerable amount of wear to the edge of the template. When using the apparatus to finally shape the work, a fixed tool (Fig. 38) is the most useful of its kind to employ, as it is rounded at the point and cuts on the sides, which causes it to remove the material on either side as it ascends and descends the different curves contained in the template.

From the profile of many of the curves, it will be at once observed that the cut cannot at all times be traversed continuously in both directions. Fig. 159, for instance, would require the rubber to be traversed from the largest diameter to the smallest, or in other words, down-hill. If the cut is made in the reverse way, the depth of the curve will act as a stop and prevent further traverse in that direction. When the work is reduced to the form required, resulting from the template employed, it may be decorated by any of the revolving cutters. Fig. 1, Plate 6, is an example of the kind of work produced by the aid of the vertical cutter combined with the curvilinear apparatus, and is one of the most simple to execute. After the material has been roughly shaped by hand, the apparatus is mounted on the slide-rest and the template (Fig. 158) adjusted, and, with the round-nosed tool, Fig. 38, before alluded to, it is turned to the shape required. In the figure under notice, it will be seen that the resultant curve differs in appearance from the template. This is simply from the fact of its being reduced considerably below the diameter of the latter.

The material being thus shaped up, the fixed tool is removed and replaced by the vertical cutter; and here a very important adjustment is necessary. It will be noticed that the centre of the tool in the cutter presents itself to the work in a totally different position, and until this is corrected it will not follow the same course as the fixed tool that turned the outline; to adjust this a very fine pencil-line should be marked on the work, preferably, at the most prominent part, and at the precise centre of the fixed tool. This done the slide-rest must be moved bodily along the bed, until the centre of the tool in the vertical cutter coincides with the pencil-line; the slide-rest is then again clamped to the bed. It will now be found to traverse the same path as the tool it has replaced; the cutter is set to a radius of $\frac{8}{10}$, and the 96 division arrested at every 12 employed, giving eight segments. The exact depth of cut required is ascertained by trial, and the finishing cuts should always be made in the same direction ; by preference from right to left.   Work of this kind requires the support of the popit-head, while that of large diameter can be done without it, unless exceptionally long.   The lateral adjustment of the slide-rest above alluded to will not be found at all a difficult matter, but will require care.

The universal cutter (Fig. 122), however, does away with the necessity for it, as the centre of the tool when clamped in the receptacle is coincident with the axis of the spindle which passes through the square stem; it will therefore represent the same centre as the fixed tool. This is the case whether set vertically or horizontally.

From a strictly theoretical point, the cutter, whether fixed or revolving, should equal in size the rubber that bears against the edge of the template, that is, for a precise reproduction of the curve employed. This cannot at all times be so, and, although an alteration in the curvature of the guides will effect a facsimile, it is not considered necessary, as sufficient precision is obtainable without.

The variation is more observable when the cutter is set to revolve horizontally, and, the more the tool is extended with regard to its radius, the more perceptible will be the difference in the profile of the work when cut, especially at the larger diameters, either concave or convex, as that portion is nearer at a right angle to the axis of the material. For some reasons this cannot be deemed an objection, as many different curves may be cut from the same template.

Fig. 2 is illustrative of the work produced by employing the drill, or, rather, both it and the vertical cutter. The same template was used; the form turned in precisely the same way as Fig. 1, leaving a projection at the centre of the concave portion ; the fluting-stops were then adjusted to cut the flute the length required; a round-nosed drill, $\frac{1}{100}$ in. in diameter, was then placed in the drill-spindle and traversed from right to left until

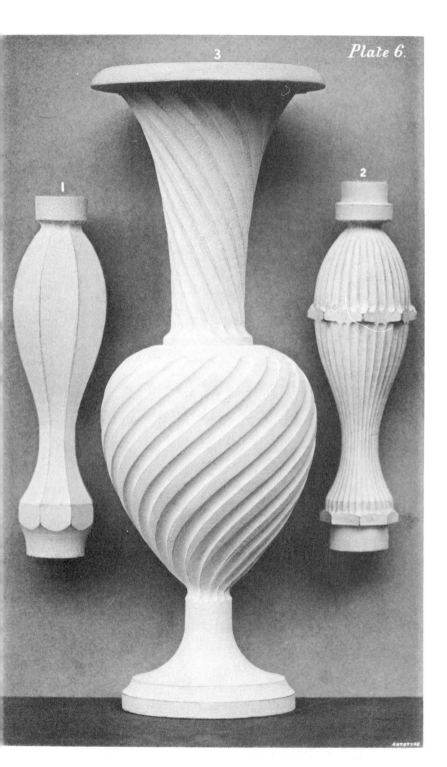

Plate 6.

arrested at the desired points by the fluting-stops. Thirty-two consecutive cuts were then made; and the fluting-stops moved to decide the terminal points on the other side. The short cylindrical part was then cut with the same drill, the depth being ascertained by trial cuts just to bring up the edges sharp; the vertical cutter then takes the place of the drill, and the rim round the centre cut into eight equal parts, the small end of the same figure being cut in a similar way. The flutes gradually diminishing in width at the smaller diameter renders most graceful lines.

Fig. 3 represents the results of the curvilinear apparatus used in conjunction with the spiral apparatus. This vase is made in two pieces, the body and foot being in one, while the top forms a separate part. When reproducing this, the form is first shaped approximately by hand and, finally with the templates (Figs. 156 and 157); the spiral apparatus is then arranged, and being fitted to the back of the lathe-head, the work is placed on the mandrel nose, without the necessity for interposing the spiral chuck in front.

The wheels employed were 144 on dividing chuck on the mandrel, gearing into a pinion of 18 on the double arbor, a wheel of 120 on the same, gearing into a pinion of 20 on the socket below, acting the same as when geared to a wheel on the slide-rest screw, when the apparatus is fitted to the front of the lathe-head. The fluting-stops are adjusted to arrest the traverse on each side, but the latter should always be made in the same direction, as referred to in the chapter devoted to spiral turning. In the instance of the figure under notice, the cuts were made from right to left, terminating at the small part of the figure. The tool is withdrawn and traversed back to the right hand fluting stop for each succeeding cut. The spiral chuck is then moved 6 divisions and the second cut made. The depth being decided by the two first cuts, it only remains to proceed in the same way entirely round the figure. The curves produced by this combination are very graceful, and may be altered to any extent by using different templates and varying trains of wheels.

To produce the top portion of this figure, the template (Fig. 156) was used, and it will be observed that the spiral grooves run in the reverse direction.   The only thing necessary for this, is to place the intermediate arbor with a 30 wheel on it, between the 144 and the 18, the gearing in other respects being precisely the same.   It is, of course, needless to say that figures of a similar class may be produced, with spirals crossed in both directions; the result of this being a series of square or diamond-shaped pyramids, the precise figure of the same being determined by the twist or pitch of the spiral.

CHAPTER XXI.

THE eccentric chuck may be considered the first of the series of ornamental chucks, and for the simple face or surface patterns, its productions are similar to those produced by the eccentric cutter. With the chuck the patterns are cut with a fixed tool in the slide-rest, and the eccentricity obtained by the slide of the chuck being set out from the centre, according to the pattern desired, and the radius given to the tool by the main screw of the slide-rest, the amount determined by the number of turns or divisions of the micrometer, the worm-wheel in front of the chuck forming the necessary means of dividing the cuts equidistantly.

With the eccentric cutter the radius is obtained by the movement of the tool-carriage from its centre, and the eccentricity by a corresponding adjustment of the slide-rest; the division-plate on the pulley being used for the sub-division of the work. The two are frequently used in combination, both for surface patterns and for the ornamentation of solid forms of various characters, by which very beautiful and curious effects are produced.

It has been suggested by numerous influential patrons, that a preliminary explanation of the manufacture of the various chucks will be of interest, especially to those amateurs whose inclination and time are devoted to making tools, in preference to using them, and it is hoped that the details which the author has great pleasure in publishing, will also render the mechanical actions of the various apparatus more intelligible.

The eccentric chuck illustrated by Fig. 162 is seen in a vertical position to the lathe-bearers; and when the back-plate is screwed to fit the mandrel-nose, it should be so adjusted by turning off the face that bears against the mandrel, in order that it may assume this position when the index point is placed in any one of the starting points on the arc on which the divisions are drilled, also the adjusting nut of index midway on the screw. The object of the latter is to admit of the more accurate adjustment of the chuck, by elevation or depression of the index, whichever is required.

Fig 162

The front face of the plate is then turned true and flat, and a small hole about $\frac{1}{16}$ in. in diameter drilled in the centre for the convenience of centering the front plate to it, which also has a hole drilled in it the same size. The steel double chamfered bars should be either planed or filed up in one piece and separated afterwards. The front plate should then be surfaced, and the angular grooves planed out.

The bars must then be fixed to the back-plate by two steel screws, the front being the first to fix. The two plates are placed together with a small pin fitting into the holes in the centre, which gives their approximate position in one direction. The bar is then placed against the V-grove, in which it is to work, and held parallel to the side of the chuck, while the position for the holes to receive the screws are marked, thus giving the position for the first or front bar. The centre-pin is then removed and the opposite bar fixed in the same way. The front one should have, in addition to the screws, two steel steady-pins, fitting tightly into the steel and passing into two corresponding holes in the metal plate. The object of these is to prevent any movement, which would destroy the axial truth of the chuck when completed. The off side is provided with two set-screws, the heads of which project so that the steel bar can be set up to the slide in the plate. The holes in this bar are elongated to allow it to move forward with the pressure of the set-screws. The reason for placing the latter on the off side, is to leave the front free from obstruction, as it is often required when using a square to set the chuck to the position seen in the engraving.

The two plates should not be in contact, but fit only between the angles of the bars. When the slide is thus far fitted and parallel, it may be well worked together with a little fine oilstone powder, but not under any circumstances should emery of any kind be used. When finally corrected the front plate should be set as near central as possible, and the hole to receive the steady-pin drilled. This, it will be seen by the engraving, is indicated in the lower left hand corner, the hole is broached slightly taper from the back, the pin being well fitted. It is generally placed in this position, as it is more readily removed and less in the way; the pin projecting at the back, is not seen.

The chuck should now be placed on a true surface-plate by the side opposite the set screws, and the necessary centres for drilling the hole to receive the main screw obtained. This is done with a scribing-block set to the centre, and a line marked across each end. This, with the division of the two plates, will give the centres.

Th e hole, which is ½ in. in diameter, is then drilled from the top to about 1 in. past the centre.

The chuck must now be taken apart, and the top end of the front plate cut out to receive the nut in which the main screw is to work, and by which the slide is actuated, the recess is made with a circular cutter about ⅝ in. in diameter, and ¾ in. long, sunk into the half of the hole drilled to admit the screw, the second half of which is in the back plate. The nut is simply a short cylinder of a corresponding size to the cutter; to ensure its accuracy it should be turned on the main screw, it is then soldered to the recess so that the screw will lie perfectly parallel with the face of the slide.

The screw in this, as in all other chucks, must be ten threads to the inch; a shoulder about ¾ in. in diameter is left on it when forged, which is fitted to the recess countersunk in the top of the back-plate, and is retained there by the coupling in front of it, fixed by two screws. The main screw has a square filed on its end to receive the micrometer, which is fitted to it, and pinned across to prevent it coming off when the chuck revolves at speed.

It will now be discovered that the nut, from the extra diameter necessary to fit the recess, will not slide in the back-plate, it must therefore be reduced on the projecting side to pass freely in the semi-circular groove, which is in the back-plate, and is practically the second half of the hole drilled for the main screw. The nut is reduced with a file, care being taken not to remove more than necessary, and to see that it works quite freely up and down the groove; the metal bearing is then fitted to the top of the back plate, by which the main screw is kept in its place. Thus far the slide and screw may be considered complete, and the worm-wheel and tangent-screw will form the next part to proceed with.

The wheel has ninety-six teeth, and is cut first with a single-tooth cutter, set to an angle in the universal cutter-frame to correspond with the rake or pitch of the screw; this is inserted about half the depth of the thread. The single-tooth cutter is then replaced by a router or hob, which is a counterpart of the screw itself, and is fluted to cut like a master-tap. The cutter-frame is then set perfectly vertical, and the wheel cut up to what may be termed a full thread, the hob or cutter being worked gradually into it. The metal turning slide-rest (Fig. 18) is the most suitable to employ for such a job. The correct diameter for the wheel is 3·18, and the pitch of the screw ten threads to the inch. This the author has now adopted in preference to that of 9·45, and it may be said that the latter is gradually becoming obsolete.

The chuck should now be carefully put together, with the steady pin in its place, and the projection on the front plate turned accurately to fit the recess in the back of the wheel. This is a most important point, the ultimate truth of the chuck to a certain extent depending upon it, both diametrically and facially. This done, the slides must be taken apart and the front plate carefully re-chucked by the fitting, and there is nothing better for this purpose than a well seasoned piece of boxwood. A recess is then turned out sufficiently deep to allow the screw-head and washer that hold the wheel in its place, to go below the main screw, which passes over it when the chuck is finally put together. The recess should be about 1 in. in diameter and perfectly true, the wheel having to turn evenly between the front face and bottom of the recess. Any inaccuracy will cause the wheel to be free during one part of its revolution and tight at others.

The steel frame to hold the tangent-screw is made from a forging of the required shape, and has a pivot on one end, which is fitted to a hole in the front plate, so that the screw, when placed in gear, is square across the front of the chuck and tangental to the wheel. The hole in which the pivot of the frame is fitted is then countersunk at the back to receive the head of the screw that holds it. The screw is fitted tightly against the end of the pivot, so that the frame may move round without undue freedom. The end of the tangent-screw is then filed square to receive a metal micrometer, which is divided into eight equal parts, also for the convenience of using a key or winch handle to adjust the wheel to the division on its periphery.

The screw being frequently thrown out of gear, a steel spring must be fitted into a mortise hole in the front plate, under the flange of the wheel, so that its point will press against the under side of the frame at the end where the micrometer is fitted. By this it will be seen the screw is kept out of gear with the wheel, so that it can be turned to any division required. To replace the screw in gear, a steel cam, made as seen in the engraving (Fig. 162), having two flat sides and a rounded edge, is held to the plate by a screw, in such a position that the curve will throw the frame into gear, and the square edge hold it firmly, and when turned the reverse way, the spring operates on the frame and releases the tangent-screw. The cam has a short projection for the thumb to press it either way. This particular action was designed by the author in place of the plain eccentric with a long lever, as sometimes made, and found to be in the way. In that now illustrated, there is no possible chance of the cam being unintentionally moved when the work is in progress.

For the convenience of reading the division on the periphery of the wheel, two steel indices are fixed in the front plate, one just below the micrometer, and one on the opposite side. Each of these agrees with the divisions on the wheel, so, that whatever position the chuck may be in, the reading may be taken with equal facility. The wheel is divided at every tooth with figures at every 6 and a mark at every 3, the micrometer being, as before stated, divided into eight equal parts.

A portion of the front plate, at the top, above the cam, is filed away to form a straight line, and from this the back plate is divided at every turn of the main screw to agree with the micrometer on it, which is divided into ten equal parts, and again subdivided —having in all twenty equally divided lines, capable of reading to two hundredths of an inch.

The lines on the face of the back plate are at all times more convenient for denoting the amount of eccentricity given to the slide, when a complete turn of the screw is required.

The front wheel is sometimes made in the form of a ratchet, having also ninety-six teeth, with a detent and spring. This, for patterns requiring the process of double counting, is preferred by some amateur turners, but it has many defects : one in particular, is, that if the chuck that holds the work receives any undue pressure, it becomes fixed, and the force required to remove it causes the detent to slip out and the wheel to move round, thus destroying, or at least damaging the teeth; to avoid this, a steel pin may be placed under the detent. The worm-wheel, however, may be said to have entirely superseded it, since, by the aid of the cam and spring, the screw is conveniently placed in and out of gear when the wheel is required to be partially revolved, and it has also greater facilities for subdividing the work by the micrometer on the tangent-screw: the ratchet-wheel is therefore seldom made.

Having thus detailed the process of manufacturing this chuck, and, as previously stated, determined to pass over the group consisting of mere fine line surface ornamentation, the more interesting subjects, comprised in compound solid figures, both of a simple and complex nature, to be executed by this chuck, will form the matter for the following chapter.

CHAPTER XXII.

Cylinders Decorated by the Eccentric Chuck.

It is possible with the eccentric chuck alone to produce some very beautiful designs, but when used in co-operation with others, such as the ellipse and dome chucks, more elaborate works are produced. And many references will be made to them in describing the specimens contained in the autotype plates, some of which may be deemed worthy of reproduction.

Plate 7 contains a few examples of ornamented cylinders of the first series or type of decorations as applied to this particular form, and it will be noticed that in some instances the result is simply a number of discs placed eccentrically one to the other, which particular formation is generally known as the geometric staircase, and may be made extremely useful in many ways. Others are more or less of a spiral form, the pitch or twist being varied by the increased eccentricity of the slide, and alteration in the movement of the dividing wheel; the width of the tool employed also exercising great influence over the result.

This particular style of work may also be applied to the tubular cylinder, which, for many kinds of work, is most beautiful. The effects of it will be seen by reference to Figs. 3, 4, and 7, and in this, as in the solid figure, there is practically no end to the variety.

To reproduce Fig. 1, Plate 7, the work is held in a small metal cup chuck and mounted upon the nose of the eccentric chuck. It is then turned to a perfectly true cylinder rather less than 1 in. in diameter, the end being faced off also perfectly flat and true, the latter proceeding being necessary for it to receive the centre of the popit-head, all work of any length requiring its support.

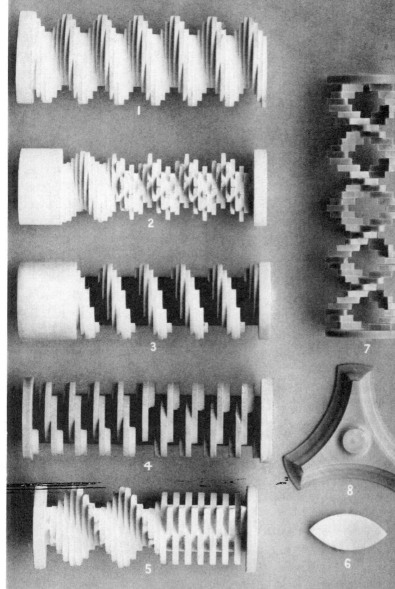

Plate 7.

The slide of the eccentric chuck is then moved out one turn of the screw, the wheel of the chuck is set to 96, and a fixed tool $\frac{5}{100}$ in. wide employed in the slide-rest.   When adjusting the tool previous to starting the pattern, care should be taken that it is set to the desired point, when the zero of the micrometer agrees with the reading line on the end plate of the slide; any of the divisions may be employed as a zero, but it is likely to confuse the operator in the various movements.   It is therefore better to make a rule of starting from 0; should the two points not agree, the slide-rest may be moved bodily along the bed of the lathe till they do, but the adjustable micrometer obviates any necessity for this trouble, and may be at once set to the required point, irrespective of the lateral position of the tool.   The slide of the chuck being moved out, and all the other settings arranged, the popit centre should be placed in contact with the work to prevent vibration, and the first disc turned, the tool is gradually advanced until all the eccentricity is removed and the material at that point again reduced to a concentric state $\frac{3}{4}$ in. in diameter; the stop screw of the top slide is then fixed, which will determine the depth of cut and consequent diameter of each succeeding disc.   The tool is now moved exactly its own width by one half turn of the main screw, or $\frac{5}{100}$ in; the popit centre is withdrawn, and the wheel turned towards the operator twelve divisions; the centre is replaced and the second cut made, and it only remains to repeat these movements throughout any length of material that it may be desired to ornament.   Thus the settings are, the movement of the tool precisely its own width, the dividing wheel 12 divisions forward, the eccentricity of slide remaining the same for each cut, the popit centre being withdrawn while the wheel is turned, and replaced before each succeeding cut is attempted; the end of the material will therefore have eight consecutive centres.   This will be found anything but a difficult operation, and forms a very interesting study indeed.

Fig. 2 was cut in precisely the same way, but is smaller in diameter; a few of the original discs are left on the end to show this.   Having cut through the desired length in this way, the fixed tool is replaced by the vertical cutter with a tool the same width, and adjusted very carefully to cut over the same surface; the tool is set out to a radius of $\frac{7}{10}$, and the work held stationary by the index in the division-plate. The tool is then advanced, so that when cut at every quadrant of the dial-plate, the corners of the disc are left sharp, each one representing a square with slightly concave facets, and, it will be observed, entirely altering the appearance of the work. This style of decoration may be varied in many ways by the employment of bead and figured tools in the vertical cutter.

Fig. 3 represents a still further variation. The ivory is first bored out to a $\frac{1}{2}$ in. hole and fitted on to a hard wood plug, mounted on the eccentric chuck; it should be carefully fitted, and fixed with very thin glue, the exterior is then turned to a true cylinder, $1\frac{3}{16}$ in. in diameter. The slide of the chuck is then moved out one turn, or $\frac{1}{10}$; the width of the tool in the slide-rest is $\frac{5}{100}$, and the dividing wheel moved 12 divisions for each successive cut; that is, the first cut is made with the slide-rest set at zero, and the wheel at 96. For the second, the tool is moved precisely its own width by the screw of the slide-rest, which will require one half-turn, and the wheel moved forward 12 divisions, and the tool penetrated till a true circle is turned; this process is repeated throughout the length required.

When the work is finished the wood plug can be removed, and at times this is not altogether unattended with difficulty. To dissolve the glue, it should be soaked in warm water ; but the wood having a tendency to expand, it sometimes creates a risk of breaking; this, however, with care and patience is overcome. Having removed the core, the hole may be filled either with an ivory polished cylinder, or black wood, the latter being very effective, as seen in the illustration.

Fig. 4 is a still wider extension of this particular style of decoration, being cut half its length in each direction, right and left. The settings for this particular figure are as follows :—The hole is bored out $\frac{1}{2}$ in., and the external diameter left $\frac{7}{8}$ in., the tool being $\frac{7}{100}$ wide, and the wheel divided into four. The object of this alteration is to illustrate the difference in the twist of the spiral, caused by the diameter having only half the number of discs cut on it. Having adjusted all the different settings, the tool is made to penetrate just deep enough to again turn a true circle; the tool moved precisely its own width, and the wheel moved one quarter round. This is repeated one-half the length from the popit-head towards the mandrel; arriving at the centre, the wheel is moved in the reverse direction, which causes the twist to turn in the opposite way.

It will be observed that the spiral form of Fig. 3 is more distinct and appreciable. This beauty is lessened in Fig. 4, consequent upon its having, as before intimated, only four discs in place of eight, in one complete turn. It is not exhibited as a form of beauty, but simply to more clearly define the two results obtained by this means.

Fig. 5 shows another distinct variation. The chuck is moved out to $\frac{4}{10}$ eccentricity, the tool $\frac{7}{100}$ in. wide. The first cut is made at 96, the tool made to penetrate deep enough to cause the termination of the cut to pass out each side at the centre of the diameter of the cylinder. The wheel is then turned round to 48, or the exact half, and a corresponding cut made; the shape of that part left by this process is seen by Fig. 6, which is intended to show the result of the two consecutive cuts. The tool is then moved precisely its own width laterally, and the corresponding incision made with the wheel set to 24 and 72. These operations it will be seen have been repeated alternately along a portion of the cylinder.

The remaining half is again cut differently, the same tool and equal depth are employed, consequently the form of the discs is still identical with those previously cut, and the only difference in the settings for the production of this part is, that the wheel is moved 6 divisions forward, the second cut for each being made at the opposite side, thus: 96 and 48, 6 and 54, and so on. This movement of the wheel it will be observed causes the work to take a spiral form, which may be varied in a number of different ways.

By reference to Fig. 7 it will be seen that a still further advance is made in the application of the eccentric chuck, and although very much more beautiful in effect, it was cut in precisely the same way as the preceding one. The only thing necessary to create the double strand spiral form, as seen, is to bore the ivory out to a tube. The following details, although in some measure a repetition, will not be out of place :—The ivory was first bored out to a tube with $\frac{1}{2}$ in. hole, it was fitted to a boxwood plug in a metal chuck, and then mounted upon the eccentric chuck, the cylinder was then turned to $\frac{7}{8}$ in. in diameter, the tool exchanged for one exactly $\frac{7}{100}$ in. wide, the slide of the chuck moved out $\frac{4}{10}$ by four turns of its main screw, the dividing wheel set to 96, and the first cut made; this is repeated with the wheel turned half way round to 48 ; the tool is then moved laterally exactly its own width, the wheel moved forward 6 divisions, and cut again ; the wheel is then turned to the opposite which will be 54, and the second cut to complete the figure made ; by this it will be seen, that each consecutive disc requires two separate operations, and by moving the wheel 6 divisions for each one, an elegant spiral is formed, which may be varied like Figs. 3 and 4 in endless different ways, either by increased or diminished eccentricity, or more or less movement of the wheel, the width of the tool employed having also again considerable influence over the result.

This specimen, as will be noticed by reference to the autotype, is also cut in two directions, that is, half with a right-hand twist, while the other is in the opposite way. The first, or that nearest the popit-head, is formed by the wheel being turned towards the operator, for the reverse, the wheel is moved the opposite way.

Patterns of this character may be varied to a large extent by making a certain number of cuts each way, that is to say, eight or ten, with the wheel moved from the operator, the same number being repeated with the wheel turned the other way, these alternate movements create so many complete parts in the two directions, thereby destroying the spiral twist, but with a result which may be considered equally beautiful.

Such work may also give more trouble in removing the wood core, which is occasioned by the delicacy of the parts, and the tendency of the wood to expand. When the plug is removed, the tube may be filled with either an ivory polished cylinder or, if preferred, black wood, each giving great finish to the appearance of the work. Left open, as seen in the illustration, it is sometimes more effective, as both sides of the work are visible, but should it be intended, as a pedestal, to support any other object, its strength will be increased by the interior being filled.

To illustrate all the different forms to be produced on a cylinder by the movements referred to, would necessitate a large number of plates; the foregoing remarks will show the manner in which to proceed, and it is hoped enable those who read them to not only reproduce, but to improve upon them.

All works operated on by this, or similar chucks should be placed on hard wood cores that have been previously driven into metal chucks, as those composed of wood only, are likely to move round on the nozzle of the dividing-wheel, and thus destroy the accuracy of the work, as the slightest alteration in this respect will be detrimental; it should be made a rule to use nothing but a metal chuck.

We have now considered the application of the eccentric chuck as applied to the decoration of cylinders. It is also much used to shape and embellish compound solid forms of many distinct characters; surface solids, for instance, are shaped in several ways (Fig. 8), representing a simple and effective base in the form of a curved triangle with moulded edges. The material for this was first roughly shaped, and surfaced on one side, by which it was glued to a true surface on a chuck attached to the eccentric chuck. It was then reduced to the desired thickness and polished, the slide of the chuck moved out to $1\frac{1}{2}$ in. eccentricity, and the radius of the fixed tool set to the necessary distance to leave the terminals the desired width. The drilling instrument is then placed in the tool box with a moulding drill, the latter is made to revolve at a high speed, and the work moved partially round by the left hand, or, preferably, by the worm wheel and tangent-screw of the segment apparatus. Having cut the three concave curves of the triangle, the slide of the eccentric chuck must be returned to the centre, and the steady-pin replaced. The drill is then set to a radius suitable to the diameter of the material, and by gradual penetration the same figure cut on the ends, which will mitre at the corners and form a very elegant finish. Such moulding may be made to form an entirely different figure by employing the division and index, and cutting seriatim, the space for each cut being determined by the movement of the division-plate, the formation of the pattern depending upon the figure of the tool employed.

Many examples of this class of work are contained in the different forms of claw-footed bases, of three, four, six, or practically any number of feet, which are arranged by dividing the worm wheel to the number required, and adjusting the radius of the tool to suit the same, duly considering the external diameter of the material. Many such forms are to be executed with the eccentric cutter, the work being placed on the mandrel nose ; or, for further combinations, on the eccentric or other chuck of a similar nature, in which case the various curves may be operated upon with the revolving cutters to effect further decorations than can be obtained with the eccentric cutter only.

When the work is mounted on the chuck, that may be selected, either eccentric or rectilinear, the combined right line movements of it and the slide-rest, admit of the production and decoration of solid forms composed of curved and straight lines together, and by this arrangement both curious and beautiful results are obtained. A deal of unnecessary changing of tools is saved by using the moulding tools similar to Figs. 82 to 93, which may be equally well applied in all the instruments. At times, however, it is desirable to use a series of separate tools to effect the same purpose, as it is not always possible to place the eccentric cutter in contact with the work, in consequence of the projecting right angle slide. These are points that the nature of the work and the particular tool employed will lead the operator to decide which is the most appropriate.

CHAPTER XXIII.

The Ellipse Chuck.

This has, for some reason not yet explained, been commonly known as the oval chuck. It is entirely wrong to call an ellipse an oval. The latter is a distinct figure, shaped like an egg, being wider at one end than the other. An ellipse has two unequal diameters, the longest being the transverse or major axis, the short one the conjugate or minor axis. Reference will be made to these as the major and minor axis.

The details necessary for the manufacture of this chuck are similar to those embodied in the description of the eccentric chuck, but with further additions. That now under notice is illustrated by Fig. 163, and is the latest pattern, containing all the most recent improvements. It will be observed that the front worm-wheel and tangent-screw are in every way the same as in the eccentric chuck.

In the present case, the V-grooves are planed in the back plate, which is screwed to fit the nose of the mandrel, and is the narrow one. The double chamfered steel bars are fixed to the front or broad plate. Two steel pallets are then fixed across the back of the chuck, being attached to the steel bars, and set-screws are provided to adjust them to their relative positions in reference to the movable ring upon which they operate.

The sliding ring, which is cast in the solid with a metal frame, is attached to the face of the headstock by two steel centre-screws, the points fitting into corresponding centres in the headstock, and when fitting up the frame, it should be chucked by the centre-hole and the ring turned inside and out; it is then re-chucked by the periphery of the ring, and the back turned as far as the projecting bosses through which the centre-screws pass will allow; it must be then surfaced, and the holes tapped to receive the centre-screws. It is necessary that these holes should be in a parallel line with the face, and, to ensure this, the holes are tapped with a tap having a long plain pin turned to the size of the bottom of the thread, the plain part entering one hole, while the tap itself cuts the thread in the opposite one. The screws should be parallel and well fitted.

To fix the frame in its position on the head, it must be temporarily placed on a metal plug on the mandrel nose by the

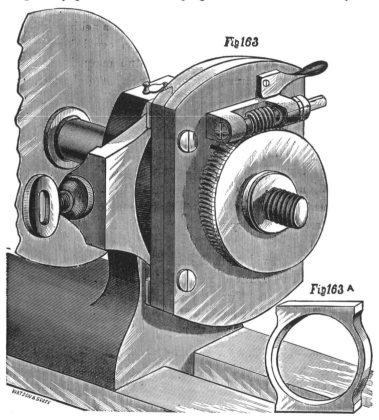

centre hole, and set square across the face; by which process the centres are obtained, and when marked, the ring is removed, and the holes drilled and countersunk to correspond with the points of the screws. When countersinking the holes, they should be placed so that the screws when tightened, will draw the frame firmly to the face of the head.

When the metal plug is removed, it is very probable that the ring will be found to have slightly deviated from actual concentricity to the axis of the mandrel; to correct this a cutter is used, and this is fitted into a chuck made for the purpose, and is set down on to the ring as required, the mandrel being rotated slowly by hand until the ring is again cut perfectly true.

The top of the metal frame is then filed perfectly level with that of the head, and before moving the ring, a line mnst be carefully marked square across both, to denote the position for the purpose of replacing it at any future time; the centre hole is then elongated to allow the ring to be adjusted to the necessary eccentricity, a graduated scale, 1 in. long and divided into 20 equal parts, is then engraved on the top of the frame from the zero line previously marked.

The movement of the ring from the centre is governed by the two centre screws, which, being radial, draw the frame transversely across the face of the head, the front screw being released and the opposite one screwed up a corresponding amount. The off-side of the frame should have a set-screw fitting through the side of the boss, so that when the ring is moved, which it often has to be, the centre-screw may be fixed, and the front one only released, thus ensuring the return of the ring to its original position, this can, however, be readily determined by the division on the frame. By the engraving it will be seen that the screws are made in the shape of thumb-screws with elliptical heads, and when the ring is fixed, the pressure of the hand is sufficient to secure it. It is not desirable to use a lever, except with the utmost caution, as an overdue strain is likely to spring the plate, and destroy the accuracy of the ring.

When adjusted by the division on the frame to the zero, the pallets should be carefully set down to bear upon the ring. The simple revolution of the chuck will then have no effect, but when the steady pin is removed and eccentricity given to the ring, the revolution of the steel pallets round it, will cause the slide to oscillate, thus combining a straight line and rotary movement, which produces an ellipse, and the difference between the two axes will be as follows :—The minor axis will be twice the amount of the radius given to the tool by the slide-rest, and the major axis the same, with twice the eccentricity of the ring added.

So far we have the mechanical principal of the ellipse chuck, but in following a course of ornamental turning, it will require manipulating in various ways. A few examples of the combined movements of it and the slide-rest will be of service in further illustrating its powers.

The number of varied patterns to be produced by the application of this chuck to face work, by shallow fine lines grouped and arranged by the different adjustments, is without end. The primary movement will be at once understood by the few woodcuts which have been prepared with reference to the movements of the chuck for the necessary degrees of difference between the two axes, and the position of the figures.

Fig. 164 illustrates the result of the following settings : The slide-rest set at right angles to the mandrel, and a double angle tool (Fig. 26) of 50° fixed in the tool box. The tool is then set precisely to the height of the lathe axis ; it is also set correspond-

Fig. 164.

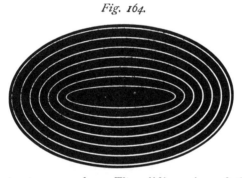

ingly accurate, transversely. The sliding ring of the chuck is then set out $\frac{6}{10}$ and the tool moved to a radius of $\frac{7}{10}$. The first cut is then made very shallow, and the depth screw adjusted. The eccentricity of the ring remains unmoved, and the successive cuts are made at every turn of the main screw of the slide-rest : and when the point of the tool is returned to the centre, it cuts a straight line. It will be observed that the ellipses in this figure are all parallel to one another.

Fig. 165. This figure may be said to be the opposite in character, and requires the movements reversed; the slide-rest still set in the same position, the radius of the tool identical, and for each successive cut the eccentricity of the ring is reduced $\frac{1}{10}$, the tool remaining in the same position throughout. This shows clearly that the reduction of the eccentricity only, decreases the difference between the two axes of the ellipse, and when the ring arrives at the zero, or concentric to the axis of the mandrel, a plain

Fig. 165.

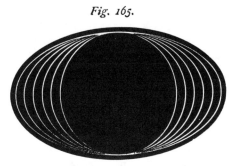

ring is cut. By these two figures we have clearly defined the two opposite movements, namely, the reduction of the radius of the tool only, in the first instance, which produces a series of parallel ellipses terminating in a straight line, and the decrease in the proportion of the figure at the major and minor axis by the corresponding reduction given to the eccentricity of the ring alone, terminating in a concentric ring at the final cut.

Fig. 165a.

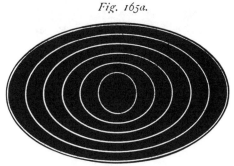

Fig. 165a shows the result of the two movements employed in combination, by which a series of ellipses are cut of equal proportions. Reference to the following instruction will show that this figure is produced with equal facility : The slide-rest in the same position, the eccentricity of ring $\frac{5}{10}$, the radius of tool $\frac{7}{10}$ for the largest ellipse, and for each successive cut, reduce both equally, and when the ring is concentric to the mandrel a circle is again the result.

Fig. 165b. This figure illustrates the use of the dividing, or worm-wheel, on the front of the chuck, which may be employed to produce an unlimited number of beautiful line patterns. This particular group being, as before stated, practically passed over, only those that are required to show the movements of the chuck will be illustrated, and Fig. 165b, it will be seen, has a series of ellipses standing at right angles to each other. In this instance, the ring had an eccentricity of $\frac{5}{10}$, the radius of the tool being adjusted to the same amount; the worm-wheel, set to 96 for the first cut, which is the largest of the series; the wheel is then turned to 24 to place the next ellipse at right angles to that already cut. It will be observed that if the wheel is turned to 48,

Fig. 165b.

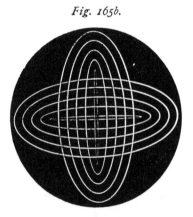

the same course is again travelled as when it is set to 96, consequent upon the equal movement of the slide of the chuck on each side of the centre.

Having cut an ellipse with the wheel set respectively at 96 and 24, the radius of the tool is reduced by one whole turn of the screw of the slide-rest for the second, so that for every turn of the screw the wheel is held alternately at the two numbers, indicated by the figure on the periphery of the wheel. The latter may be divided into almost any number, as previously stated, by which complicated patterns are executed; but the more simple illustrations, as in Fig. 165b, are better adapted to clearly show the movements required for its manipulation.

Fig. 165c is an example of employing the ellipse and eccentric chucks in combination, by which the figures are placed in various positions, that illustrated being quite a simple example, at the

Fig. 165c.

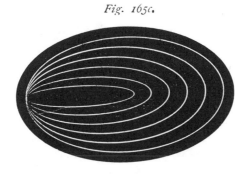

same time fully showing the movements and adjustments required. The two chucks are also largely employed in the shaping and decoration of compound solid forms.

The ellipse chuck is placed on the mandrel nose, and the eccentric chuck upon it, adjusted to stand perfectly parallel one to the other; the sliding-ring is then set out to $\frac{5}{10}$ eccentricity, the radius of the tool to $\frac{6}{10}$, and the first, or largest ellipse cut. The slide of the eccentric chuck is then moved out $\frac{1}{10}$ by one turn of the screw, and the radius of the tool reduced a corresponding amount by one turn of the slide-rest screw; these two movements being carried out for each cut, result in the figure seen, which is similar to the ordinary shell-pattern cut with identical movements of the eccentric cutter and slide-rest; the two adjustments being equal, cause all the cuts to pass through the the same line at one extremity.

By these movements in conjunction with the front dividing wheel, which, as already stated, facilitates the adjustment of the ellipse to any angular position, as seen by Fig. 165c, unending variations may be made. The few examples will, however, suffice to illustrate some of its powers, and enable amateurs to prosecute their researches further.

When practising ornamental turning with this chuck, there are several points in its manipulation found by practical experience to be of great importance, which, being referred to here, will be of valuable assistance, more especially to those uninitiated in such work.

First then, it is necessary in ellipse turning to use a slow motion, as a quick speed causes such vibration that the chuck, from its oscillatory movement, cannot perform its function correctly; secondly, a metal chuck should always be used in place of one composed of boxwood, the latter being likely to turn round upon the screw of the wheel, if it receives undue pressure during its preparation. Should this occur, the angular position of the ellipse will be changed; the deviation, if discovered in time, may be rectified by the worm-wheel and tangent-screw. The use of the metal chuck, however, will prevent this, and it should therefore be employed in all cases. Thirdly, and a most important point to consider, is the centering of the tool to the axis of the mandrel, and any tool in the slide-rest, that is substituted for another, must be carefully tested to see that it is identical in this respect with the one it has replaced.

Work of a large size, that from its unequal surface will require considerable reduction, such, for instance, as an ivory hollow, suitable for the body of a box or other purposes, will be more easily brought to a smooth surface by using the metal turning slide-rest (Fig. 18), with a strong tool or cutter-bar fixed in the tool holder. Works of more delicate nature may be operated upon with the ornamental slide-rest with a satisfactory result. In turning out a deep recess with the latter, the cutter bar (Fig. 20) will be found of valuable assistance, as a continuous cut may be taken with the main screw in place of a series of consecutive incisions with the top slide, when set at right angles to the lathe axis. The capacity of the depth screw is also insufficient for work of large size.

The sliding ring should always be removed during the process of reducing the material to a concentric state, the steady pin being then in its place; if the ring is allowed to remain on, the steel pallets revolving continually round it in the same position become worn in the centre, but when the ring is set out, to even a small amount of eccentricity the pallets have a lateral movement, which causes the wear to be equalised; and when from constant use they are free, the adjusting screws will set them down on to the ring again; it is also essentially necessary to keep both well lubricated.

The supplementary ring (Fig. 163A), is a very considerable improvement to the ellipse chuck. It will be seen that it admits of a broader surface bearing for the pallets to slide on, instead of working only on the periphery of the metal ring, to which the steel ring itself is fitted, giving a smooth and even action to the slide, thus preventing any tendency to vibration whatever; the wear to the ring and pallets is also minimised. The advantages of this introduction will be so apparent that no further details will be required.

To follow the style of Grecian architecture, by the employment of semi-elliptical arches, will be found useful in the construction of temples, clock towers, watch stands, &c., and will be found a most interesting study, and, by the combined movements of the ellipse and eccentric chuck, aided by the segment apparatus, may, without difficulty be produced, and subseqently ornamented to a varied extent, either by continuous mouldings, or by numerous consecutive cuts, the work being arrested for each by the index, or segment apparatus, while the depth-screw of the slide-rest determines the penetration of each. In some instances the front dividing wheel is employed for a similar purpose.

When decorating elliptical cylinders, the various positions in which the work presents itself to the tool during its rotation must not be lost sight of. Having adjusted the eccentricity of the ring and reduced the material to the desired form, the fixed tool may be replaced by the drilling instrument, the chuck is then set to a vertical position, and, the drill being radial to the axis of the tool, will cut equally deep on each side of the centre at the opposite points of the major and minor axis.

As the chuck is partially rotated for the next cut, it will be observed that the upper portion of the quadrant of the figure comes in closer proximity to the tool than the lower, thus cutting deeper, and the variation of each cut will be found to increase in this respect until nearing the major axis, when it decreases, eventually cutting equally when the ellipse stands horizontal to the lathe-head, thus presenting the major axis radial to the tool. Continuing the process, the cut will be seen to be deeper on the reverse side of the following quadrant, gradually again decreasing till the minor axis is reached, when the depth of cut will be found to be coincident with the first. Of course, the larger the amount of eccentricity given to the ring, the greater the difference in the above respect will be. The deviation is not so detrimental when a plain round-nosed tool is used, but when a bold moulding tool is applied, it will destroy the contour of the figure entirely.

All the revolving cutters are more or less applicable to the ornamentation of the elliptic cylinder, the vertical cutter and drill spindle, however, are generally used and are most to be recommended. The universal cutter is also of great service, especially when the ellipse chuck is used in conjunction with the spiral apparatus, which it can now be, with the author's arrangement of the latter to the back of the lathe-head, suggested to him in the first place by General G. C. Clarke, who is acknowledged to be one of the best amateur turners of the present day, and this particular arrangement of the apparatus is universally approved of and admitted to be superior in all ways. It will be found fully explained in subsequent chapters especially devoted to it.

So far we have considered the various instruments as applied for the ornamentation of the elliptic cylinder, it will now be necessary to give here a brief outline of their employment for the same purpose on the surface, and the autotype of miniature or photograph frame (Plate 8) will suffice to show more clearly the result of their various adjustments.

When about to make such a frame, the first thing will be the selecting of the material; and in doing this, it may be mentioned, that it is not necessary that it should be of any definite proportion, unless for any specific purpose. It must be cut from the hollow end of a tusk. This done, a piece of well-seasoned boxwood is driven firmly into a metal cup chuck, and turned as short as possible, it is then faced over and the ivory glued to it. The sliding-ring is now adjusted to suit the proportions of the material, so that it may be left as large as possible. The rebate at the back is then turned out to receive the picture and glass; this should be about a quarter of an inch deep, and quite half an inch larger than the aperture, so that a good face is left for the picture to bear against. It may now be removed from the chuck by being soaked in warm water to dissolve the glue.

A second chuck is then turned to fit the rebate, and again glued to it. When fitting it, care should be taken that the chuck is exactly the depth of the recess, so that the face of the ivory will bear against it, the inner pattern being cut through at each penetration, as seen in the illustration.

The slide-rest must in all cases be employed in turning ellipses, and such a frame may be roughed into shape by using both the main and depth screw in conjunction, the lever of course being dispensed with, and the top slide placed under control by the bridle; thus, by working both hands together, curves, either concave or convex, and mouldings of any shape may be worked up approximately. The fixed tool must then be replaced by the revolving cutters.

In proceeding to ornament the frame now under our notice, the horizontal cutter is the first of the revolving cutters employed, having in it a double quarter-hollow tool (Fig. 98), set accurately to the centre, the slide-rest is set parallel to the lathe-bearers, and the 192 circles arrested at every hole, thus creating 192 consecutive cuts. The tool is inserted sufficiently deep to bring the points up sharp, and passed slowly over the part to be cut; the slide-rest is then turned to an angle to bring the tool to the centre of the following concave curve, and the horizontal cutter replaced by the drilling instrument, having in it a round-nosed fluting-drill, $\frac{25}{100}$ in. wide. By reference to the illustration, it will be seen that the incisions made by the drill are in the centre of the points left by the horizontal cutter, and in order to adjust the work to place them thus, it is necessary to use the adjusting index, for the reason, that having been cut at every hole in the division, there is no half to set the index to for this purpose. The work is moved round by the adjusting nut of the index to the desired position, and fixed by the lock nut; the drill is then made to penetrate deep enough to leave each cut the exact width of the points left by those preceding it.

When the division employed can be equally divided, the necessity for the adjusting index is dispensed with, and it is only to move the plate round to half the number taken for the first cut, and continue as before. The object of explaining this, is merely to give an instance of the service of the adjusting index.

The projecting beads will be the next part to proceed with, and it will be seen that these are equally divided, and as this was accomplished without special apparatus, a few hints in connection with it will, it is hoped, be of value. There are forty-five consecutive beads. When turning that part of the work on which they are to be cut, it should be left rather wider than required, for the purpose of future adjustments, if found necessary; the ellipse chuck is then set perfectly vertical by the segment apparatus, which also affords the means of equally dividing the work; the drill-spindle with a bead-drill $\frac{25}{100}$ in. wide, and astragal at the end, is then set to the centre of the lathe axis, which is, of course, the same as the tool previously employed, it is arranged to cut also in the centre of the space left to receive the beads; the drill is then inserted very lightly, only in fact to disclose its extreme diameter; the work is then moved round by the tangent-screw of the segment apparatus until the edge of the drill comes exactly in contact with that of the previous cut. This trial of distance should be carried entirely round the work, and in all probability it will be found that the space will be either too great, or insufficient

Plate 8.

for the last bead; the error being discovered before the beads are cut, it may be corrected in the following way. The drill is moved either to or from the centre, according to the deviation, and it is for this compensation that the part on which the beads are to be cut should be left wider than required. The substance of the method is simply this:—Supposing the entire surface, from the centre at which the drill is set will not hold accurately, say, forty-five beads, by extending the radius of the drill to a larger diameter it can be made to do so, and by exercising care, the result is perfectly satisfactory; by using a drill of rather less dimension the same object is attained. It may be mentioned that these means would only be employed in the absence of the legitimate apparatus, which is specially made for the equal division of the ellipse, and will be fully explained in the following chapter.

The beads are all cut in the first instance with the drill set radial to the surface, the astragal drill is then replaced by a pointed one of the same size, and as the beads, when finished, are more like a ball than a hemisphere, the top-slide must be moved round by its quadrant to an angle, so that they may be undercut, the adjustment of the slide must be the same on each side of the centre, and the drill also set to its desired position, by the main screw of the slide-rest. The projecting points between the beads are the result of the angle on the point of the drill, and not a second operation; a small round-nosed drill is afterwards inserted between the beads, on both sides.

The plain continuous bead was cut with a fixed tool, and to turn this correctly, with a really polished surface, the chuck must be rotated slowly, and the penetration be slight and even. If once the tool is allowed to cut roughly and unevenly, considerable difficulty will be experienced in getting it quite smooth again. This is most important, as work of this class must be left untouched from the tool, except to be polished with whiting on a brush.

The following seriated moulding was cut with a large quarter-hollow drill, inserted at every hole of the 96 division. There are two ways of placing the drill in contact, either by the depth screw of the top slide, or by moving it laterally by the main screw of the slide-rest, which is arrested at every cut by a fluting-stop.

For the final pattern on the inside, the eccentric cutter was employed, having in it a narrow parting tool $\frac{3}{100}$ in. wide fixed at a radius of $\frac{3}{20}$, and passed entirely through the ivory on to the box-wood, the same means for the equal division being adopted as for the beads, viz., the segment apparatus. Care should be exercised when cutting through work of this character, as there is some liability of the extreme points breaking off, the result of which would be, the destruction of many hours' labour. The present subject may be considered complete, and although a comparatively simple example, it is both effective and useful.

Various other references will be made to the combined uses of the ellipse chuck and revolving cutters as applied to the specimens in the various plates, but the foregoing are sufficient to illustrate its capabilities in this respect.

CHAPTER XXIV.

COMPENSATING INDEX FOR THE EQUAL DIVISION OF THE ELLIPSE.

THIS instrument forms a most valuable addition to the lathe, and by its aid, all works executed with the ellipse chuck, are rendered more perfect, and beautiful in effect. [Reference has been made to the equal division of the ellipse in the details of the miniature frame illustrated in Plate 8 in the preceding chapter, which gives sufficient evidence of the advantage of a mechanical means of effecting the same purpose, and the following details, combined with the very clear and distinct illustration contained in Fig. 166 will, it is hoped, render the whole apparatus easily understood. Although it may be considered a difficult instrument to manufacture, it is comparatively easy to manipulate, and, as now fitted by the author on an improved plan at the back of the lathe mandrel, as suggested by the Rev. C. C. Ellison, it is more perfect and convenient in every way, and forms a distinct apparatus, being removed intact from the mandrel when not required for use. When fitted to the front of the driving-pulley in the original way, the two discs and wheel have to remain on the mandrel, which is a decided objection, the wheel having a tendency to catch in everything that it comes in contact with, and also to collect dirt, shavings, &c.

A metal sleeve, to which is attached in the solid, a dial-plate 7 in. in diameter, is fitted to the mandrel in the same way as the dividing chuck of the spiral apparatus. On the sleeve two discs are fitted, to which radial arms are attached, so that they work as if hinged thereto. The arm at the back, or nearest the dial-plate has an index-point fixed to it, as seen in the engraving, which moves up and down with the arm when in action. The second radial arm is held stationary by a steel blade, the lower extremity of which is fitted to the arm of the spiral apparatus, the top of the blade being slotted, and open at the end, so that the binding screw may be passed into it, by which it is fixed in the desired position.

To obtain the required motion, a wheel of sixty teeth is fitted to the sleeve in front of the arm. This wheel is provided with the means of adjustment in either direction, and is fixed by three screws,

Fig 66

the holes through which they pass being elongated, so that when finally set, the screws can be tightened by a key. A second wheel of sixty teeth is then fixed to the radial arm, to revolve and gear with that on the sleeve. This is also geared to a wheel of thirty teeth, which is attached to the axis of a slide that revolves between the two radial arms. The nut of this slide is actuated by a screw of ten threads to the inch, which has a micrometer on its end, and passes through a steel stud, which works in an oblong slot in the arm nearest the dial-plate; on the top of the slide a scale, divided into twentieths of an inch is engraved, the zero being precisely opposite the axis of the wheel that has thirty teeth. When the index is set to this point, and the mandrel rotated, the slide between the two arms simply revolves, while both arms remain stationary, but when the nut is moved towards the mandrel, it carries the stud in the arm with it; the consequence of which is, that the arm moves up and down with the revolution of the mandrel, the exact amount being determined by the eccentricity given to the nut of the slide. When fitting up an instrument of this kind, the work should be so far completed as described; it is then set up on its place with the slide and index precisely radial to the mandrel, when the ellipse chuck is standing in a vertical position, as seen in Fig. 163. When thus adjusted, the two arms and slide will all be in parallel lines, and once made, this adjustment is permanent and will not require further attention.

The index in the arm nearest the dial-plate is then used to describe an arc on the plate, from which the zeros or starting points for the divisions are drilled, thus enabling any one of the several circles to be employed without any further adjustment. The top of the index is provided with the means of altering the position of the pointer, if for any reason it should be found necessary, but, the divisions being drilled with the starting points on the arc, the point may be transferred from one to the other, in the same way as the index to the division on the pulley-face.

When fitted to the lathe in this way, the whole apparatus may be removed in one piece, and, when replaced for future employment, it only requires to be set perfectly radial to the mandrel. This is simplified by marking a line on the lower blade, to correspond with one on the metal radial arm to which it fixes, the lower arm in which the blade is held at its base may also be placed at the same distance, by which the readjustment of the apparatus is more readily effected than when fitted to the front, and it is clearly and distinctly the most convenient method to employ for such an instrument.

When adjusting the index for use, it will be necessary that its movement should correspond with that of the ellipse chuck, and in which ever position the chuck is set, either vertical or horizontal, the slide between the arms must be radial to it.

The slide must be set parallel with the line on the arms, when they are attached to the discs on the sleeve, and, if the ellipse chuck does not stand precisely vertical, the sixty-wheel on the sleeve may be released and the mandrel rotated until it does, when the wheel is again fixed. The eccentricity to be given to the slide of the compensator will depend upon the difference between the two axes of the ellipse, and may, of course, be altered to suit the material.

It has been found impossible to give any definite rule by which the movement of the eccentric ring of the ellipse chuck may be governed by that of the compensator, for the reason that the radius of the tool in the slide-rest has considerable influence over it; therefore absolute accuracy can only be obtained by trial. It may be mentioned, however, that all ellipses of the same definite proportions will be found to require the same amount of eccentricity in the slide of the compensator. The following table of adjustments will give a few of the approximate settings, showing the amount of movement necessary to the slide, for various proportions of ellipses :—

Proportion of ellipse.	Movement of slide of compensator.
5 to 6	$1\frac{1}{4}$ turn
$4\frac{1}{2}$ to $5\frac{1}{2}$	$1\frac{1}{2}$ turn
4 to 5	$1\frac{3}{4}$ turn one division
$3\frac{1}{2}$ to $4\frac{1}{2}$	2 turns one division
$3\frac{1}{2}$ to $4\frac{1}{2}$	$2\frac{1}{4}$ turns
3 to 4	$2\frac{3}{4}$ turns
$2\frac{3}{4}$ to $3\frac{3}{4}$	$2\frac{3}{4}$ turns
$2\frac{1}{2}$ to $3\frac{1}{2}$	3 turns
$2\frac{1}{4}$ to $3\frac{1}{4}$	$3\frac{1}{4}$ turns one division
$1\frac{3}{4}$ to $2\frac{3}{4}$	$3\frac{3}{4}$ turns
$1\frac{1}{2}$ to $2\frac{1}{2}$	$3\frac{3}{4}$ turns
$1\frac{1}{4}$ to $2\frac{1}{4}$	$4\frac{1}{4}$ turns
1 to 2	5 turns

These will be sufficient to illustrate the movement of the apparatus, and it must be pointed out that a very slight deviation in the proportion of the ellipse will necessitate a readjustment of the slide, according to the variation in the figure.

Fig. 165*d* will perhaps still more clearly demonstrate the advantage of equally dividing this class of work. The shells cut round one portion of the ellipse, it will be seen, are all cut equi-

Fig. 165d.

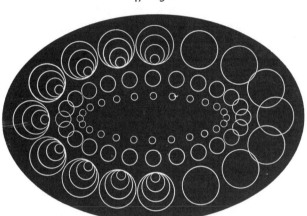

distantly, and were done in the following way :—The apparatus, Fig. 166, placed on the back of the mandrel, as seen in the engraving; the ellipse chuck set vertically, and the slide of the compensator set radial, and held by the thumb-screw to the lower steel blade; the index point then placed in the zero of the 192 circle on the dial-plate of the compensator, and the slide between the two radial arms moved towards the mandrel $3\frac{1}{4}$ turns, the eccentric cutter placed in the slide-rest, and the tool moved to a radius of $\frac{3}{10}$. The dial-plate is then moved to every 12 for each consecutive cut, so that if carried throughout the figure, there would be sixteen consecutive circles ; the radius of the tool is then reduced $\frac{5}{100}$, or half a turn of the screw, and the slide-rest moved a corresponding distance, for the second circle.

The latter movement of the tool nearer to the axis of the work, creates a further difference in the proportion of the ellipse, and will therefore necessitate a readjustment of the slide of the compensator, the same being required for each alteration of the distance to or from the centre. The shells are thus equidistantly placed round a portion of the figure, the remaining space being left, so that the result of employing the stationary index may be more clearly portrayed. By referring to the print (Fig. 165*d*), it will be seen that the circles become gradually nearer to each other as they approach the major axis, while the difference is increased in the opposite direction as the minor axis is neared. To cut the seven plain circles, above alluded to, the chuck is again set vertically, and the tool in the eccentric cutter returned to the same radius as employed for the first series—the 96 circle of divisions on the pulley-face also used—and arrested at every sixth hole.

This deviation in the proximity of the cuts is perhaps more clearly illustrated by the two inner circles of smaller rings, which, from the increased difference between the two axes, are more distinctly visible.

CHAPTER XXV.

The Rectilinear Chuck.

This chuck in its improved form may be said to have entirely superseded the straight line chuck, which, from its inability to perform a rotary movement, is limited to work of a straight line character only, and although a necessary adjunct to a rose engine, and usually supplied with such a tool, is seldom made to the modern ornamental turning lathe, therefore its construction may be passed over, being of small interest to those who study the art, and practise the same, with the modern apparatus; and as the chuck illustrated by Fig. 167 is one of the most important, and will perform a rotary and straight line movement in combination, it is rendered of considerable service for the ornamentation of compound solid forms, all the various instruments being used in conjunction with it, according to the results desired.

It may be classed as an extra large eccentric chuck, and its process of manufacture is similar to it, with exceptions and additions. The body of the chuck is planed up and surfaced, it is then held on a true surface chuck, and a recess turned in the back, $1\frac{1}{4}$ in. in diameter, $\frac{1}{4}$ in. deep, this is for the purpose of receiving a supplementary or false back, on which it is held during its progress in manufacture, by four strong steel screws. The back is sometimes cast in the solid with the plate and screwed to fit the mandrel nose; either way is equally true. The particular advantage of the false back is found in the fact that the chuck can be made in the absence of the lathe-head on which it is to work, except for a few hours while the back is fitted. A standard steel chuck should be made for the purpose, which ensures its ultimate accuracy.

When fixed to the back a light cut must be taken over the surface with the slide-rest set perfectly true, and the steel double chamfered bars then fixed, as described for the eccentric chuck,

Fig 167

but with three screws in each, instead of two, on account of the extra length of the bars; the front plate is then adjusted, and the slide ground up. The steady-pin is then fitted, being placed at the top of the plate, the lower end being reduced as much as possible, in order that the slide may be extended as far from the centre as possible.

From the extra length of the chuck it is obvious that the front slide is capable of a much more extended movement than the eccentric chuck, and its facilities are also considerably advanced by the slide moving to each side of the centre. When it is set vertically, it will move two inches above, and three inches below the centre, thus creating a vertical traverse of five inches.

The main screw, like all others, is ten threads to the inch, and is carried through the entire length of the chuck, having a coupling at each end; a separate steel collar being fitted on one end to form an equal bearing with the other; both ends are then squared to receive a key and a micrometer. The latter are both divided from corresponding zeros into ten equal parts. This improvement was introduced by the author, and its advantages will be apparent, as the slide can be moved with equal facility from either end, so that when, during the progress of cutting various patterns, the chuck assumes such an angular position as to render it difficult to manipulate the slide from one end, it can be worked from the opposite; and the micrometers being coincident, the setting can be read from either. This arrangement of the screw is admitted to be superior to the short one, movable from the top only, and adds much to the value of the chuck. When used in conjunction with the segment apparatus and revolving cutters, it becomes in reality a shaping machine, and a deal of beautiful work, such as Gothic arches, moulded bases, and polygonal figures, is easily produced.

The front worm-wheel must now be fitted, and, unlike the eccentric and ellipse chucks, it has 120 teeth. The tangent-screw and frame in other respects are the same, also the cam for actuating it, the wheel being divided on the periphery at every turn of the tangent-screw, and figured at every 10, with a dot at each 5.

MANIPULATION OF THE RECTILINEAR CHUCK.

Although to a certain extent resembling the eccentric chuck, it has distinct advantages, which consist in its extended capacity, and the traverse of the slide on both sides of the centre, and, being a stronger tool, it carries the other chucks with less tendency to vibration; it is seldom used in complete revolution, except while the work is turned true upon the wheel, being generally fixed in a vertical, horizontal, or angular position, and retained so by the segment apparatus, and it is when held at such an angle that the screw-head cannot be readily got at, that the advantages of the screw working from either end is apparent. It is largely employed in cutting and decorating compound solid, and polygonal figures of any number of facets, &c. A few words upon the manner it which it is manipulated will assist amateur turners in working out its capabilities. As an example, we will assume it is required to cut a square base 3 in. wide, with a thickness of $\frac{1}{2}$ in.: the chuck is set to a vertical position, the slide-rest parallel with the lathe-bed, the eccentric cutter (Fig. 62) is placed in the tool-box, but the eccentricity need not be extended beyond what is necessary to cut out the width of the base; the cutter is then revolved at speed, and the work moved above and below the centre by the main screw to cut out the length of the square; the wheel is then moved round 30 divisions, or one fourth, and the second side cut, the remaining two sides of the square receiving the same treatment at 60 and 90 respectively. The work, thus roughly shaped, may be moulded into endless shapes, and to effect this, various means are used: first, the moulding tools (Figs. 82 to 87) may be placed in the eccentric cutter; secondly, a moulding drill may be employed, also, the different tools may be placed in the vertical cutter (Fig. 95) or the universal cutter (Fig. 122), set to cut in various positions.

To cut out a bold concave curve at the base of a square pedestal or similar object, the horizontal or universal cutter, set to cut horizontally, will be found a ready means to employ; the tool is set out to the radius required, and revolved at a high rate of speed, the work being carried up and down as before, with the slide of the chuck.

The variety of mouldings, as before stated, are practically without end, and a very effective result is found in the same being pierced seriatim, the cutter revolving as before, but the work held stationary, and moved by the main screw of the chuck to the required distance for the succeeding cuts, the figure resulting, being dependent upon the nature of the cutters used for the purpose. The slide-rest, set transversely across the lathe-bed, affords the opportunity of producing a large variety of patterns upon the face of the work, and many may be composed of curved and straight lines in combination.

In the latter instance, having cut the straight recesses the required length, for which purpose a square-end drill, sharpened on both sides, is employed, the eccentricity of the slide is adjusted so that the convex curves terminate at their extremities, and the partial rotation of the mandrel is arrested each side by the segment stops.

The production of Gothic arches also forms an important feature in this tool, and they may be executed on a large scale, their formation and decoration with the various moulding tools being also practically unlimited, either by continuous moulding, or seriated cuts at intervals, decided in some instances by the partial rotation of the mandrel under the influence of the segment apparatus; at other times the movement is under the control of the dividing-wheel or slide-rest, either by lateral or horizontal movements.

The formation of large boxes or caskets, of square or oblong shape, by being put together, is also an interesting study, as the sides may be elaborately decorated by the combination of curved and straight recesses; and for such work the different pieces of which the box is composed, will represent simply flat plates, which are glued to a surface while being operated upon; and for this it is preferable to use a metal chuck with a large surface of wood attached to it, as it is most important that the work, having been once set to the position, either vertical or horizontal, should not be liable to move on the nozzle of the chuck.

By reference to the autotype (Plate 9) it will be observed
that the rectilinear chuck may be employed for another and still
more important branch of turning, which is, the cutting of convex
curves round cylinders, and the result of such work, it will be seen,
so closely resembles rose-engine turning, that it is generally
supposed to be such by those who have not been instructed in the
use of the chuck for such work.

The subject now to be considered was designed and turned by
the Earl of Sefton, to whom the author is greatly indebted for the
privilege of illustrating and describing it, and the thanks of
amateurs are also due to his lordship for initiating this particular
pattern, as it was from his long experience as an amateur
turner that it emanated. To reproduce the example illustrated,
the following instructions will assist the turner, and lay the
foundation of a class of work that may be enlarged upon to a
very considerable extent.

A piece of ivory $2\frac{3}{4}$ in. long, and 3 in. in diameter, is turned
out perfectly true inside, and lightly glued to a boxwood chuck
or plug; the exterior is then turned to a true cylinder, when
mounted upon the wheel of the chuck. The latter is then set horizontally, and fixed by the tangent screw of the segment apparatus;
the slide is moved out from the operator to sufficient eccentricity to
describe the curve that will be contained in the thickness of the
material; the drilling instrument is then placed in the slide-rest,
with a square-end drill sharpened on each side. That used for
the present example was $\frac{16}{100}$ in. wide. The segment stops are
now arranged so that the partial rotation of the mandrel may be
carried in each direction, in order that the drill may cut entirely
through the ivory into the wood plug, and in this process, great care
is necessary, to avoid breaking away the ivory as the cut passes out.

Having by two trial cuts determined the position of the
segment stops, the succeeding cuts may be made with the hand on
the pulley by which its movement is governed; but the safest plan
to adopt is to rotate the mandrel by the tangent-screw, as it is
more certain in its motion, and not so likely to cause a fracture to
the drill or work.

Plate 9.

The same process is performed six times, the driving wheel being turned round twenty divisions for each cut; for the second series, the drill is moved by the main screw of the slide-rest precisely its own width; the wheel of the chuck turned round fi ve divisions, and a cut made at each twenty of the wheel fr om that point, and this process is continued throughout its whole length, retulting in a series of segments of circles being plac ed round a cylinder in a spiral form, and when the inside is filled with black wood or other material, it forms a most effective pattern. The amount of twist contained in the spiral may be varied according to the movement of the wheel for each succeeding series.

The foregoing description is of a pattern which may be varied in many ways. Work of the same class may be carried out on a similar object without being cut through, and the formation of the curves is not confined to a spiral twist. For example, suppose a cylinder of ivory the same size is to be cut into similar curves, but not through, nor in a spiral line. This being the case, the space occupied by the drill passing into the wood plug, as in Plate 9, may be usefully employed, and dispersed amongst a greater number of curves around the cylinder. The following few remarks will at once illustrate this description of work, the manipulation of the chuck being in many respects similar.

In the first place the chuck is set horizontally, and the necessary eccentricity given to the slide, the dividing wheel set to 120, a drill of the same description, but $\frac{10}{100}$ in. wide, employed; the segment stops arranged to allow the mandrel to rotate past each side of the centre, and the trial cuts made. This pattern will require rather more care than those that are cut through, and the first cut must only be allowed to penetrate towards each end of the curve, without touching the extreme diameter of the cylinder. The tool must be gradually advanced by the guide-screw of the top slide, and it may happen that this proceeding will clearly indicate that some altera-tion in the eccentricity of the slide is necessary. This is a matter that is important, and may be readily effected, and when so adjusted, and the necessary depth is decided by the stop-screw to complete the

M

curve, the remaining cuts of the first circle may be finished at every ten divisions of the wheel, leaving twelve consecutive curves in all. The drill is now moved its own width by one turn of the main screw, the wheel moved five divisions, or half the distance, and the second circle of curves cut in the same way, at every ten. It will be seen that this movement will equally divide the cuts, so that each alternate series starts from the centre of that preceding it, the result being, that instead of a spiral formation, the curves range in a straight course throughout its length.

There are many points connected with the working of this chuck that will be at once apparent to the operator when using it. In such a pattern as that last described, it will be found that the curves do not meet absolutely, and, when this is the case, a projection is left at the termination of each cut, formed by the curve contained in the diameter of the drill; this adds, rather than detracts from the general appearance of the work; long taper forms are very handsome when cut in this way, and for such specimens it is necessary to support the end of the work by the popit-head centre, which must be removed each time before the wheel is turned round, and carefully replaced before the succeeding cut is made, in the manner referred to in Plate 7, descriptive of work executed on the eccentric chuck.

CHAPTER XXVI.

The Dome or Spherical Chuck.

This chuck also forms a very important addition to the apparatus employed for ornamental turning, and by the aid of the following details it will not be found a difficult instrument to manufacture. The chuck illustrated by Fig. 168 is one of the most complete description now made, having improvements which render its manipulation more easy than heretofore. It is composed of a strong oblong metal body with a projecting boss at one end, which is screwed to fit the mandrel nose; it is then carefully faced with the slide-rest, when set accurately to a right angle, and the sides are filled up parallel, after which the oblong mortise is got out true and square to the body.

A circular metal disc with a tenon attached to it, is fitted by the latter to slide from end to end of the mortise, one end projecting through the plate, so that it can be fixed at any desired position by a steel nut and washer. On the top of the disc a worm-wheel with ninety-six teeth is fitted, so that it will revolve. This is achieved by a screw countersunk into the wheel, and screwing into the lower disc; the worm-wheel is actuated by a tangent-screw working in a metal frame, fixed also to the lower disc by two screws. On the top of the wheel a third circular plate is fixed, to which is cast in the solid, the horizontal arm that carries the worm-wheel upon which the work is placed when the chuck is in use; the end of the arm is turned out to fit the external diameter of the tangent-wheel, which is also cut to ninety-six teeth. On one side of the arm a projection is left, so that the tangent-frame can be fitted on an improved plan lately introduced by the author. It will be seen, perhaps, more clearly, by reference to Fig. 168*, that the

screw and frame are made so that the former can be move
in and out of gear; the frame is hinged to the side of the
arm by a screw seen on the left-hand side, and a milled-head
thumb-screw passes through a curved slot in the opposite side;
the screw entering the frame, so that when it is required to move
the wheel, it is released, and the wheel turned independently,

FIG 168   FIG 168*

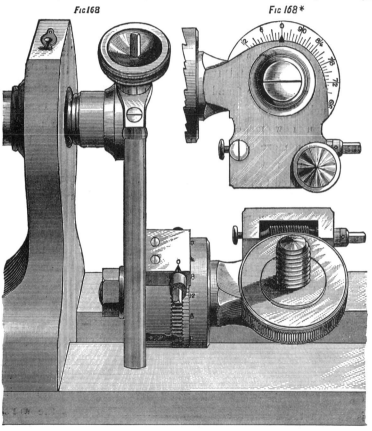

the tangent-screw [is then returned to gear and fixed by the
thumb-screw.

As an instance of the advantage of this improvement, it may
be presumed that it is desired to cut a square base; as one turn
of the screw moves the wheel through the space of one tooth, it will
require twenty-four complete revolutions to move it one quadrant

of its circle; this cannot be deemed anything but a monotonous proceeding, and it is entirely obviated by releasing the screw, and
moving the wheel from 0 to 24, 48, and 72 for the respective
cuts, fixing the wheel each time by the thumb-screw. To ensure the
worm-wheel being as free from vibration as possible, it is held in
its place by a screw, under the head of which is fitted a steel
washer $1\frac{1}{4}$ in. in diameter; the back of the wheel is divided into
96 equal parts and figured at every 6, with a long line at each
third division; these are read by a steel point fixed to the arm,
the micrometer of the screw being divided into eight equal parts,
so that the divisions of the wheel may be sub-divided if necessary.
Through the body of the chuck a steel screw of ten threads to the
inch is fitted, and in consequence of the length of the plain part,
and the support derived from its passing through the tenon which
forms the nut, there is no necessity for the end of the screw to
pass into the metal at the opposite extremity. On the top of the
body of the chuck, a metal plate is attached by two screws, the
latter bearing against the collar of the main screw, the end of which
is filed square to receive a key, and a micrometer with milled-
head, which is divided into ten equal parts, and figured at each
alternate line—0, 2, 4, 6, 8. This division, it may be mentioned,
is seldom of much real service in adjusting hemispherical objects,
the work being generally reduced approximately to form while
revolving on the mandrel nose, and when transferred to the dome
chuck it is adjusted to suit the sphere, without reference to
any particular starting-point or division of the micrometer on the
screw.

The worm-wheel attached to the base of the horizontal arm,
forms an important addition to this chuck, as it enables the work to
be moved to an oblique position, by which various compound shapes
are formed, that cannot be obtained by any other means. The
ellipse chuck may be placed on the mandrel nose, and the dome
chuck attached to it; and for further combinations, the eccentric
chuck may be interposed between them.

The following instructions will, it is hoped, assist the amateur
to manipulate, and develop the resources of this chuck. It

differs from others in many ways; it holds the work at right
angles to the mandrel nose, and unlike the ellipse and eccentric
chucks, it is seldom required to make a complete revolution, its
partial rotations being governed by the hand, or placed under
control of the worm-wheel and tangent-screw of the segment
apparatus, the latter being in most cases preferable.

The work is first turned as nearly as possible to the desired
curve, and if from absence of superfluous material, extreme
accuracy is necessary in its adjustment, it will be expedient to
employ a transfer chuck. Of this particular adjunct there are
two kinds: a steel chuck is fitted to the wheel of the dome chuck,
and turned out perfectly true to receive the plain end of a spring
chuck, and the latter having been turned on the mandrel nose, will
cause the work to assume the same axial truth, when replaced on the
dome chuck, with the transfer intervening. Another plan is to
have a metal chuck screwed to fit the mandrel, and turned out to
fit the stem of the worm-wheel, which is removed from the chuck,
while the work is approximately shaped in the transfer, on the
mandrel; the wheel is then replaced in the dome chuck, so that
the work may receive further decoration. The latter process
is not to be recommended, as it occupies a deal of time, and the
former arrangement is equally correct in its result; the use of either,
however, is not always required, as the adjustment of the chuck
can be arranged to suit the work.

As an example of comparatively simple work, the body of the
pepper-box (Plate 4), which has already been noticed, will serve
to demonstrate the action of the chuck for the decoration of
spheres, &c. The material was first turned as near as possible
to the desired form on the mandrel nose, on a wood plug, driven
firmly into a metal cup chuck, the diameter of the latter being
less than that of the material to be operated upon; it was then
placed on the dome chuck, while adjusted to stand in a vertical
position, as seen in Fig. 168.

When turning the work to the desired form in the first
instance, a minute projection should be left at the centre of the
hemisphere, for the purpose of testing the height of the centre, also

the lateral position of the same. The slide-rest is then set parallel
with the lathe-bearers, with a point, or double-angle tool (Fig. 26)
fixed in it; this is very carefully adjusted to the precise height,
the point of the tool is then moved laterally by the main screw of
the slide-rest until it coincides with the same test point, and to
ascertain the accuracy of this, the chuck is moved to a horizontal
position by turning the tangent-screw of the segment apparatus
forty-five whole turns, or the screw may be released and the chuck
moved round by hand, and the screw again moved into gear and
fixed by the cam.

Having thus adjusted the tool to the two respective centres, the
winch-handle of the slide-rest should be removed from the screw
to prevent the possibility of its being accidentally shifted; the
tangent-screw of the segment apparatus may now be released, and
the chuck allowed to hang vertically, which, from its weight, it will
do, and, as a series of rotations is required to adjust the arm
holding the work, it is not necessary to refix it each time. The
steel nut is then loosened, and the horizontal arm moved by the
main screw, to adjust the work to touch the tool as nearly as
possible at all parts of the curve, and if the work has not been
turned to a correct sphere it will not be possible for it to do so,
therefore, if the tool is made to cut equally at the circumference
and centre, the partial rotation of the chuck will reduce those parts
that are not true, to a perfect hemisphere, or any portion of the
same; the arm is then fixed by the nut at the back.

The drilling instrument now takes the place of the point-tool,
and has a quarter-hollow drill (Fig. 132) placed in it. This drill it
will be seen has the curve brought quite to the centre, and is
made sharp at the point, so that the reeds, when cut, are close
together. It will be found more convenient, in executing work of
this kind, to arrange the slide-rest, so that the top slide is under
control without the use of the lever, both hands being then more at
liberty. This is to be highly recommended for all work, but is
especially necessary in the present case, as the left hand is required
to govern the semi-rotation of the mandrel, while the right hand is
fully employed in manipulating the slide-rest, &c.

The tool is then made to penetrate deep enough to bring the top of the reeds up to the shape of the drill, which is ascertained by a series of trials upon the two first cuts; the distance for each being determined by moving the tangent-screw of the chuck the required number of turns, which, at the same time, must be some definite number that will divide into the ninety-six teeth of the wheel—for the pattern under notice three turns of the screw are made, leaving thirty-two consecutive cuts. Having made all these adjustments, the partial revolution of the chuck is arrested at each point, by the pins placed in the side of the worm-wheel of the segment apparatus.

This specimen has been referred to in the details of the universal cutter (Fig. 122), as being executed with that instrument, employing a double quarter-hollow tool. As far as the arrangement of the dome chuck is concerned, there is no difference whatever, and if it can be conveniently worked, a fly cutter is preferable to a drill; in some cases the termination of the cut will not admit of the former being used, in consequence of the radius of the cutter causing the frame to come in contact with projections on the work; this must be decided by the operator during the progress of the work, and the instrument which is most suitable for the purpose employed; under any circumstances a drill, or revolving cutter, renders much better work than a fixed tool, which can, however, be employed for a like purpose, but does not cut the incisions so cleanly as the former. The shape of the reeds or ribs produced, will depend upon the form of the tool, and the distance the wheel is moved for each cut. A very decorative result is obtained by the wheel receiving sufficient movement to leave an interval of polished surface between each reed; the plain portion can then be further ornamented by being either pierced seriatim with a round-nosed drill, or studded with pearls, for which purpose a bead-drill (Fig. 130) of the desired size is necessary, and as the width of the space between the reeds gradually diminishes towards the centre, a series of drills of corresponding diminution is necessary to correctly embellish such a form.

Having selected the drills, the wheel of the chuck must be adjusted to the precise half of the distance it was moved for each reed. The first bead, which will be the largest of the series, is then cut near to the circumference, on each intervening space; the dome chuck is then partially rotated and fixed, either by the index-point or the segment wheel, at the desired position; the drill is exchanged for one of rather less dimensions, and by carefully adjusting the distance for each, and using correctly graduated drills, such a pattern is to be made extremely elegant.

It may be mentioned that when it is desired to leave any portion of the hemisphere untouched by the drills or cutters, or free from any decoration whatever, the work must be carefully and accurately turned and highly polished, prior to its being placed on the dome chuck, as it cannot be so finished after the cutting has been executed.

The foregoing remarks have reference to the spherical chuck as employed for the decoration of the hemisphere only, from which it may be said to derive its name of dome-chuck.

It is to be used for the production and ornamentation of many different shapes, such as square or polygonal bases, pedestals, &c., each separate moulding or face of which may be further operated upon by any of the various instruments, as all of them can be employed in conjuction with the chuck.

The dome or hemispherical top of any particular object may be made flatter than the actual hemisphere, by extending the radius of the tool from the axis of the worm-wheel upon which the work is placed; with the tool thus moved, the work will be carried through a portion of the quadrant without touching it, as that part reduced to a flat dome represents a segment of a larger circle; the work for many such like purposes will require further adjustment in the slide of the chuck.

Fig. 1, Plate 9A, illustrates two distinct applications of the spherical chuck to the decoration of a square, and the production of polygonal solid forms, which may contain any number of facets to be moulded in one continuous figure, or incised seriatim, also that different flat surfaces may be panelled out and further decorated. To produce such a result as seen in Fig. 1, the following instructions should be followed: The dome chuck is set accurately to a vertical position, to obtain which it must be tested with a square, the ordinary back-square being most suitable for the purpose; the chuck is thus held by the worm-wheel and tangent-screw of the segment apparatus during the process of cutting the different facets of which the figure is composed.

The object, whether pedestal, box, or other design, is first turned on the mandrel nose approximately to the desired circular form, after which it is mounted on the dome chuck while in the before-mentioned vertical position, and the transfer chuck intervened to secure its axial truth; the slide-rest is adjusted transversely across the lathe-bed, and the eccentric cutter is employed, with a round-nosed tool, to shape up the facets of the figure—that now under notice being a square pedestal, first had the body reduced on each surface. The radius of the cutter is extended to cover the space between the base and cornice; the work being adjusted by the screw of the chuck to bring the centre of the facet opposite the axis of the mandrel of the lathe; the cutter is then revolved at speed, and passed over the surface by the screw of the slide-rest, the penetration being adjusted to bring the corners up square and sharp, maintaining the limit of the square as large as the diameter of the cylindrical form will allow. If the height of the pedestal is greater than can be covered by one cut, consequent upon the somewhat limited extension to be obtained in the eccentric cutter, the work must be raised or lowered by the main screw of the chuck, and the process repeated; the first face reduced, the wheel is turned to each quadrant of the wheel for the remaining three sides. Having cut the body deep enough, the base and capital must be reduced to the same shape, and, as there is a great deal less depth, the radius of the tool in the eccentric cutter should be reduced to suit it, and the work raised or lowered by the screw of the chuck. The two projections thus roughly shaped may be considered ready to receive the mouldings. This may be done either with separate tools in the eccentric cutter, by the moulding-tools selected from the series 82 to 93, or by a moulding-drill. If

the latter is employed, the work must be brought to closer contact for the succeeding cuts required to complete the figure, by again raising or lowering the arm of the chuck, but when the eccentric cutter is used, this may be avoided by increased radius being given to the tool. The base and capital of Fig. 1 were cut at the same time by a moulding tool in the eccentric cutter. Mouldings of this kind are also cut with the tool revolving horizontally in the universal cutter, Fig. 122, and the radius of the tool adjusted to best suit the material and its various proportions. In some cases this is perhaps the most convenient means to adopt, the frame of the instrument, from its construction, being less likely to come in contact with other projections on the material which may be in close proximity to that under treatment.

It is, when cutting mouldings of this nature, that mitre at the corners, that the accuracy of the vertical adjustment of the chuck is certified, any error in this point being fatal to the production of excellent work, and consequent finish. To ensure its being correct, it is better to test it each time the chuck has been partially rotated for any specific purpose, and when the tangent-screw is replaced in the worm-wheel of the segment apparatus, this can be quickly done should it be necessary.

If it is desired to further decorate the four facets of a square pedestal, each one may be so embellished with a variety of patterns, any of those to be produced by the eccentric cutter being available for the purpose. The work is placed in position by the vertical movement derived from the main screw of the chuck, and to produce the pattern illustrated by Fig. 1, Plate 9A, the tool in the eccentric cutter is first adjusted to the centre of the facet by the lateral movement of the slide-rest, and the screw of the chuck in the vertical line; the adjusting index is placed in the 96 division, the eccentric cutter extended to a radius of $\frac{2}{10}$, and the slide-rest moved $\frac{2}{10}$ forward, then cut round at every twelve holes, a double-angle tool of 45° being employed.

A second side of this figure it will be seen has been cut in a different way. The same moulding tool that cut the base and cornice is employed, the eccentricity being reduced to cut the recess

to the desired width. The dome chuck is set to the horizontal
position by moving the worm-wheel of segment forty-five turns of the
tangent-screw, the slide-rest remaining in the same position. The
fluting stops are fixed to arrest the traverse on each side of the
centre. The cutter is then revolved at a high speed and traversed
gently through the length.

If it is desired to cut out a panel with square terminals, the
work must be raised and lowered for the two ends, and the sides
cut with an even traverse of the work by the screw of the chuck
when set vertically. This description of panel may be cut also with
a number of consecutive cuts seriatim, and this is a kind of decoration where the divisions on the micrometer on the main screw of the
chuck are of service. For instance, if the ends have been cut, say at
every one or two turns of the screw of the slide-rest, the sides should
be cut in equal proportions, therefore the vertical movement must
coincide with that of the slide-rest, the length and breadth having
been arranged to receive so many cuts each way.

For works of extra size it is preferable for many reasons to
build up the subject of separate pieces, especially when composed
of ivory, as the reduction of the circular form to a square pedestal,
involves the loss of a considerable amount of material.

Fig. 2 illustrates a still further and distinct mode of
decoration, and consists of a reeded spherical top, with the same
figure carried through the diameter of the cylinder. This specimen
represents a match-box, and may be made both usefnl and ornamental. The box is first turned out inside, and the lid fitted; it is
then turned to the desired proportions while on the mandrel nose;
then mounted on the dome chuck, in the transfer; while the dome
is adjusted by the slide of the chuck, and the reeds on the
curved top first-cut; the slide-rest being set parallel with the lathe-
bed; this requires three turns of the tangent-screw for each
individual penetration, the universal cutter (Fig. 122) turned to
90° to cut vertically being employed with a double quarter-hollow
tool (Fig. 98) $\frac{16}{100}$ in. wide. When the top is thus cut, the slide-
rest is set at right angles to the bed, the dome chuck set to the
horizontal position, and the universal cutter turned to zero,

which will bring it to the position in which the tool revolves horizontally. The cut being carried throughout the entire length of the work, it is not necessary to use the fluting-stops, but the penetration of the tool must be very carefully adjusted to agree with the incisions already cut on the dome. This is not by any means a difficult class of work, but at the same time it requires considerable care.

The moulding at the base of this figure, it will be seen, has been worked up in a different way, by cutters varying in form and the manner in which they are applied; the manipulation of the chuck also receiving fresh treatment. The square is first roughly shaped, having the sides removed by a saw, it is then faced over on one side, and a hole about $\frac{3}{4}$ in. in diameter turned in the centre; by this hole it is fitted to a short plug or chuck, so that the surface of the work will bear against its face, which must be less in diameter than the sides of the square when finished, it is then held by glue to ensure its maintaining its position, and the top turned to the desired thickness.

The work is then mounted on the dome chuck, which is accurately set to the vertical position, the slide-rest is set at right angles to the lathe head, and the eccentric cutter fixed in it with a round-nosed tool; the radius of the tool is extended just to cover the width of the base, and the four sides are cut to the same depth, which is decided by the stop-screw of the top slide. Having cut the four sides, the tool is changed for one with a square end about $\frac{10}{100}$ in. wide. the work lowered so that the material may be further recessed, leaving the lower extremity $\frac{2}{10}$ deep. It is then again lowered by the slide of the chuck, and recessed at the top to remove the material, so that the bead-tool, which is next used, shall not have more to do than is absolutely necessary.

The universal cutter, Fig. 122, now replaces the eccentric cutter, and is arranged for the tool to revolve horizontally; a bead-tool, Fig. 105, of suitable size is then employed to cut the moulding, and this, it will be observed, is a more distinct figure than when cut with a quarter-hollow tool. For many types of work this may be used with considerable advantage; a round-nosed tool is then used to cut the concave curve at the top, a square fillet intervening between it and the bead. The base is then decorated with a series of consecutive cuts, which particular class of work forms another interesting feature of the chuck, and these may be executed in two ways; the simplest, however, is the following, and that by which the specimen under notice was produced.

The chuck still remains in the vertical position, and the universal cutter is turned to 90° to cut vertically, the slide-rest in the same position; the tool is exchanged for a double-quarter hollow (Fig. 98) of suitable size; the point of this tool is then set accurately to the centre of the square, by the lateral traverse of the slide, the micrometer at the same time at zero; the work is then spaced out by this means to receive so many cuts on each side of the centre. Having arranged this to suit the work, the first cut is made, the tool revolving at a high speed, and the work passed up and down through the space to be cut, by the main screw of the chuck, for which purpose the nut at the back is released to allow the horizontal arm to move without undue freedom or shake; in the base of the match-box, there are twelve consecutive cuts in each facet; the depth is ascertained in the usual way by trial cuts, and the tool moved laterally $\frac{2}{10}$, or two turns of the slide-rest screw.

The incisions may be cut in a number of different designs, by having spaces left between each, to afterwards receive another style of ornament; they may be produced also by moulding drills; in fact there is practically no end to the variety of elegant decorations to be obtained by varying the tools used.

The same result may be produced in the following manner :— The dome-chuck is mounted upon the rectilinear chuck, which is adjusted to stand vertically when on the mandrel nose, in which position it is securely held by the tangent-screw and worm-wheel of the segment apparatus; the dome chuck is then set accurately to the horizontal position by the adjustment of the worm-wheel of the rectilinear chuck; the universal cutter being again turned to zero for the tool to cut horizontally.

The tool is set to the centre of the square as before, but in this case the work is spaced out by the movement of the slide of the rectilinear chuck, which, to obtain the same distance, would require two turns of its main screw, while the slide-rest screw is used to pass the tool through the material. Although for many classes of work the interposition of the rectilinear and ellipse chucks is absolute necessary, it is not so in the case of the figure under notice, but at the same time it serves to point out the action of the chuck, should it be required for similar works.

The chuck illustrated by Figs. 168 and 168*, is further improved by the length of the horizontal arm being extended, as it now admits of a square base six inches across the corner being revolved on the wheel; and although the extra length tends theoretically to vibration, it has no existence in practice, when the chuck is substantially and well made.

Fig. 3 demonstrates the mode of employing the dome chuck to decorate the concave curve, and this, of increased diameter. The form is first approximately turned by hand, also the convex curve forming the rim ; it is then mounted on the dome chuck, and the tool allowed to follow a curve of the diameter contained in the figure ; the chuck that holds the work must be as shallow as possible, so that the axis of the work may be placed as far as possible from the centre of the lathe mandrel, away from the operator. The chuck is then set to the horizontal position, and fixed by the worm-wheel of the segment apparatus, the slide-rest parallel with the lathe-bearer, and the universal cutter (Fig. 122) placed so that the tool revolves vertically, a double quarter-hollow tool (Fig. 95) being used.

The tool must be extended to a radius of $\frac{9}{10}$, so that the full depth of the curve may be cut without the frame reaching the edge of the work. The point of the tool is then set accurately by the movement of the slide-rest screw, to agree with the test centre, which, when first prepared, should be left on the work for this purpose. The horizontal arm is then adjusted along the body of the chuck until the tool will pass as nearly as possible over the curve, the two usual trial cuts are then made to decide the depth. As there are forty-eight reeds in the specimen illustrated, the worm-wheel of the chuck is moved two divisions for each succeeding cut.

The partial rotation of the mandrel is arrested at the centre by one of the pins placed in the side of the worm-wheel, and in arranging this, the radius of the tool must be considered—it should just cut out at the centre; therefore when the radius of the tool is allowed for, the dome chuck will not assume the exact horizontal position each time the tool reaches the centre. The tool passing out at the diameter, it is not necessary to employ the second stop pin, except to prevent the chuck from completing the revolution, should the hand be released. For work of a very bold character, it is always advisable to rotate the mandrel by the tangent-screw, thus preventing such an occurrence. A corresponding result may be obtained by employing the drilling instrument with a quarter-hollow drill (Fig. 132), but a revolving cutter is the better mode to adopt.

In consequence of the dome chuck requiring to be extended so far from the centre on the one side to trace the concave curve, the convex curve forming the outer rim will necessitate an equally distant adjustment on the opposite side, and from the limited movement of the horizontal arm in this direction it is not possible to trace a curve of so large a diameter without interposing a deep transfer chuck to carry the work nearer towards the operator. The radius of the tool may now be reduced, but it must be adjusted laterally by the slide-rest screw most carefully, so that the tool will follow precisely the same course as that previously cut on the concave curve. When these adjustments are made, the same movement of the worm-wheel of the chuck is required, and as the cut is carried out in each direction, the segment-stop will not be required, except to prevent the entire revolution of the chuck, as above described.

Fig. 4. To reproduce this example, the material is first shaped by hand-turning, after which it is mounted on the dome chuck when set vertically on the mandrel, the slide-rest set parallel with the bed of the lathe, and the universal cutter (Fig. 122) or the ordinary vertical cutter (Fig. 94) placed in it, with a broad double-angle tool of 50° set to a radius of $\frac{5}{10}$; the tool is set accurately to the centre, for which purpose the usual test-point is left on the work, and the depth of cut determined. To adjust the latter, the cutter is placed over the concave curve, and the work moved up to it by the main screw of the dome chuck, and when deep enough, the tool is withdrawn by the guide-screw of the top slide; the worm-wheel of the chuck is then moved by two turns of the tangent-screw, and the second cut made; by these two trial cuts, the penetration is adjusted till the edges are made quite sharp : each consecutive incision is then made by the movement of the top-slide, arrested by the stop-screw, the horizontal arm being fixed when the depth is determined.

Having cut all round in this way, the tool is withdrawn to the edge of the material, that it may cut in precisely the same radial line, to produce the points; and here again the depth is obtained by the two first cuts, and when so arranged, the nut of the horizontal arm is loosened so that it can be moved by the screw, up and down, and by it, the work is moved past the tool while the latter revolves at a high speed, the result being as seen in the autotype, a series of angular points each accurately placed as a terminal to the reeds cut on the concave curve.

The chuck which holds the work is now placed in a deep transfer to extend the convex curve further from the axis of the lathe mandrel, and as the particular shape of the tazza is required to be a portion of a large circle, the work is adjusted by the screw of the chuck to the position required, the same tool being set to follow accurately the figure cut on the previous curve; one stop-pin should be placed in the worm-wheel of the segment apparatus to prevent the cut passing the centre, the second is also used to protect the points already cut from accidental damage, if the mandrel should be turned beyond the required distance, which, especially under the guidance of the hand only, it is likely to be. Many very beautiful decorations may be placed on different curves, by a careful selection of the tools employed.

CHAPTER XXVII.

The Segment Apparatus.

THIS apparatus has been referred to in the previous chapter, wherein its employment in combination with the various ornamental chucks, especially the dome chuck, is clearly detailed, but although it has been so explained, and repeatedly noticed with regard to many of the examples contained in the autotype plates, it is necessary that the entire details connected with its manufacture and further uses, should be described, so that if desired, the more simple form may be first added to the lathe, and afterwards completed by the addition of the worm-wheel and tangent-screw.

The plain form consists of a gun-metal disc, which is attached to the back of the pulley, and has a wide rim on its face, through which seventy-two holes are drilled equidistantly, and afterwards made taper with a broach of the necessary form. These holes are to receive the steel pins which act as stops, to decide the length of the segment of the circle to be cut.

On the periphery of the disc a line is marked across the full width, opposite every sixth hole, and figures engraved to denote the same, thus: 72, 6, 12, 18, 24, and so on, round the entire number. A stout steel post is fixed to stand vertically on the lathe-head, and is sunk into the mandrel frame at the base, and fixed by a strong screw; at the top it is turned to a right angle, and has through the projection a capstan-head screw, on each side, upon which, when employed, the pins that fit into the holes in the plate take effect. The screws are made to adjust in each direction, so that any distance less than the space of one hole may be obtained, and it is necessary to be sure that the screws are

partially withdrawn, so that their movement may be available for
this purpose.

Many very elegant patterns are, with the aid of this apparatus,
cut on the faces of different objects, such figures consisting of arcs
of circles, grouped and arranged to form various designs; and to
enlarge upon this particular style of work, it is necessary at the
same time to employ the eccentric or other of the ornamental
chucks, in order that the different cuts may be placed in positions
varying from concentricity to the axis of the work.

The foregoing remarks are sufficient to show how the simple
form of segment apparatus is made, and attached to the lathe-
head, but in this form it can only be considered quite a primary
attachment, which has been much improved by the addition of the
worm-wheel and tangent-screw.

This is illustrated by Figs. 1, 2, and 169, the latter being the
engraving of a complete lathe-head; and it will be seen that the
metal disc and steel vertical post, with its capstan-head adjusting-
screw, are in every way similar to that already described for the
plain segment apparatus. The periphery of the disc is then cut to
a worm-wheel of 180 teeth, and this is actuated by a tangent-screw,
which is fitted into a strong metal frame, hinged on centres in a
frame at the back of the lathe-head, and moved in and out of gear
by a steel cam, which is worked by a square that receives a key, a
steel projection being let into the casting upon which the cam
works. Towards the front, two steel pillars are screwed into the
head, and filed away to the half, so that the metal frame moves
within them, and is thus prevented from any movement, except
that required to raise and lower it.

This particular action has rather a disadvantage, inasmuch as
it is likely to be accidentally raised, and thus damage the teeth of
the wheel, if the mandrel should be rotated. To avoid this the
author has now introduced a spring underneath the frame which
keeps the screw from inadvertent displacement. The following
arrangement is also an improvement, as it admits of the screw being
firmly retained, either in or out of gear. The cam is dispensed
with, and the end of the frame made to correspond with the arc of

N 2

a circle described from the centre-screws at the back. A block of steel is then fixed to the lathe-head, with a projection to fit the metal arc; through the front an elongated hole is made, a screw passing through it into the steel block. The tangent-screw may be raised to gear with the wheel, and there secured by the fixing-screw, and, when freed from the same, it may also be fixed, and be prevented from accidentally coming in contact with the wheel, and spoiling the teeth.

It will be obvious that by the introduction of the worm-wheel a slow speed is obtained, by which the mandrel is rotated between the limits of the two pins, when adjusted for any length of segment; and while cutting deep mouldings this is most essential, as the hand has not sufficient command over the pulley to ensure smooth and perfect cutting.

As previously stated, the various chucks, such as the eccentric, rectilinear, dome, &c., are adjusted to, and held in the required position, and the weight of the latter, from the fact of the horizontal arm extending so much on one side of the centre, renders the worm-wheel almost indispensable.

The benefit of this addition is not confined to the advantages already described. It will be seen by reference to the engraving, Fig. 169, that on the end of the tangent-screw a micrometer is fitted, and divided into ten equal parts; the worm-wheel and screw may be used in place of the index-point and division on the pulley face, and for many purposes it is more appropriate. When employed as the means of dividing, and sub-dividing the work, it must be remembered that the wheel has 180 teeth, therefore one complete rotation of the tangent-screw moves the mandrel through precisely the $\frac{1}{180}$ part of its diameter, and that the number of cuts or spaces upon the work result from the revolutions of the screw, or partial movement of the same, indicated by the division on the micrometer, read from a line on the frame; for instance, two turns of the screw give ninety consecutive cuts, while four result in forty-five equal spaces. Against these movements, it will be obvious that one half-turn of the screw gives 360 divisions.

Fractions of turns of the screw are obtained by the addition of extra micrometers divided to 8, 9, 11, 12, and many others, any one of which numbers may be employed, and the apparatus may in consequence be used as a dividing engine for wheel-cutting; and again, with the worm-wheel and tangent-screw in gear, combined with the rectilinear and dome chucks, the whole becomes, so to speak, a complete shaping-machine, by which the various subjects previously alluded to are produced.

As a dividing engine, the author was honoured with the order to fit one to a lathe made by him for the Earl of Crawford and Balcarres, and this was fitted to work at the top of the worm-wheel, and by an arrangement of arbors to carry wheels similar to those used on the geometric chuck, a most complete dividing and wheel-cutting apparatus was produced, the position for each succeeding cut being indicated by a detent falling into a notch on the collar of the spindle, and by various collars having different numbers of notches, combined with a full set of change wheels, the addition was a complete success. A scale of the movements of the tangent-screw to produce from 360 to almost any number of lines may be worked out, but this will be of small value to ornamental turners, as the segment apparatus is seldom used for such purposes, and the value of its movement is found in its employment as described, in connection with the dome and other chucks, for the production and decoration of compound solid forms.

CHAPTER XXVIII.

THE SPIRAL APPARATUS.

THIS apparatus may be fairly considered as indispensable to a complete ornamental turning lathe, and as it can be attached in two ways, it is considered necessary to fully explain both methods, in order that the distinct merits of the improved plan, as at present fitted to the back of the lathe-head, may be clear and appreciable.

The engraving (Fig. 168A) represents the apparatus as fitted in what may now be considered the old plan—at the front of the

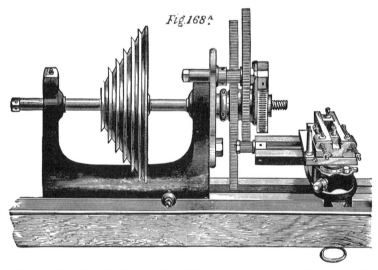

Fig. 168ᴬ

lathe-head. A radial arm, it will be seen, is arranged to partially rotate in a circular groove cut in the front of the lathe-head, concentric to the mandrel axis, and is held by a steel binding bolt, which passes through a curved slot at the lower extremity of the arm. The head of the screw is made hexagonal to fit a spanner, which, for all such screws, is 1 in. across the flat; it is also drilled to receive the point of a bent lever, which, in many instances, is more convenient than the spanner to loosen it, when it is necessary to raise or depress the arm. The long mortise slot is then filed out perfectly parallel and square, so that the arbors which carry the wheels, will slide from end to end, and fix at any desired position.

The bodies of the arbors are made of gun-metal, having a flange on one end to bear against the side of the arm, and are screwed at the other to receive a tubular nut, also made of gun-metal, and passes over that part which projects through the arm. When the screw is cut, the sides are filed away equally, till the body will fit into the mortise and move freely; the end of the nut is then filed to fit the standard spanner.

Through the body of the arbor, a steel spindle, with a collar $1\frac{1}{4}$ in. in diameter in the centre, is fitted, the hole to receive it being tapered about $2°$. The spindle must be well fitted and the face of the collar bear against the flange of the metal. A steel screw is then fitted into the end to keep it in its place, the head of the screw being rather less in diameter than the width of the parallel slot through which it has to pass when fixed to the radial arm.

The projecting end of the steel spindle is then turned to fit the small wheels, which are termed pinions, the holes in which are $\frac{1}{2}$ in. in diameter; it is then screwed at the end to receive a steel nut similar to those previously described, but only $\frac{3}{8}$ in. thick, and this has a thin steel washer before it. The double and single arbors are identical in every respect, with the exception of the total length of the spindle from the face of the collar, the former being long enough to receive two wheels, which are used in double gearing; the latter holding one only for a single train, in which case the wheels all run in the same plane. It is necessary that the spindle which passes through the metal body should be always kept close to the flange, as it is upon this that the wheels revolve, when in action.

The intermediate or reversing arbor is made in a different way, being composed entirely of steel; a wheel of thirty teeth is fitted to work permanently upon it; it is also filed to fit the parallel slot and has a corresponding steel nut to fix it. This arbor is of very considerable importance, as its intervention reverses the action of the apparatus for the production of left hand screws and spirals. Its application will be referred to in connection with the various specimens of spiral work. In fitting up these arbors, care must be taken that the diameters of the various parts do not prevent the thirty wheel on the intermediate one, being placed in gear with the small pinion on the double arbor.

The dividing chuck forms a most important part of the apparatus; it is made from a solid casting, the body of which is long enough to admit of the wheels being arranged upon it to run in the same plane as those on the arbor, when fixed in the arm. It is screwed to fit the mandrel nose, and the external diameter turned to fit the holes in the large wheels, which are $1\frac{1}{4}$ in. in diameter; the body of the chuck is turned away at the back until the wheels are all in one plane. It is then screwed with a fine thread, and a circular steel nut and washer fitted, to bind the wheels securely to it; the edge of the nut is drilled to receive the end of the lever by which it is tightened. This is preferable to the original plan of drilling small holes in the face of the nut, which necessitated the use of a pin-wrench, and was found at times inconvenient, and consequently discarded.

The front of the chuck is bored out to receive the stem of the worm-wheel, which must also be well fitted, and have a substantial face bearing on the front; it is held by a steel screw, fitted into the stem of the wheel, and is passed up the hole where the chuck is screwed to fit the nose of the mandrel, and the bottom of the hole being turned perfectly true, the wheel revolves between it and the front face.

A metal frame with steel tangent-screw is then fitted so that it can be moved in and out of gear, and to obtain this action a steel screw is fitted firmly into the lower side of the frame and has a plain part larger than the thread, which is screwed tightly to the latter, the head just bearing against the face of the projection on the chuck, thus forming a centre, or hinge; a milled head-screw is fitted to the opposite end, the plain part of which moves in a curved slot, long enough to obtain sufficient movement, and by this it is fixed in either position as required. This action is the most convenient for the chuck under consideration, as it is at times necessary to place the slide-rest in such close proximity to it, that the cam, as advocated in other chucks, is somewhat in the way.

The worm-wheel and tangent-screw has many advantages over the original, and now obsolete ratchet-wheel and detent; one particular disadvantage in the latter being, an inclination to slip, which may arise from any undue amount of force being required to remove a metal chuck from the nose. This defect has been referred to, as applied to the eccentric and ellipse chucks of ancient patterns. Another important advantage derived from the worm-wheel is, that it can be divided into any fractional part of a whole turn of the tangent-screw; and this, for various necessary adjustments is of much importance.

For all screw-cutting and spiral turning, 96 equal divisions are sufficient, and practically more than are likely to be required, but the worm-wheel, for the reasons given, is vastly superior; the ratchet has, therefore, long been discarded in modern lathes.

The worm-wheel is divided on the edge at every complete turn of the tangent-screw, and figured at every 6, the collar on the screw is divided into eight equal parts, a steel reader or index being fitted on each side to read the divisions on the periphery, which agree with the zero on the screw head. The end of the slide-rest screw is fitted with a socket to carry a wheel, as explained by the illustration (Fig. 13), that is, for the purpose of holding the various change-wheels used in the train, when in action. Here again the hexagonal nut takes the place of the round one, which, like the large one on the chuck, was originally drilled on the face for a pin-wrench.

Thus far it will be seen that the apparatus as fitted to the front of the lathe-head, consists of the radial arm, double, single, and intermediate, or reversing arbors, sixteen change wheels and pinions, and the dividing chuck; the number of teeth contained in the several wheels are 144, 120, 96, 72, 60, 60, 53, 50,

48, 36, 30, 24, 20, 18, 16, 15. The wheels that have large holes, are, when required to be placed on the arbors, filled with a metal bush, which fits on to the arbor, and has a thin steel washer in front to extend beyond the diameter of the aperture.

Having described the apparatus as fitted to the front in this way, the following details of its arrangement at the back of the head, with its additions and improvements will, it is hoped, clearly illustrate the benefits to be obtained by its aid when thus employed, and establish its superiority over the original and comparatively defective plan.

The engraving (Fig. 169) represents the apparatus as arranged ready for use, the train of wheels being those which produce a twist of one turn in 7 in. approximately. It will be observed that the radial arm in this case is attached in precisely the same way, but to the opposite end of the ltahe-head. The three arbors are also similar, being simply reversed in the arm, so that the wheels revolve on the left, instead of the right side of it.

Thus far the only alteration consists in reversing the arm and wheels to the position seen in the engraving. The dividing chuck, however, is of quite a different character, and is composed of a strong metal body of a tubular form, with a projection at the end. It is bored to fit on the end of the mandrel, the base of the hole being cut out to fit over the projection on the end, which is generally used for holding the screw-guide and steel cap or sleeve from moving round, when in operation. A hole is then bored through the end to allow the screw to pass into the end of the mandrel, which retains it in its necessary position. The body is then turned on the mandrel, or a supplementary arbor (the former being preferable, as it ensures perfect accuracy). The exact size of the tubular fitting cannot be given, as it varies according to the diameter of the mandrel.

The outer diameter of this part should be turned slightly taper, about 2°, and left as strong as possible. The worm-wheel is then bored out to fit it accurately, after which it is transferred to a separate arbor, and the periphery cut to a worm-wheel. This, like all wheels of a similar character, has 96 teeth, and is divided

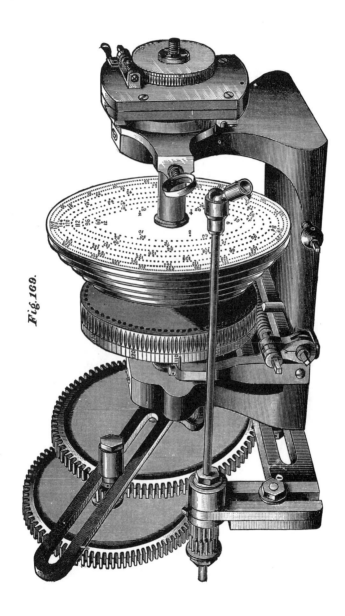

Fig. 169.

as seen by Fig. 169* on the back face, into ninety-six equal parts, with a long line and numerals at every 6.

The steel tangent-screw is fitted into a metal frame, which bears against the projecting flange of the body of the chuck, the screw by which it is held forming its centre of action, and the milled head screw on the right side (*vide* Fig. 169*) used for clamping it when in or out of gear with the wheel. This screw passes through a short curved slot in the flange, and, when screwed up, brings the frame in close contact with it; thus, it will be

Fic.169*

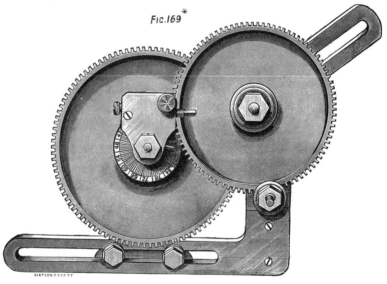

observed, that when it is required to move the work round any desired portion of the entire circle, the milled head is released, and the tangent-screw raised; the mandrel is then moved round, carrying the work with it, also the body of the dividing chuck, and when the steel index points to the number required, the screw is lowered into gear, and the fixing-screw tightened.

At the base of the headstock a straight arm (seen in Figs. 169 and 169*) is fitted to move transversely, having a long parallel slot, and is fixed in its necessary position by two steel bolts with hexagonal heads, which, like that used for fixing the radial arm, are drilled to receive the bent lever.

On the front of this arm, a metal frame, with a projecting boss on each side, is fitted, and slides on a steel fillet, fixed to the arm, so that it may be raised and depressed as required. It also affords a ready means of adjusting it to the height of the centre of the slide-rest screw. The cylinder boss is bored out to receive a steel socket, which revolves freely in it, and is retained in its place by a nut and washer. The projecting end of the socket is turned down to receive the pinions, which are $\frac{1}{2}$ in. in diameter, and are also held by a nut and washer. It is an advantage to have this fitting long enough to hold two wheels, therefore it should be 1 in. long in the plain part, and when a wheel is fixed to it, it bears the same reference to the train of wheels, and the pitch of the spiral cut, as when, in the preceding arrangement, it is fixed on the end of the main screw of the slide-rest.

Through the centre of this socket a long steel connecting-rod is fitted, being held at any distance by a fixing-screw, the point of which fits into a groove cut the entire length of the rod. On the end of the connecting-rod an improved double, or universal joint is attached, the end of which fits over the projecting socket on the slide-rest screw, and a screw passes through both to hold it in its place ; and when the wheel on the arbor is placed in gear with that on the chuck, and the arm lowered so that the wheel also gears with that on the socket, the action of the whole train is obtained by turning the winch handle of the slide-rest screw.

The universal joint, improved and introduced by the author, and applied to this particular purpose has the advantage of allowing the slide-rest to be set to an angle, to turn a cone or a long taper spiral without the interposition of the extra surface spiral apparatus, with its round edge and bevel wheels—to be described in the following chapter.

The object of the adjustment in the lower straight arm is to allow the connecting rod to be moved to or from the centre, to suit the various positions of the slide-rest for work of large or small diameters, and the vertical movement of the socket bears the same reference to the height of centre of the slide-rest screw when set above, below, or at the centre of the lathe axis.

Fig. 169B illustrates a still further edition and improvement by the author, and is for the purpose of increasing the length in the twist of spiral. It is simply an additional arbor which can be fixed to the frame through which the socket holding the connecting rod passes, and will carry two extra wheels to gear with the train already described; this arrangement also disposes of the surface spiral apparatus, which must be used for the same purpose when the apparatus is fitted to the front of the lathe head.

Before giving the details of the various specimens illustrated in connection with this apparatus, it will be expedient to point out

Fig 169B

the advantages claimed, and due to it, as attached to the lathe in the form we have just considered.

First then, the extra length of the spiral chuck in the front is dispensed with, and the chuck which holds the work is placed direct on to the mandrel nose; this decreases the tendency to vibration, and allows the work to be executed in closer proximity to the mandrel; the undue length of the chuck in front being at all times a disadvantage.

Secondly, the work remaining on the mandrel nose, does not require to be again turned, which is necessary when the apparatus is fitted to the front, as in Fig. 168A.

Thirdly, the greater part of the whole apparatus may be left on its place ready for future employment, thus saving a considerable amount of trouble and time.

Fourthly, the cutting of taper spirals can be effected by the aid of the universal joint, without any additional apparatus; and

Lastly, it enables the ellipse chuck to be used in conjunction with it, which combination renders some very beautiful work indeed; and, as the ellipse and spirals can be combined in no other way, it must be, as it is admitted, a very great improvement and advantage.

The original idea was suggested, as before stated, by General G. C. Clarke, and its evident advantages induced the author to study it in all its details, and after some years' experience in working it, to bring it to its present complete form.

CHAPTER XXIX.

The Surface Spiral.

THIS is also an addition to the spiral apparatus, and is employed as a means of transferring the various spirals from the cylinder to the surface; it is also necessary for the same operation on cones, when the apparatus is fitted to the front of the lathe-head.

The apparatus (Fig. 170) consists of a cast iron pedestal similar to the hand-rest for plain turning, but longer in the base, and is fixed to the lathe-bed, when required in the same way, by a dove-tail slide; a steel stem is then fitted to the pedestal, on which is fixed a metal barrel holding a socket, on one side of which the change-wheels and pinions are fixed, and through which a long steel rod is fitted, similar to that already explained; on the end of the rod a collar is fixed, to which a mitre or round-edged wheel is attached, when required to connect the movement of the slide-rest with that of the other wheels of the train, and consequently that of the mandrel.

When setting up the apparatus, the rod should stand parallel to the lathe-bed and the wheels as required, but generally speaking the mitre-wheel of thirty teeth is fixed to the rod, while that containing sixty teeth is attached to the end of the slide-rest screw, when it is placed at right angles to the lathe-bed, but when used for ornamenting cones, the round-edged wheel and pinion are substituted. The rod having a longitudinal movement, the wheels may be geared, when the slide-rest is set at varying distances from the mandrel nose, to suit the different depths of the chuck and material to be operated upon, while the transverse adjustment admits of work of large or small diameter being accommodated, and when these are finally and satisfactorily adjusted, the stem is fixed by the binding screw in the pedestal, and the point of the screw placed in the groove of the sliding-rod, thus retaining the various fittings in their several places.

Fig. 170A illustrates a new method recently designed by the author for effecting the same purpose as the surface spiral apparatus referred to; it will be observed that the mitre and round-edged wheels are entirely dispensed with, and the motion is obtained

Fig 170

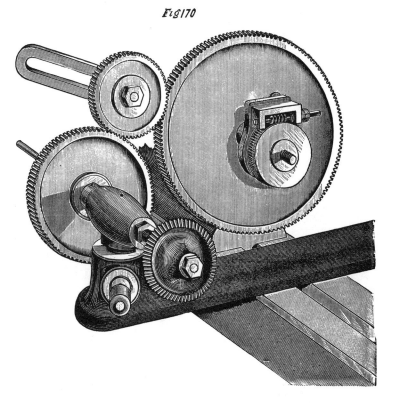

by the application of two double universal joints, one of which is attached to the rod A, which passes through the barrel in the pedestal, while the second, C, is fixed to the socket on the end of the main screw of the slide-rest, the two being connected by the socket on each, secured by the screw, D. By the aid of these joints the slide-rest may be set to any degree between the parallel and right angle.

O

This comparatively simple arrangement works perfectly, and is now fitted to the lathes of many amateurs; it is less trouble to mount, and relieves the spiral apparatus of the inherent loss of

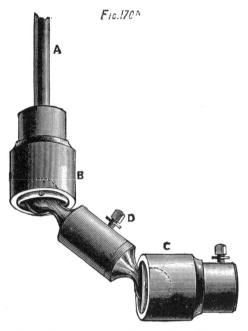

Fig. 170ᴬ

time derived from the extra wheels; and further, the work produced by the different trains of wheels employed upon cylinders, may be transferred to the surface, without differing in any way by the introduction of extra gearing.

CHAPTER XXX.

THE RECIPROCATOR.

THIS instrument affords the means of obtaining a still wider variation of effect, and it may also be considered a very important addition to the spiral apparatus. It can be applied to either the cylinder or surface, with equal facility. It will be seen by reference to the engraving (Fig. 171), that it is composed of two steel arms with circular ends, the short one which has the series of holes drilled in it, is made to fit on the dividing chuck, and is attached there by the same nut and washer that hold the wheels ; the longer arm of the two is fitted to revolve on a metal bush with a plate on the front; the bush is made the same width as the pinions, $\frac{1}{2}$ in. wide, and it will be observed that it has two holes bored through the face which are marked A and B, the former having an eccentricity of $\frac{3}{20}$, while the latter has twice the amount. On the opposite side of the centre, the holes are made to fit on the double arbor, and are therefore also $\frac{1}{2}$ in. in diameter.

At the opposite extremity of this arm a movable joint is arranged, the end being turned down and the latter fitted to it; this is retained in its place by the point of a small screw fitting in a groove turned in the pin. The joint has an open slot, into which the arm with the holes passes freely, being connected by a milled head screw with a plain part fitting the hole.

When adjusting the instrument for use, the following directions should be carried out. The short arm is placed on the dividing chuck and fixed by the circular nut, the long arm is then attached to the double arbor with a wheel in front of it, which must be selected to suit the work. For example, say the 120 wheel, the aperture

in which must be filled up with the metal bush, and both it and
the arm fixed by the nut and washer; the two arms are then

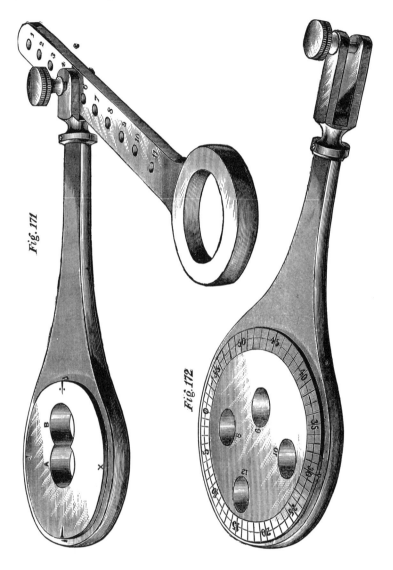

connected by placing the pin through the hole that may be selected;
the radial arm is then lowered to gear the 120 wheel with that on

the slide-rest screw or socket, according to the manner in which the apparatus is fitted.

Upon turning the handle of the slide-rest, it will be seen that the mandrel performs a backward and forward motion, while the tool or cutter in the slide-rest travels laterally the necessary length of the work to be decorated, when it is arrested by a fluting-stop on each side.

The partial rotation of the mandrel in either direction, combined with the lateral traverse of the tool in the slide-rest, produces waved, or undulated lines, which are varied by the alteration of the train of wheels; and again, by the difference in the fixture of the two arms in relation one to the other, by the holes, which are figured from 1 to 11, the latter denotement being nearest the axis of the mandrel.

When the arm is placed on the arbor by the hole A, which has the smallest amount of eccentricity, and the second arm attached to it by hole 1, the least height of wave is the result, while with the eccentricity B on the arbor, and hole 11 employed, the greatest is obtained, the length of the wave being entirely governed by the wheels used in the train; the effect of the curve produced is also much influenced by the diameter of the material upon which it is cut. It will be useful to many amateurs to give a few of the different wheels that are available, and more generally employed to effect waves of given lengths:—For one of $\frac{2}{10}$, 18 on slide-rest with 36 on arbor; for $\frac{3}{10}$, 16 and 48; $\frac{4}{10}$, 15 and 60; $\frac{6}{10}$, 16 and 96; $\frac{8}{10}$, 15 and 120, &c., the smaller wheel being always placed on the slide-rest screw or socket, as before mentioned.

To change the arm attached to the arbor from one eccentricity to the other during the progress of the work, produces some very beautiful results, as the waved lines are cut in the reverse direction; but, at the same time, it is perhaps the most difficult operation to perform accurately, in consequence of the slide-rest screw requiring to remain without the least movement, while the eccentricity of the arm is adjusted. It will be seen that the face of the bush is divided at every quadrant, thus: ·|· | |· ×.

If the eccentricity A is fixed to the arbor with ⊹ opposite the indicator the wave will begin at the opposite side to what it will if the bush is turned round until the mark ❘ be in the same position; but if the arm is fixed to the arbor by eccentricity B, this will be reversed, in consequence of the two eccentricities being on the opposite sides of the centre of the bush.

The relative positions of the various waves following each other round a cylinder or on a surface, are determined by the movement of the dividing chuck, in a similar manner to that in which numerous strands are cut with the spiral apparatus.

Fig. 172 illustrates a considerable improvement in the reciprocator, by which its capabilities are greatly increased; the metal bush on which the arm works is enlarged to 3 in. in diameter, and through it four holes are bored to fit the arbor, in the same way as those in Fig. 171; but these, it will be seen, have their eccentricities extended to six, eight, ten, and twelve-tenths, by which the partial rotation of the mandrel is increased in each direction. But, so far, the only difference resulting from this is, the increased depth of the wave; but the inventor of this improvement (Mr. Ashton) desired to create at the same time a greater length, in combination with the depth, which produces such extremely graceful curves, and, in order to effect this, it is essential that the lateral movement of the tool should be increased in equal, or even extended ratio, with the eccentricity. For this movement it is necessary to employ a second pair of wheels, which, in the instance of the spiral apparatus being fitted to the front of the lathe-head, are made to operate in an extra arm fitted across the end of the slide-rest, with the power of adjustment to suit different sized wheels; but, when the spiral apparatus is fitted on the improved plan, the same result is obtained by employing the extra arbor (Fig. 169B). This is much to be recommended for the purpose, and disposes of the extra arm on the slide-rest.

Before entering upon the details of the manipulation of the apparatus contained in the preceding pages, it will be an advantage to have a table of the various wheels required to produce certain screws and twists. The following is considered the most suitable for the purpose, and will be readily understood—the words mandrel, screw, and pitch, signify the manner in which the wheels are geared, and the screw they produce :—

TABLE OF PITCHES DERIVED FROM SINGLE GEARING.

MANDREL—144.		MANDREL—120.		MANDREL—96.	
SCREW.	PITCH.	SCREW.	PITCH.	SCREW.	PITCH.
120	8·33	144	12·	144	15·
96	6·66	96	8·	120	12·5
72	5·	72	6·	72	7·5
60	4·166	60	5·	60	6·25
53	3·68	53	4·416	53	5·52
50	3·472	50	4·166	50	5·208
48	3·33	48	4·	48	5·
36	2·5	36	3·	36	3·75
24	1·66	24	2·	24	2·5
20	1·388	20	1·66	20	2·0833
18	1·25	18	1·5	18	1·075
16	1·11	16	1·33	16	1·66
15	1·0416	15	1·25	15	1·5625

MANDREL—72.		MANDREL—60.		MANDREL—53.	
SCREW.	PITCH.	SCREW.	PITCH.	SCREW.	PITCH.
144	20·	144	24·	144	27·16
120	16·66	120	20·	120	22·64
96	13·33	96	16·	96	18·11
60	8·33	72	12·	72	13·58
53	7·361	53	8·833	60	11·32
50	6·944	50	8·33	50	9·433
48	6·66	48	8·	48	9·056
36	5·	36	6·	36	6·792
24	3·33	24	4·	24	4·528
20	2·77	20	3·33	20	3·773
18	2·5	18	3·	18	3·396
16	2·22	16	2·66	16	3·088
15	2·0833	15	2·5	15	2·83

MANDREL—50.		MANDREL—48.		MANDREL—36.	
SCREW.	PITCH.	SCREW.	PITCH.	SCREW.	PITCH.
144	28·8	144	30·	144	40·
120	24·	120	25·	120	33·33
96	19·2	96	20·	96	26·66
72	14·4	72	15·	72	20·
60	12·	60	12·5	60	16·66
53	10·6	53	11·04	53	14·72
48	9·6	50	10·417	50	13·88
36	7·2	36	7·5	48	13·33
24	4·8	24	5·	24	6·66
20	4·	20	4·166	20	5·55
18	3·6	18	3·6	18	5·
16	3·2	16	3·33	16	4·44
15	3·	15	3·125	15	4·166

This table it will be seen bears no reference to the double gearing, which employs four wheels instead of two. It is, therefore, necessary to indicate this by a second table, which is practically the most useful in following the art of ornamental turning, as it is the longer twists that are generally used, and are the most decorative. The expressions in this case bear the same reference to the arrangement of the wheels as in the previous table, the double arbor being always used in place of the single one. When the apparatus is fitted to the back of the lathe-head, the reference to the screw bears the same relation to the socket, which has a corresponding influence, and it is connected to the slide-rest by the universal point.

TABLE OF PITCHES OBTAINED BY DOUBLE GEARING.

MANDREL.	ARBOUR.	SCREW.	PITCH.	MANDREL.	ARBOUR.	SCREW.	PITCH.
144	24			144	36		
	60	72	·5		120	16	3·
144	15			144	15		
	30	48	·6		60	18	3·2
144	72			144	15		
	60	16	·75		60	16 .	3·6
144	15			144	30		
	30	36	·8		120	15	3·48
144	24			144	24		
	72	48	·9		120	18	4·
144	36			144	24		
	60	24	1·		120	16	4·5
144	15			144	24		
	60	48	1·2		120	15	4·8
144	16			144	20		
	17	48	1·35		120	16..	5·4
144	72			144	20		
	120	16	1·5		120	15	5·76
144	15			144	18		
	60	36	1·6		120	16	6·
144	15			144	18		
	30	16	1·8		120	15.	6·4
144	36			144	16		
	120	24	2·		120	15	7·2
144	16						
	60	20	2·7				

CHAPTER XXXI.

MANIPULATION OF THE SPIRAL APPARATUS.

THIS apparatus, although capable of producing screws of various pitches, from more than fifty threads in the inch, to one complete turn in seven inches, is seldom employed for the purpose of cutting fine threads to be used as screws, and it differs from the slide and screw-cutting lathe only in the manner in which it is employed, the principle of connecting the guide-screw to the mandrel by a train of wheels being maintained.

As it is now to be considered, the mandrel is connected with the main screw of the slide-rest, and as thus arranged, it is in theory exactly the same as the slide-lathe, but is more suitable for ornamental turning, and the production of spirals of long pitches, which are generally known as Elizabethan twists. By reference to the illustration, Fig. 168A, it will be seen that to make the necessary connection between the mandrel and slide-rest, a wheel is placed on the dividing chuck, and gears into another on the double arbor, a larger wheel on the same, gearing to one on the end of the main screw of the slide-rest; a great number of different pitches may be cut with a train of three wheels only, geared in one plane, in which case the intermediate wheel bears no influence over the screw produced, but is simply a means of communicating motion from the wheel on the chuck to that on the slide-rest; the screw or pitch produced being dependent upon the multiplication or division of the main screw of the slide-rest, by the fraction given in the number of teeth in the two wheels—that on the chuck, and on the slide-rest screw.

It will be seen at once that should two wheels only be used, the slide-rest having a right-hand screw, the twist produced will be a left-hand one, caused by the two wheels turning in opposite directions, therefore the intermediate wheel is necessary to the production of a reverse direction, as it guides the wheel on the mandrel and that on the screw of the slide-rest in the same direction, the result being a right hand twist.

Spirals of both characters, however, are largely used in the practice of ornamental turning; and when it is necessary to change the direction from one to the other, the intermediate arbor with the thirty-wheel is interposed between the wheel on the chuck and that on the arbor, and this, it may be repeated, does not alter the pitch, but simply changes the direction of the traverse of the slide, and in the case of large diameters, also facilitates the movement of the slide-rest further from the axis of the mandrel, which is very often necessary. At times, however, even a greater range is required, in which case a wheel of larger size is placed upon the single arbor, and takes the place of that referred to. This latter arrangement is seldom required, from the fact that double gearing is mostly used for ornamental purposes, as the longer twists are much preferred, and are the most suitable for such work.

Double gearing is again illustrated by the engraving, Fig. 169, which shows the apparatus as now fitted on the new principle, at the rear of the headstock; it employs four wheels, as shown in Table 2, and, as seen in the engraving; the wheels are 144 on the dividing chuck, gearing to a pinion of 16 on the double arbor, a wheel of 120 teeth being on the same, which gears into a pinion of 15 on the socket, which is the same as when placed on the slide-rest screw; if the apparatus is fitted to the front, as in Fig. 168A, it will be observed, by reference to Table 2, that these wheels produce a twist of 7·2. Spirals consisting of more than two turns in 1 in. always necessitate the use of the double arbor, and any spiral beyond one turn in 7 in. involves the use of a third pair of wheels, which are usually mounted on the surface spiral apparatus, and connected by a pair of round-edged wheels of 30 and 60 teeth ; but when the apparatus is fitted at the back of the lathe-head, the introduction of the double arbor, Fig. 170A, renders the surface spiral apparatus unnecessary for this purpose.

As seen by the engraving, the third pair of wheels is fitted on a steel arbor, which revolves in a socket, fitted to slide in a metal frame, which is fixed to the boss on the lower arm that carries the connecting-rod. The two extra wheels thus placed at the end of the train, have the effect of producing a twist twice as long as that obtained without their addition, and as it can be taken off and refixed without delay, it forms a most important improvement to the apparatus. Spirals used in ornamental turning, are generally of a multiple nature, such for instance, as, 2, 4, 6, 8, or any other number of grooves or strands, being cut round the cylinder or form that is being ornamented, and it is for this purpose that the dividing chuck is employed ; the dial-plate on the pulley cannot be used, from the fact that it is always rotating during the process of cutting the work. The height of the centre of the tool must also claim great attention from the operator; the slightest deviation from accuracy in this respect will entirely alter the result of the pattern produced, and if not adjusted precisely to the axis of the mandrel, more material will be removed from one side than the other.

The tool should always be carried through the cut in one direction, it does not matter in which ; but as a rule a right hand twist is cut from right to left, and a left hand from left to right. The way in which the tool is made to revolve must depend somewhat upon the grain of the material to be cut; sometimes it will cut more smoothly one way than the other. In all such spirals as those illustrated in Plate 10, the apparatus is worked by the winch-handle on the slide-rest screw, the driving-band to the pulley being of course removed. The necessity for always making the cut in the same direction is caused by the unavoidable back-lash in each of the several wheels when geared, and it will be evident that when the handle is turned the freedom between the wheels will allow the tool to move laterally before the work begins to rotate, thus causing it to cut more on one side than the other; this, however, may not be fatal to the work, and, if the cut is carried through in both directions with a step-drill, the result will be, that the recess so cut is made wider than the diameter of the drill, and, provided the strand is cut right through at each end, it will not at times be a disadvantage, but where the spirals terminate within the cylinder at each end, through the traverse being arrested by the fluting-stops, every successive cut must be taken in the one direction only, otherwise the circular ends will be distorted.

In such spirals as Fig. 4, Plate 10, where the universal cutter is used, with a double-angle tool, the cut can only be made in the one direction, for the reason, that if the cut is increased in width, the figure of the tool would be lost, and a space left at the bottom, instead of the actual shape of the tool.

When the universal cutter is thus employed, it is necessary that the tool should be set to an angle, so that the plane of revolution will agree with the pitch of the screw or spiral it is desired to cut. The amount of angle required to be given to the tool is easily decided by trial, as it will be seen when a fine cut is first taken, if it is correct; the angles, however, which are given for the following examples will be sufficient to direct the attention in this respect. When a variety of cutters is used, the instrument must be retained at the same angle throughout the work, and one important point is to always set the tool back to the same radius, should it have to be removed for sharpening; this is decided in the same way as explained with regard to this instrument when used for the pattern illustrated on Plate 3.

The production of spirals by this apparatus may be extended to a very large degree, and the variety of patterns to be so turned is practically unlimited. A very useful and decorative style is found in hollow spirals, which may be filled with material of a different substance and colour. An ivory exterior with its strands twisting gracefully round a black wood interior, forms a very elegant combination.

A further development is derived from an ivory cylinder being bored out to a tube; it is then carefully fitted to a boxwood plug and cut through with a long twist; a second ivory tube is then fitted accurately to it. This again is fitted on a plug and cut to the same pitch, but in the reverse direction, the result being that two spirals in opposite directions are combined.

Spirals may also be cut with a compound twist, that is, one within the other, leaving a solid pillar through the centre. This form is illustrated by Plate 11, for the privilege of publishing which the author is indebted to Captain R. Pudsey Dawson, who has made this particular style of turning a considerable study. The settings for this will be explained as the subject is approached.

To adjust the spiral apparatus for such work as the examples contained in Plate 10, the radial arm is first placed in the circular groove at the back of the lathe-head; and it may be here mentioned that all references to the various adjustments will point to it as arranged in this way. The radial arm fixed, the wheel of 144 teeth is placed on the dividing chuck and fixed by its circular nut and washer; the double arbor is then placed in the oblong slot, and a pinion of 16 teeth, with a wheel of 120 teeth attached in front of it; the arbor is then moved in the slot till the pinion of 16 teeth gears with the 144 on the chuck; and they should be so placed as to work quite freely, to avoid any likelihood of an irregular motion; a pinion of 15 teeth is then fixed to the socket through which the connecting-rod passes, and the radial arm lowered till the 120 wheel gears with it. This combination, as before stated, gives a twist of one turn in 7 in. approximately. The engraving, Fig. 169, shows the way in which this is arranged. The connection is then made to the slide-rest by the rod being moved laterally till the socket of the universal joint will pass on to the end of the main screw, to which it is fixed. In this way the apparatus was arranged to cut Fig. 1, Plate 10, the material being first turned to a cylinder; the drilling instrument is then placed in the tool-box of the slide-rest, having in it a bold step-drill, the dividing chuck set at 96 on the worm-wheel, and the cut made from the popit-head towards the chuck. The worm-wheel of the chuck is then moved twelve divisions for each consecutive cut. This being a deeply cut pattern, it requires about three separate cuts, and for a finishing one, the drill should be taken out and carefully sharpened. Although a very simple example, it is a most effective style of ornamentation, and one that may be usefully employed for a variety of work.

For Fig. 2 the same wheels were employed, the universal cutter (Fig. 122) being used instead of the drilling instrument; and in order that the tool should follow the same plane as the twist, the cutter was set over to the right 30°; a round-nosed tool, $\frac{16}{100}$ in. wide, was used to excavate the recess in the first place. The dividing chuck in this case is adjusted consecutively to 96, 24, 48, and 72, thus leaving four strands. Having removed as much of the superfluous material as desired, a square-end tool takes the place of the round-nosed one, by which the bottom of the recess is made flat instead of concave. The drilling instrument is then used in place of the universal cutter, and in exactly the same way as for Fig. 1; the universal cutter is then again employed to round the top of the strand, a bead-tool replacing that previously used; the angle of the instrument being unchanged.

Fig. 3 represents the difference in effect obtained by using the reversing arbor with a thirty-wheel on it. The material was first turned to a true cylinder, the same train of wheels arranged, and the universal cutter, with a double angle tool of 50°, set to the same angle of 30° for the right-hand twist, the dividing chuck set at 96, and a cut made at every six. The penetration of the tool is governed by the precise figure required. Having cut all round in this way, the radial arm is raised without moving the wheel on the socket, the double arbor moved away from the 144 wheel, and the reversing arbor interposed; the arm is then lowered to again gear the 120 wheel with the 15 on the socket. The universal cutter is set over to the other side 30°, and the face of the tool reversed; the cuts are then made from left to right, or in the opposite direction to those previously cut, the result being as seen, a series of diamond-shaped facets.

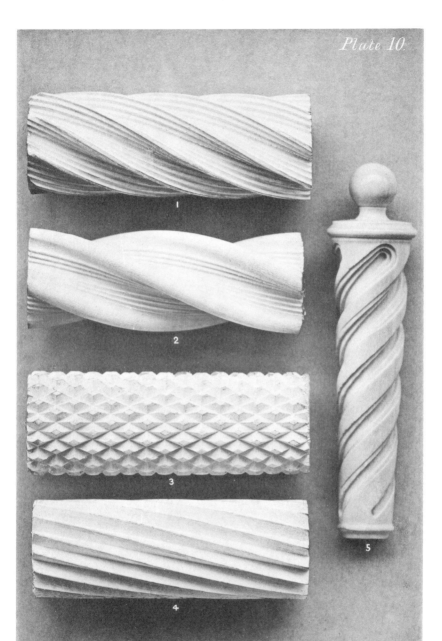

Plate 10.

The succeeding figure affords an opportunity of illustrating the advantage derived by using the extra arbor (Fig. 169B), which is for the purpose of making the twist or spirals of an increased length; the most that can be achieved with the wheels as already described, is one turn in 7 in. approximately; with the extra arbor the twist can be doubled, and by replacing the thirty-wheel by one of 15, a still further elongation results. There is a very great advantage in being able to attain this end, as the extra length of twist gives a very beautiful appearance to the work.

Fig. 4 was cut with the following arrangement: the wheels being 144, gearing to 16 on double arbor, the 120 on same, gearing to a 30 on the extra arbor, while the 60 on the same spindle is geared to the 15 on the socket. This combination gives a twist of about one turn in 15 in., the universal cutter is set over to 15° on the right, and the cut made from right to left with a double angle tool of 50°. The wheels thus arranged are even in number and cause the spiral to be left hand. To obviate this, the reversing arbor with the thirty-wheel is interposed between the 144 on chuck, and the 16 on the double arbor, thereby reversing the direction, with the result seen in Fig. 4.

Fig. 5 shows the result of combining the spiral apparatus with the ellipse chuck, from which very beautiful results are obtained. That now illustrated is quite a simple example, but serves to establish the fact that the two can be combined.

Plate 11 represents a distinct style of spiral turning. It will be seen that the stem or pillar has two series of spiral strands, one inside the other, but, at the same time, cut from the solid ivory. This may be termed compound spiral turning, and is now much practised by amateur turners. The length of the specimen under notice is 5 in., and the diameter $1\frac{1}{8}$ in.; the wheels employed in the train to produce the twist are, 124 on the chuck, 20 and 120 on the double arbor, and 16 on the socket.

The ivory for such a subject should be carefully selected, with the grain as straight as possible; it is then chucked in a wood or metal chuck, preferably the latter for such a purpose, and turned to a true cylinder. It the apparatus is fitted to the front of the lathe-head, the ivory must be turned true when the chuck holding it is placed on the spiral dividing chuck; the necessity for this affords a further opportunity of pointing out the advantage of the whole of the apparatus being fitted to the back, in which case the work is turned on the mandrel nose, the same as for any ordinary work, thus saving the unnecessary length of the chuck.

It must be assumed that the apparatus is fitted on the improved plan, therefore the work is turned to a perfectly true cylinder on the mandrel nose, and then highly polished. A round-nosed fluting-drill, in size suitable to the space required between the strands of the spirals, is selected; the slide-rest must now be raised above the centre by the elevating ring, till the thickness of the strand is determined. This done, take a deep cut at 96, 24, 48, 72; it is an advantage to raise the point of the drill slightly, by a thin piece of packing under the front of the stem in the tool box; this enables the drill to cut through the ivory with greater facility. Should it be desired to ornament the exterior of the strands, it must be done before the drill is carried completely through, because, when the strands are released they are too delicate to admit of its being done, even to the extent of the plain flute seen in the illustration, as the solid material which supports them has been removed by the drill, and the latter, prior to passing through, should be keenly sharpened. This process having been repeated four consecutive times, the first series of spirals is finished.

The solid cylinder left in the centre by the cutting of the first series, must now be operated upon in a similar way. Having selected a small drill suitable to the diameter of the cylinder, the slide-rest is lowered till the point of the drill is exactly between the strands first cut; this is more accurately adjusted by means of the tangent-wheel of the dividing chuck, and now that the ratchet-wheel is obsolete, there is no necessity for releasing and resetting the radial arm to assist in the adjustment. When thus arranged, it is only to proceed as before, the result being a small

Plate 11.

cylinder left within the second series of strands.   The drill should be driven at a quick and regular speed, and the lateral traverse of the slide be as even as possible ; it is far better to use a series of different sized drills, to follow each other.   Work of this character, but of greater length, will require the aid of a slender guide to support it as the tool traverses, but with care 6 in lengths may be safely executed.

CHAPTER XXXII.

THE SPIRAL APPARATUS AND ELLIPSE CHUCK IN COMBINATION.

PLATE 11A illustrates a further application of the spiral apparatus, used in combination with the ellipse chuck, and is one of the great advantages derived from the present arrangement of the apparatus, by which varied and beautiful work can be displayed. The body of the casket was turned from a large hollow piece of a tusk of ivory, the sliding-ring of the chuck being set out to suit its proportions, without waste; it was then turned out inside, and afterwards chucked on a boxwood plug its entire length, well fitted and glued.

The first process is to turn it to a perfectly true elliptic cylinder; a large round-nosed drill is then used to excavate a considerable depth before the figure is attempted; the wheels used are those which produce a long twist—viz., 144, 16, 120, and 15; the ellipse chuck is set vertically, the drill accurately to the centre of the lathe axis, the first cut made at 96 of the dividing-wheel, and repeated at every 12, by which eight consecutive flutes result.

An ogee moulding-drill now replaces the routing-drill, to shape the figure on each side of the separate strands; these cut, a small moulding-drill is carried in deeper at the bottom of the recess; to cut cleanly a depth similar to this example, requires a number of cuts, and the tool to be sharpened many times; in all such work, the drill should be most carefully looked to for the finishing cut.

The eight moulded strands being finished so far, the top of each alternate one is cut to a bead, and for this purpose the universal cutter (Fig. 122), with an astragal bead-tool $\frac{12}{100}$ in. wide, is employed, and the instrument set to an angle of 30°; when the four

Plate 11 A.

strands of this character are cut, the tool is changed for a round-nosed one, with which the four intermediate mouldings are cut. Deep and bold cutting of this nature may be ultimately polished with a soft lamb's-wool buff running at a high speed, which gives a beautiful finish to it. The base and top are separate pieces taken from a tusk of large dimensions, the former is cut out each side with a round-nosed drill; the latter has a deep eccentric pattern cut on the surface, and a hollow underneath to correspond with the bottom; the lid, which is hinged at the back, is composed of a series of moulded and plain parts, the final being an elliptic knob. Caskets of this stamp should be lined inside with satin; it is a great improvement, and at times assists in hiding from view a bad place in the material, to remove which would reduce it to a size unsuitable for its purpose.

CHAPTER XXXIII.

EXAMPLES OF SURFACE SPIRALS AND RECIPROCATOR.

PLATE 12 illustrates a few patterns produced on surfaces, by interposing the apparatus (Fig. 170), by which the motion is conducted to the slide-rest when set transversely across the lathe-bed; and if the spiral apparatus is fitted to the front, it is also necessary, as already intimated, to the application of it to cut work upon cones; but with the apparatus fitted at the back of the lathe, illustrated in Fig. 169, this is avoided, as the universal joint allows all such work to be done better without it. Curved surfaces are also to be decorated with the slide-rest in this position, when the curvilinear apparatus is used, and by this very beautiful results are obtained; the revolving instruments are all applicable to this as well as cylindrical forms. The strands may be also cut in either, or both directions, and, when crossed and cut with a step-drill, a series of gradually decreasing pyramidal points, renders the effect most decorative and interesting. To attempt to describe even a limited number of results to be obtained would occupy a book in itself, but those now shown in the autotypes, will serve to explain the way in which the apparatus is applied, and to demonstrate the more simple results, which will lead to far greater attainments, and it is needless to say the variations may be carried on *ad infinitum*.

Fig. 1 is quite a primary application of the apparatus. The wheels employed were 144 on dividing chuck gearing, into 16 on double arbor, 120 on the same, running into 15 on the socket, thus producing the twist. The surface spiral apparatus (Fig. 170) is then placed so that the end of the socket is connected to the universal joint, the mitre-wheel with 30 teeth is fixed on the end of the

Plate 12.

sliding-rod and geared to the 60 wheel of the same form, which is fixed to the end of the slide-rest screw.

The universal cutter (Fig. 122) was then placed in the tool-box of the slide-rest, and turned to 90° on the right, to operate as a vertical cutter, and a round-nosed tool placed at a radius of $\frac{6}{10}$, the dividing-wheel of chuck set to 96, and a cut made at every 12, the penetration being about $\frac{1}{20}$. Having cut thus eight times, the wheel of the chuck is moved six divisions, the radius of the tool reduced $\frac{2}{10}$, and the depth of cut decreased, so that the second series of cuts takes place between those already executed; the fluting-stop is fixed on the right side of the tool-box to arrest the tool at the centre, the cuts being made from the margin to that point.

Fig. 2 is cut with a step-drill in place of the vertical cutter, and being, as will be observed, of a longer twist, the extra arbor (Fig. 169B) is employed, therefore, the train of wheels is as follows:—144 on chuck, 120 and 16 on double arbor, the 144 gearing into the 18, the 120 into the 30 on the extra arbor, the 60, which is on the same spindle, gearing to the 15 on the socket. The mitre-wheels are the same in every respect. The step-drill is then inserted to the depth required, and arrested short of the centre by the fluting-stop, so that at that point the figure is represented by a pyramid, resulting from the shape of the drill. In this example there are sixteen cuts, every sixth division of the wheel being employed, the gradual diminution of the strands towards the decreasing diameter being very effective.

Fig. 3 represents the twist or strands cut in both directions, the same drill being used. This particular result would lead any one to suppose that it was produced by other means, as the crossing of the spirals at various points so destroys the continuous line, that the effect is quite altered; it may also be varied in many ways. The wheels to give this result are very different to those employed for the two previous subjects, the extra arbor (Fig. 169B) is removed, and those used are 144 on the chuck, gearing to 18 on arbor, 120 on the same, gearing to 72 on the socket, in place of the 15.

The right hand spiral is first cut from the margin towards the centre, and arrested about $\frac{1}{10}$ on the left side by the fluting-stop, the wheel of the chuck is then moved from 96 to 48, which is the opposite, or half of the entire revolution, the second cut is then made; the slide-rest is returned to the margin, the radial arm raised, and the intermediate or reversing arbor introduced between the 144 and 18; the arm is then lowered to gear the 120 and 72, and the two cuts repeated in the opposite direction, for which the wheel on the chuck is set to 24 and 72 respectively. A very distinct figure is the result of this arrangement, and when worked out on large diameters the effect is much improved. All such work may be cut from the centre and stopped at the margin, if for any reason it is found preferable to do so, for which it is only necessary to place the second fluting-stop to operate on the opposite side of the tool-box. Particular attention must be given to the reduction in the loss of time caused by the freedom inherent to so many wheels in gear at the same time. The correct way to overcome this is, when the tool is returned to the starting-point, no matter in what direction it is (although from margin to centre is generally most suitable), it should be traversed past that point and returned to it, the number of divisions on the micrometer necessary for the purpose being noted ; and the division at which the reading line points when so returned, will be the position at which the drill or cutter is to be inserted for each succeeding cut. When the terminal point is reached, care must be exercised that no portion of the return journey is commenced until the tool is withdrawn from the work.

Fig. 4 displays a still further advance in this class of surface spiral decoration; the train of wheels again differs, inasmuch as the extra arbor (Fig. 169B) is again employed to increase the length of the twist, the train consisting of the following wheels : 144 on the chuck to 18, 120 to 30 on the extra arbor, 60 on the same, gearing to 15 on the socket, the connection to the slide-rest transversely being the same. The ivory is first chucked in a boxwood chuck and by plain turning carefully surfaced, then with a short parting tool, $\frac{5}{100}$ in. wide, a series of incisions is made, the first nearest the margin, and about the width of the tool from that point; the depth of the cut is arranged according to the substance of the material and the style of decoration desired. When the first incision is thus made, the stop-screw must be adjusted, and for each successive cut it must be carefully brought to precisely the same place by the guide-screw; the tool is then moved twice its own width, which will be one turn of the main screw, and the second cut made; the same process is repeated throughout the distance required. The ultimate beauty of the work, when cut on the other side, depends entirely upon the accuracy of these incisions, and too much care cannot be exercised in the production of them.

The work must now be re-chucked, and, when preparing such a subject for this process, the periphery should be turned slightly taper to facilitate this object; a well-seasoned boxwood chuck is the best for the purpose; it should be turned out to fit the work as accurately as possible, and the bottom left perfectly flat and true; the work is then gently tapped into it, against the inner surface, until by the sound it is proved to touch it at every part. As a rule, all work held in a chuck of this kind should not touch the bottom of the chuck, but for this particular purpose it is necessary, as the work to be cut on the front must be absolutely true to that already executed, and the close contact of the two true surfaces is the safest means to adopt. Thus held, the material is turned to the desired thickness between the bottom of the recesses in the back, and the surface to remain uncut.

To cut the front, in this instance, a large round-nosed drill (Fig. 127) was first employed, and the superfluous material cleared away at every quadrant of the wheel of the dividing-chuck, thus: 96, 24, 48, 72; a drill with a square end was then used to finish the surface, and to just expose the cuts in the back, but not deeper than is necessary for this, or the excellence of the work is destroyed. An ogee moulding tool, with a fillet, is then used to shape the projections that now stand on the top of a series of rings; the material having been removed to such an extent, the moulding-tool will not reach the figure, therefore the part to be shaped must be brought in contact with it by turning the tangent-screw of the dividing chuck sufficiently to obtain the necessary depth to complete the figure, when each side of the four projections may be finished. Before any alteration is made, the number of divisions that the wheel is moved from the original zero should be noticed, and the wheel then moved to exactly the corresponding number on the opposite side, so that the other side of the figure may be treated in the same way ; the drill is then moved by the screw of the slide-rest, to present it to the outer diameter, the same depth of course being maintained. When the drill is advanced, the work is slowly rotated by hand, or by the tangent-screw and worm-wheel of the segment apparatus ; this completes the shaping of the projections left on the surface, and it will be seen that from the combination of the spiral line and the circular one, the points all mitre at different angles, but correctly, and render the effect pleasing for many purposes.

Fig. 5, Plate 12, illustrates the result of employing the reciprocator in connection with the spiral apparatus, as explained in the details of the instruments, Figs. 171 and 172. To produce the figure as seen, the reciprocator (Fig. 171) was placed on the double arbor by eccentricity B, the largest amount, a wheel of 120 in front of it, geared to one of 18 on the socket ; the arm on the chuck was then fixed to that on the arbor by the first hole, and a step-drill used to cut the figure. The gradual tapering of the waved line gives very excellent results, and may be varied in a great number of ways.

Fig. 6 represents a few of the variations to be obtained, and the manner in which the different settings are arranged to produce the figures, as seen in the illustration. As there are seven distinct classes of wave on this one disc, they are numbered consecutively, from 1 to 7.

No. 1 is produced by a train of wheels consisting of 144 on the double arbor, to which the reciprocator is also attached by its eccentricity A, the lesser amount ; the 144 is geared to a 15 wheel on the socket, and the arm on the dividing chuck is fixed to that on the arbor by hole 1, that furthest from the chuck. The line

is cut with a small round-nosed drill, and as they are simple
illustrations of the difference in the curve, resulting in each case
from a re-arrangement of the apparatus, it is not necessary, in fact
it is preferable not, to use a figured drill. It will be seen that
the result in this instance is a line with a slight wave, deeper, as
in all work thus executed on the face, at the larger diameter, and
gradually decreasing in depth towards the centre.

No. 2 differs, inasmuch as the wave is deeper; the same wheels
were used, and the only change required is to attach the arm on
the arbor by the eccentricity B, or the largest amount, which
causes the mandrel to move a greater distance in its partial
rotation; the wheels being the same as those for No. 1, the length
of the wave is the same, but the extended movement of the mandrel
increases the depth.

No. 3 again employs the same wheels and corresponding eccentricity, but the arms are joined by hole 8 on the short arm; this
simple alteration again extends the rotation of the mandrel, and
creates a still further depth of wave.

No. 4, which it will be seen has increased depth of wave, and
decrease in length, by which the number of waves is multiplied
in a corresponding distance, is obtained by the same eccentricity
and the corresponding fixture of the two arms; but the wheels
are both different—96 on the arbor gearing to 15 on the socket,
which lessens the proportional traverse of the slide to the semi-
rotation of the mandrel.

No. 5, it will be observed, bears an extremely distinct appearance, which is the result of employing a wheel of 48 in the place
of the 15, and attaching the arms by hole 1 on the short one, the
eccentricity B being the same; thus a further increase in the
number of waves is the result.

No. 6 is a further variety, and to effect this particular pattern
the larger reciprocator, Fig. 172, takes the place of the smaller,
being placed on the arbor by the hole which gives an eccentricity
of $\frac{8}{10}$, the arm attached by hole 1, the wheels being 144 on arbor
to 20 on socket, thus a similar number of waves in a corresponding
given length, as No.4, is the result, but of a considerably greater

depth; and by removing the short arm and attaching it by hole 8 in the short arm, the effect is as seen in the waved line, No. 7, which is of further increased depth only, and represents a figure, considerably altered in appearance, although of the same description. These few examples are sufficient to indicate the innumerable variations that may be made with comparatively simple alterations, and will also show clearly the manner in which the reciprocator is employed for figures to be produced on the surface. The motion is conducted to the slide-rest in each case by the mitre-wheel of 60 thereon, being geared to the 30 on the sliding-rod of the surface spiral apparatus; or the newly-designed double joint (Fig. 170A) may be substituted.

We now come to the same instrument employed upon the cylinder, dispensing altogether with the intermediate connecting apparatus. The slide-rest in this case is set parallel with the lathe-bed and connected by the universal joint in the same way as for spiral turning, and all the waved lines previouly described, as executed upon the surface may, with equal facility, be transferred to the cylinder.

The two examples seen on Fig. 7 and numbered 1 and 2 will suffice to establish this fact, and as more elegant curves are produced by extended eccentricity and quick traverse of tool laterally, the larger instrument (Fig. 172) was used in conjunction with the extra arbor (Fig. 169B), thus employing four wheels instead of two, so that the lateral traverse of the slide-rest is increased beyond what it is when only two are used.

To cut the line, No. 1, Fig. 7, the eccentricity of $\frac{8}{10}$ is employed, the wheels being 144 on arbor geared to 30 on intermediate arbor, the 60 on latter being placed in gear with a 15 on the socket, and the arms attached by hole 8.

No. 2 of these examples is the result of the same wheels and eccentricity, but with the arms attached by hole 1 in the short arm; by which means the partial rotation of the mandrel is decreased, and a longer wave is obtained. Decorations of this kind are most useful for such subjects as whip-handles, candlesticks, &c., and a large variety of ornaments. They may be cut in both directions by adjusting the work to the opposite side, as referred to in the description of the instruments.

CHAPTER XXXIV.

IVORY CANDELABRA.

THE preliminary proceedings for a subject of this kind will consist of a careful selection of the ivory, which should be matched in grain and colour as nearly as possible; it is also advisable to have a rough sketch at hand, so that the proportion of the design may be more clearly and easily worked up. It has no doubt been observed by many turners that at times a vast deal of beautiful cutting is executed upon a piece of work entirely out of proportion, and thereby thrown away. Should the candelabra, Plate 13, be considered worthy of reproduction, the following details of its construction will, it is hoped, be of assistance in carrying it out.

The base is made from a piece of ivory $4\frac{1}{2}$ in. in diameter and $1\frac{3}{8}$ in. thick. This was first held in a universal chuck, and turned to a true circle inside, sufficient only to increase the inside of the hollow in the ivory to a circle, and by this it is again chucked on a boxwood plug, to which it is glued; the latter is not absolutely necessary, as there is not a great deal of work to be done to this part. The base is left $\frac{1}{2}$ in. thick, it is then reduced as far as the hollow, when it is again carried in square, and the front turned to an angle, the slide-rest for the latter purpose being set 30°.

Having shaped this part so far by following the design from the autotype, the slide-rest is returned to its original position parallel with the lathe-bed, and the universal cutter (Fig. 122) placed in it with a double-angle tool of 55°, the 120 division used, the tool penetrated at every hole, and deep enough to bring the points up sharp. The instrument is then set over to operate as a vertical cutter, using a tool (Fig. 109), which, it will be seen, admits of the cut being carried close up to the shoulder, which could not be effected with either of the other instruments, without extending the radius of the tool beyond what is required. The diameter of that part to be so ornamented is $3\frac{1}{2}$ in., and twenty-four consecutive cuts are made; the slide-rest is then placed at the same angle at which it turned the plain form, and a corresponding number of cuts made, only just sufficiently deep to bring the terminal points in a line with those previously cut on the edge. By using a very keenly-sharpened tool, these parts may be brought up to great perfection, leaving nothing to be desired.

A shallow recess is made on the surface of this part to receive the ring, which is next fitted; this, it will be seen, is also cut with the vertical cutter, but with twelve consecutive cuts only. The drill-spindle is then substituted for the universal cutter, and a bold step-drill employed, the index being set to the half of the number used to cut out the segments, so that the drill passes through its precise centre.

The stem or pillar upon which the branches are supported will form the next proceeding. This is made in two separate pieces, with an ornamented ring of ivory between them; the lower piece is $1\frac{3}{4}$ in. in diameter at the base, gradually tapering towards the top, the same gradation being conveyed to the upper portion; care must be exercised to ensure the gradual tapering of the whole column, allowing for the intervening connection; the base of the column is held to the foot by a steel pin $\frac{1}{4}$ in. in diameter, being firmly screwed into it with a nut and washer on the under side; the two parts of the shaft are also connected by a steel screw of the same size, the ring being kept central by a plain fitting.

To cut the twist, the spiral apparatus is employed; the train of wheels consisting of 144 on the dividing-chuck, geared to the 18 on the double arbor, the 120 on the same gearing into a 20 on the socket; the universal cutter (Fig. 122) with a round-nosed tool $\frac{12}{100}$ in. wide, set out to a radius of $\frac{8}{10}$, and set to operate as a vertical cutter.

The work was held in the following way :—It being necessary to cut entirely through the length at each end, the hole tapped in

Plate 13.

the end was screwed to a corresponding thread on the chuck, the latter being turned down to the same diameter, so that the cutter passed clean through without fear of splintering or damaging the base; in consequence of the face of the ivory being in close contact with the chuck, the opposite end is supported by the popit-head centre; the dividing chuck set to zero, and a cut made at 96, 24, 48, 72, four cuts in all. The column now under notice was cut at one cut, to try the power of the new instrument (Fig. 122), and was left from the tool, by which the excellence of the improved instrument was at once established. Although the result of this proceeding was in every way successful, it is recommended that such work should be executed in two or three consecutive cuts.

Having cut all four segments, the radius of the tool is reduced to $\frac{4}{10}$, the dividing wheel moved to 12, and the cut continued at 36, 60, 84, the tool penetrated to bring the edge up perfectly sharp. The lower part thus cut, is removed, and the upper portion placed on the same screw, the diameter of the chuck being reduced to correspond with it; to cut this the same process is adopted. And here again considerable care is necessary not to cut below the surface, or the general tapering of the form will be destroyed, which will greatly mar the beauty of the work.

On the end of the upper portion a plain pin is left, to which is fitted the plate that holds the branches, and projecting beyond this is a screw that fits into the base of the tazza on the top, the foot of which holds all secure when finally put together. The outer edge of the ivory plate is cut out with the vertical cutter, the face has a deeply cut eccentric pattern, not seen in the autotype, and the six holes are drilled equidistantly to receive the branches.

The tazza is made in two pieces, the top being scalloped at the edge with a large quarter-hollow drill, a row of beads being cut to project above the surface, a similar effect being produced on the small projection at the centre, above which the socket to hold the centre candle is fixed. The branches to hold the sockets must next be made. These, it will be observed, are the result of rings, which, when carefully finished, are cut in halves and connected in opposite directions. They are $2\frac{1}{8}$ in. in diameter externally, and

1½ in. inside, turned in width to equal the substance remaining from the two diameters. The face of each is then ornamented on both sides with the eccentric cutter, each one differently. This, is done after the plain part has been carefully polished.

The horizontal cutter (Fig. 118) is then employed with the spindle and saw to cut the rings precisely in the centre. The saw is carefully adjusted to the axis of the mandrel by the two set screws, and by the main screw of the rest it is passed across the face, by which process the rings are equally divided, and perfectly square and flat where it is cut, so that when reversed the two halves will fit together and be parallel one to the other. To fix them together, and hold them firmly when fixed, a steel pin, having a thin piece between the joints to break the plainness of it, is screwed into the centre, and forms a more appropriate finish. To cut the six squares all exactly alike, a piece of ivory should be turned to a cylinder the required diameter, and long enough for all; each piece is partly cut through, the vertical cutter is then used to produce the four concave sides, and when this is done, they may be finally severed; being thus cut in one process, they are all made precisely alike, and in less time than if cut separately.

To attach the branches to the disc, which is fixed to the top of the column, a steel pin is also employed. This is firmly fixed in the centre of the square formed by the half of the ring, and the ivory nut which holds it has a plain part which fits the hole in the disc. This is less trouble than attaching a piece to the ring, and answers the same purpose. On the opposite end of the branch another steel pin is fixed to receive the sockets that hold the candles; at the base of each socket a round disc of ivory, 1¾ in. in diameter, is fitted, the hole in the centre being only just large enough to fit over the steel screw; it has a scalloped edge, which is cut with a pointed bead-tool similar to Fig. 105, $\frac{25}{100}$ in. wide on the cutting points. For this operation the instrument is set so that the tool cuts horizontally; there are sixteen consecutive cuts, the intervening point being the result of what is left from the angles on the sides of the tool. These should all be cut on the same chuck, and the same settings used, and, when thus far finished, they can be re-chucked by the inside of that part previously cut; this must be carefully done, so that none of the points are broken. On the top a series of small beads, thirty-two in number, is cut with a bead-drill $\frac{12}{100}$ in. wide, and the edge again cut to the same number with a round-nosed tool. These discs form a foundation upon which the base of the socket or sconces rest, and add greatly to the elegance of the whole design.

The next proceeding will be to make the six holders for the candles, and the only difficulty that will be found, is the fact of their being all required precisely alike; the six pieces of ivory should be all cut off the same length, each one is then held in a universal or die chuck, and the hole to receive the candle bored or turned out, all being made exactly the same size, in order that ultimately they may be worked up on the same chuck; the hole finished, the body and lip must be shaped and polished, the former only as far as the extremity of the concave curves is concerned; the top part is then cut out with the vertical cutter to eight concave curves, leaving about $\frac{1}{8}$ in. between each, to be cut with a drill; the face then has a series of twenty-four beads cut on it with a drill $\frac{12}{100}$ in. wide. Having carried out the same process on each one, they should be re-chucked by the hole, and as before suggested, if they are identical in size, one chuck will suffice for them all; when reversed, the lower part of the vase must be shaped and polished.

To cut the pattern on the convex curve, the eccentric cutter is used with a single-angle left side tool 60°, the slide-rest is set to an angle of 40°, and raised $\frac{1}{8}$ in. above the centre, so that the cut only takes effect on one side of the work. This particular class of work is illustrated also by Figs. 5 and 6, Plate 1; there are thirty-two cuts round this part, and being cut deeply, it is, for such a purpose, a most effective result.

The base is then cut square with the eccentric cutter, having a round-nosed tool in it. The size when finished, is $\frac{3}{8}$ in., therefore the diameter of the material must be left large enough at that part to admit of its being perfectly clean and sharp when reduced by the eccentric cutter to this size.

The centre sconce is made the same shape, but is cut on the convex curve rather differently, inasmuch as the slide-rest is adjusted to the precise height of the mandrel axis, and a double-angle tool used in place of the single-angle. The chains hanging from each arm complete the work, as illustrated. These are made in rings of different sizes, gradually tapering from the centre to the ends in each direction, and are put together by each alternate ring being split, which must be carefully done with the grain; they are then soaked in warm water, when they will open, and when dry the joint will remain quite close. They are attached to the arm by a small ivory pin with a head to it, screwed to the branch immediately under the disc.

Being strongly made, and each part firmly attached, it may be considered a useful as well as an ornamental specimen of turning, and the designs for such subjects may be carried out in a variety of ways. That now described may at the same time suggest many improvements for future operations, and assist amateurs in the development of this class of work.

CHAPTER XXXV.

The Spherical Slide-Rest.

The modern rest of this particular construction, with all its latest improvements, will be found illustrated by the engraving Fig. 173. It is composed of four slides and one rotary movement; the two slides at the lower extremity working at right angles one to the other, below the circular movement, while the two upper slides are arranged to work above it.

The movable plate, which is fitted to the third slide, has a socket cast on it in the solid, to which the stem of the plate

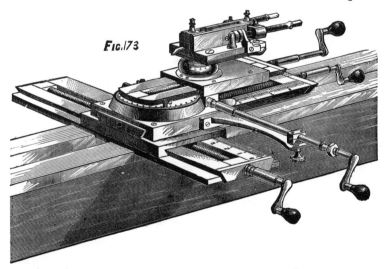

Fɪɢ. 173

carrying the tool-box is fitted, and the same is clamped in any position by a screw passing through a steel ring which encircles the socket. In proceeding to manufacture such an instrument, the following details will, it is hoped, be found of some service.

Like all such tools, it should be commenced at the foundation, therefore the first or lower slide should be chucked carefully on a

planing machine, face downward, and the tenon planed to fit freely
in the interval of lathe-bed, the base being surfaced at the same
time, where it rests on the bed.

It will be seen by reference to the engraving that this slide
is made to extend on both sides of the lathe-bed, which improvement was suggested by Mr. Ashton, and proves of considerable
service when the rest is used to turn and decorate large concave
curves. At the end overhanging the top board, that is, away from
the operator, a projection is left on the under side, through which
a long steel screw passes, and, when tightened, draws the tenon
against the inside of the lathe-bed, thereby ensuring the rest being
square to it. It is also provided with a holding-down bolt with bow-
handle and washer, to fix it firmly to the lathe-bed when in use.

The tenon and base being planed, the slide must be re-chucked
on the machine, and the face and angles planed perfectly true to
it ; and here great care must be exercised, as much depends on its
accuracy, so that when the screw is tightened to the bed and the
tenon drawn against it, the slide will be at right angles. The plate
which forms the slide is then got up to a perfect surface and the
two side-bars fixed ; these are made of gun-metal and held by
three screws, the heads countersunk in the under side, one bar has
also two steady pins, the other is adjustable by two set screws
which are screwed into the steel plate, their heads projecting so as
to create a pressure upon the metal bar. When fitted thus far,
the slides should be very carefully ground together with fine oilstone powder, but the greatest care must be taken to exclude
emery powder of any description.

On the top of the plate, the second slide is fixed, having been
first planed and surfaced. It is held firmly by four steel screws,
with their heads also countersunk in the under side of the plate ;
its position is such that one end is flush with the side of the first
plate, the whole of the extension being on the right side, as seen
in the engraving. In fixing this slide to the plate, one screw
should be first put in, the slide then set perfectly true at a right
angle to the lower one, when it will be in a parallel line with
the bed, and when so set, the other three screws are fitted with

greater facility. Having the slide thus fixed, a plate, similar to that on which it is placed, is fitted to it, with gun-metal bars, in the same way as the lower one.

The rotary movement will be the next to engage attention. The worm-wheel is made of gun-metal, and has 120 teeth cut on its periphery, and is actuated by a steel tangent-screw, working in a frame of the same material; the frame is pivoted at one end, and is thrown in and out of gear by a steel cam and spring, the action being the same as applied to the ellipse and other chucks.

The top of the wheel is turned out at its centre to receive a large screw, with $\frac{3}{4}$ in. plain part and $1\frac{1}{4}$ in. diameter in the head; the screw is then accurately fitted to it, and screwed into the top plate of the second slide. This screw should be so fitted, that when it is forced tightly to the plate, the worm-wheel will revolve without too much freedom between the face of the plate and the head of the screw, and (as seen in the engraving) is on the left side, when the slide is parallel to the lathe-bed. The worm-wheel is covered with a gun-metal ring, fitting closely round its periphery for the purpose of excluding dust and shavings; the frame into which the tangent-screw is fitted is also cut out to fit round the wheel for the same purpose. On the top of the worm-wheel, the third slide is fixed by one extremity, and held by four screws countersunk into the bottom of the wheel.

On this slide a strong gun-metal plate with a projection to form a socket is fitted, in the same way as those already described. The bars should then be removed, and the plate very carefully chucked by its lower surface, the socket then turned out to 1 inch in diameter to receive the stem of the fourth slide. When this aperture is turned out, a small air-hole should be drilled through the base, or a perfect fitting cannot be made; at the same time, the external part of the socket should be turned to receive a steel ring, through which the fixing-screw will pass, to hold the stem of the top-slide in such positions as it may be required when in use.

The fourth and last slide is, to a very large extent, a copy of the ordinary tool-box of the ornamental slide-rest, being fitted up on a steel plate with a stem attached to it to fit into the hole already turned out in the socket of the plate on the third slide. This fitting is one in which particular care should be exercised, as it must fit accurately, or the pressure of the binding screw will alter its truth in relation to the other slides. It may be well to again refer to the necessity for absolute truth in all the chuckings, as the least error in any one will eventually become a serious drawback when all the slides are finally put together. Nothing but extreme accuracy of workmanship will make such an instrument capable of working truly.

At present, it will be seen, there is no adjustment for the exact height of the tool. To effect this, the stem which fits into the socket has a screw through it, which raises or lowers the tool slide. This screw, the head of which is under the tool-box, is only accessible when the latter is withdrawn. This can very easily be done when any alteration in the height of centre is necessary. It will be seen that the steel ring which surrounds the socket has a divided scale on it. This is most useful in setting the tool round to any particular position that may be found necessary.

The slides being so far finished, the fitting of the main-screws will form the next proceeding. These, like all such screws, are made with ten threads to the inch. The ends of the slides are carefully lined out and drilled, the front large enough to allow $\frac{7}{16}$ in. screws to pass freely through, while the opposite ends are drilled to receive the point of the screws when turned down to the bottom of the threads. The front is also countersunk to receive the collar attached to the screw, which must be well fitted. Gun-metal plates are then fixed to the ends of the slides to hold the main screws in their places. On the end of each screw a gun-metal micrometer is fitted, divided into ten equal parts. These are first turned down, so that the slides will pass over them, and not made with milled heads. The latter are entirely a mistake, as they prevent the slide moving as far as may be required. This is avoided when they are turned down, and each slide, it will be seen, has a divided scale on its surface, marked at each turn of the screw, that is, every tenth of an inch. This has been found of very considerable service.

Another improvement in this instrument is of such a simple character as to scarcely deserve the name, but, at the same time, it renders the tool considerably more serviceable. It is simply the addition of two extra holes, in which the screws that hold the nut of the third slide are placed. Its importance is clearly shown by the fact that work of much larger dimensions can be executed, consequent upon the slide being allowed to pass over the stem of the winch-handle, which admits of the various instruments being brought further from the centre of the circular movement; the nut need only be fixed by these holes when required. Fixed in the centre of the plate for instance, work of $1\frac{1}{2}$ to 2 inches only could be decorated, but when fixed at the end, by the two holes as seen in the engraving, the slide is allowed to recede 2 in. or more, further from the axis of the wheel, and larger work can be done. In recognising this fact, it must be remembered that such instruments as the horizontal or universal cutter project a long way from the face of the tool-box, and thus occupy the space which is required for the work to revolve in.

Another improvement, is the adapting of the tangent-screw to receive the whole of the spiral apparatus. This is done by fixing a strong metal arm to the plate of the second slide under the centre of the tangent-screw, the object of the arm being to support the end of a spindle, which is fitted to a bearing as seen in Fig. 173, and on which the various wheels of the spiral apparatus are fitted; the bevel-wheels are used to connect the rest with the rotation of the lathe-head. The end of the arm has a curved slot, which allows the tangent-screw to be moved in and out of gear, without taking off the spindle, the end of which is made to receive a winch-handle for ordinary purposes.

The segment-stops are also another important addition. It will be noticed that a series of holes is drilled round the top of the worm-wheel; into these are placed two steel pillars with adjusting screws, in place of the now obsolete arrangement of pairs of pins of various sizes, with flat heads. The points of the screws come in contact with a projecting steel pillar, which can be placed on either side to correspond with the alteration of the third slide.

CHAPTER XXXVI.

MANIPULATION OF THE SPHERICAL REST.

THE difficulty of producing an accurate sphere by hand-turning, and of decorating curves with continuous ornamentation, has brought the simple rest, as known to Bergeron, to its present state of perfection, and made it a most valuable addition to any ornamental turning lathe. It has no less than seven movements, by means of which convex and concave curves of any degree are readily obtained, from a small bead around the periphery of a large piece of work, to a sphere of four or five inches in diameter; and when so turned, the bare form may be ornamented to any extent by replacing the fixed tool with the various revolving cutters, the termination of each cut or flute being determined by the segment-stops, which fix into the worm-wheel.

The curves produced, whether concave or convex, and their position, depend entirely upon two conditions: First, the position of the worm-wheel; secondly, whether the tool be on the far or near side of the centre of the worm-wheel. To ascertain the position of the worm-wheel, it is necessary to mark a zero line upon the first slide, which is effected in the following manner:— Turn a cylinder, mark on it a fine pencil line, place the rest on the lathe with the axis of the worm-wheel as nearly as possible under the pencil line, place the fourth slide parallel with the third by means of its index and divisions on ring, and both parallel to the first slide; place a double-angle tool in the tool-box, and by means of the second slide, bring its point exactly opposite the pencil line; throw the tangent-screw out of gear, and turn the worm-wheel exactly half way round, and by means of the first slide it is so adjusted that the tool shall just touch the line, both on the far

and near sides of the cylinder; the axis of the worm-wheel will then
be exactly under that of the lathe.   The zero line should then be
cut on the surface of the first slide.   The worm-wheel can always
be adjusted to the zero line, which will in most cases be found
sufficient for practical purposes.

Having obtained the means of placing the worm-wheel accurately in a transverse direction, it is necessary also to do this in the
longitudinal, which is affected as follows : Place the third slide
parallel with the second, and move the rest until a straight edge
placed on the face of the work coincides with the zero line which
passes transversely through the axis of the worm-wheel.

To illustrate the working of the spherical rest, let it be desired
to cut a boxwood sphere of two inches diameter ; turn the wood true
at the end and reduce it to a cylinder of the required size, mark a
fine pencil line one inch from the end; it should then be turned
approximately spherical by hand ; place the slide-rest then on the
lathe with the axis of worm-wheel under the pencil-line, and the
first slide at zero.   This done, the first and second slide must not
be moved ; any other alteration may be made as you please.   Now
if an ordinary slide-rest tool were used, the fourth slide would
come in contact with the shoulder of the work, or the chuck on
which it is, long before the tool had traversed round the sphere
far enough for even general purposes, hence the necessity for the
application of the curved tool (Fig. 178), this would completely
sever the sphere, but a stem sufficiently strong to hold it must be
left until the whole of it is turned ; it can then be detached by a
tool of a similar shape, but with an acute point (Fig. 179).

It is obviously impossible to ornament a sphere entirely from
pole to pole by one chucking only, but this can be effected by a line
marked exactly upon the equator, and after one hemisphere is
decorated, it can be re-chucked the reverse way with the equatorial
line perfectly true with the surface of the chuck, a proceeding
which will require great care, as it is a somewhat difficult processs.

Next let it be desired to excavate a hemisphere, the reverse
operation to the last.   To do this, turn the end of the work true, place
the spherical rest with the first slide at zero, and the third slide

parallel to the second, so that the zero line of the worm-wheel shall exactly coincide with the surface of the work. This is effected by means of the second slide, thus: Commence with a straight round-nosed tool, which must be let in gradually while it sweeps out the material as the excavation progresses; when the fourth slide comes in contact with the edge of the work, a curved tool must be substituted for the straight one, and the hemisphere completed. In practice the bulk of the material would be removed by hand-turning, and the hemisphere finished only by the spherical slide-rest.

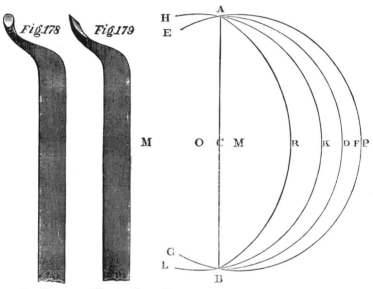

A diagram illustrating the curves, though simple, may be desirable. Let M P represent the axis of the lathe from mandrel to popit-head, c the centre of the work, and A B the diameter and back of work. (1) With tool at radius c B, and worm-wheel coincident with c, the hemisphere A D B results, and the alteration of the radius would only increase or decrease it; (2) if worm-wheel be ·25 nearer P at M, the curve E F G results; (3) if worm-wheel be ·25 nearer M at O, the curve H K L results. It is to be observed that these curves, E F G, H K L, must fall within the diameter A B, therefore this must be compensated by an increase of radius if the diameter A B is to be preserved; and again this increase of radius will necessitate another compensation E G if the hemisphere A D B has been cut, and it is desired to cut a curve A K B, passing through the point A B, and also through K, a point ·25 nearer to M; then by means of the second slide the worm-wheel must be moved from C to O, *i.e.*, ·25 nearer to M. But curve A K B falls within the points A B by, say ·05, therefore the radius must be increased by ·05; but this will bring the curve ·05 further from M beyond the point K, consequently the worm-wheel must be moved nearer to M by fully ·05, for as the worm-wheel is moved towards M, so does the curve A K B fall still further within the points A B; (4) it is obvious that as the worm-wheel approaches M, the flatter does the curve become, as A R B, provided that by increased radius the tool still travels through A B, and conversely, as the worm-wheel approaches P a greater portion of the sphere results; (5) if you regard A B as the axis of the lathe, and M P as the diameter of the work, the same reasoning applies to oblate and prolate spheroids. These may all be ornamented by means of revolving cutters, or a drill, and the flutes may, by traversing the first and second slides, be continued at right angles to the axis of the lathe or parallel with it.

A great variety of tools have been made for use in the spherical slide-rest, most of which, however, are more or less useless; the ordinary slide-rest tool will do a deal of the work, but curved tools are essential. Fig. 178 is an excellent tool for roughing-out the work externally, while Fig. 179 is employed for cutting off. There should be about four sizes to suit different diameters of work.

Whilst upon the subject of tools, the author has pleasure in bringing under the notice of amateur turners the spherical parting tools invented and patented by the Rev. C. C Ellison. They are made in sets of four (Figs. 174, 175, 176, and 177), sufficient for all general purposes. They all fit into a steel bar, which is also useful as an internal boring or parting tool. The blades vary from ·8 to 1·5 in. in width, and are as simple in appearance as they are difficult in production, being turned by a specially constructed tool to the exact radius of the curve they are intended to cut—viz., 2, 3, 4, and 5 in. diameters. By their assistance the whole of the inside of a hemisphere, either of soft wood or ivory, can be turned out in shells clean and true to shape, and ready without further labour to be chucked and ornamented; thus a very large amount of valuable material is saved. They are used thus: Suppose the material to be a solid block of ivory, turn the surface true and polish it, make five circles of 2, 3, 4, and 5 inches diameter, place the

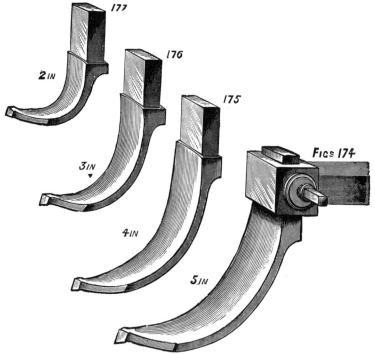

tool-box of the spherical slide-rest level with the front of the fourth slide, and fix it by both depth and stop-screw, using, of course, the bridle to the former; it is necessary that both screws should be fixed, lest vibration should occur; place the steel bar quite home in the tool-box, adjust the rest to excavate a hemisphere, and fix the 2 in. blade quite home in the tool-box, throw the tangent-screw out of gear, release the fixing-screw of socket-ring, and adjust the inside edge of the blade to touch the 2 in. circle, and the inside curve of blade to a trifle less than 1 in. from the centre of the face of the ivory; the exact position being determined by a brass gauge made for the purpose.

Place the tangent-screw into gear and tighten the fixing-screw; the tool may then be passed into the ivory by rotating the tangent-screw, and a solid 2 in. hemisphere will be cut out; readjust the slide-rest, substitute the 3 in. blade for the 2 in., proceed as before, and a hollow hemisphere will result. The same process must be repeated with the other blades. Where hemispheres of larger dimensions are required, the blade may be taken out, sharpened, and replaced with mechanical accuracy. There is one important arrangement to notice, without which some difficulty may arise when operating upon work of the larger diameter. While the blades can be made of any strength, the spherical rest, from its construction, is of necessity comparatively unstable, and to counteract the great strain in cutting a large diameter, a piece of soft wood must be placed against the face of the work and between the bottom of the blade and the top of the third slide; this prevents vibration and strain upon the rest. If it is desired to cut out shells, greater or less than a hemisphere, the axis of the worm-wheel must be moved further from, or nearer to the lathe-head.

It is not only as an inventor of tools that Mr. Ellison has excelled, but as a turner also, and by his courtesy I have on several occasions been enabled to exhibit specimens of his ornamental work, which will bear comparison with that of the best professional turners, and is the result of experience, patience, and the great attention paid to the cutting edge of the tools used.

On Plate 14, Mr. Ellison further enables me to give an illustration of one of the best specimens of spherical work yet produced, by a combination of the rose engine, ellipse chuck, and the spherical slide-rest, and it is hoped that the following details will enable any amateur possessed of the necessary apparatus to reproduce it:—The ring or moulding was cut first, and as no larger ivory could be procured, the two blocks (weighing 7 lbs. each, and measuring 7½ by 6½ inches in the rough) for the two halves of the vase had to be reduced; one block for the lower half was chucked and turned true upon a double eccentric and ellipse chuck, the sliding ring having ·55 eccentricity, a groove cut ·1 in. wide and ·2 in. deep at ·25 from the edge; the block was reversed in the chuck, and a corresponding groove cut upon the opposite side. A hole was then bored from one to the other, and by means of a frame saw, the grooves serving as guides, an oval ring, 6·8 in. by 5·8 in. by ·25 in. was severed; next a large oval picture frame was cut off, but not until the rebate and back had been turned and polished.

The block was then re-chucked the reverse way and fitted to receive half the thickness of the ring, by means of the spherical rest and inside parting tools, the inside was cut out in frames, finished off with a cutter-bar and polished. Then it was re-chucked the reverse way by the rebate, and the rose engine oscillating movement so adjusted by a spiral level, that one point of the rosette was in the same horizontal line as the longer or major axis of the ellipse; the edge of the revolving cutter was placed in the same plane and its axis in the the same vertical plane as the back of the work, where it thus cuts the full depth of the pattern. This done the rosette was moved exactly one half of its wave or pattern. The tangent-screw was moved four complete turns and the cutting repeated to the same depth; the rosette having been moved back to its original position, a similar cut was made; and so on until the pattern was completed; the other block was treated in the same way and also made to fit into the ring. For the base the ellipse chuck received ·4 eccentricity and it was cut in the same manner as the halves of the body, the rest having been adjusted to the requisite curve, the ring between the base and body received ·45 eccentricity and was cut like the ring on the top, upon the face and each edge, the finial was begun with ·4 eccentricity, gradually reduced to 0 and was cut with a vertical cutter revolving the reverse way to the lathe. The ivory in the rough weighed 18½ lbs. and was worth £14. The finished vase weighs 1 lbs. 14 ozs., and about £6 in value was saved in frames, &c.

The cutter used was designed by Mr. Ellison and deserves mention. It consists of a steel disc, 1·5 in. in diameter, ·3 in.

Plate 14.

thick, having fifteen teeth inclined over the radius at an angle of
about 15°, the face of the teeth being at an angle of about 30° to
the axis of spindle, so that the best cutting edge, perhaps, is
combined with such clearance, that the ivory shavings flow out like
a stream of snow-flakes. The rapidity of cutting is such that a
4 in. hemisphere can be fluted with only one sharpening of the
cutter, and in less time than is required by the usual fly-
cutter; the work, moreover, is left in a highly polished condition.
With a fair amount of practice, any amateur turner of average
experience can so far master the spherical slide-rest, as to produce
and ornament a vast variety of curves, in as great a number of
different positions. Such a tool can only be regarded as a most
valuable addition to a lathe.

CHAPTER XXXVII.

VASE ORNAMENTED WITH SPHERICAL SLIDE-REST.

THE vase represented by Plate 15 further illustrates the different applications of the spherical slide-rest, and the following details will, it is hoped, enable any amateur turner to reproduce it. This particular specimen was described in a mechanical journal in the year 1881, and several turners copied it with great success. It may, of course, be reduced or enlarged, as well as made from various materials. That from which the autotype was taken is made from boxwood only, which arose from the fact of its being made by the author during some experiments and improvements that were carried out with reference to the spherical slide-rest.

As a first trial, perhaps it will be as well to appropriate the same material, but for a finished specimen it should be made either in ivory, or African blackwood, one of each of which has been made by amateurs from the details as they appeared, and is considered in every way satisfactory. The first attempt to reproduce a piece of work of this nature may not result in an exact copy ; this is scarcely to be expected, as the instrument is in itself complicated, and it will require some practice to overcome the difficulties of such an intricate piece of machinery ; this, however, is modified by the explanation of the manipulation of the slide-rest in the previous chapter.

When about to turn such a vase, the proportions must claim the attention of the operator, and the material, whatever it is, must be selected with care as to the size and grain. Should it be desired to produce a fair copy, the dimensions of the original are $12\frac{1}{2}$ in. high, the tazza $5\frac{1}{2}$ inches diameter. Those portions of the material that will not turn up to the required dimensions must be discarded,

Plate 15.

and replaced by others. If the sizes of the various parts are not so maintained, the result will probably not be satisfactory. The author does not presume to anticipate that the vase illustrated may not be greatly improved by many of the experienced amateur turners who may read this work. The above remarks therefore refer to the production of a true copy only.

The material to be used must now be left entirely to the taste of the turner, but, as a basis, we will assume that ivory has been selected for the purpose. The base which is a plain ogee should be cut from the hollow end of a tusk, the body also cut from a similar part, but of smaller dimensions, the former may be held in the following way : From the unevenness of the interior, it will probably not be expedient to turn it out, in which case a boxwood chuck should be turned down to allow the ivory to pass over with sufficient freedom to admit of the external diameter being set as near true as possible, the ivory is then fixed to the face of the chuck with strong glue.

The figure is then carefully turned, and being quite plain is executed by hand-turning ; the front is next turned out to a suitable diameter, and screwed to receive the body which, when fitted, is held in its place for further operations, as the base into which it is screwed forms a permanent chuck.

The body is fluted with a large size step-drill employed in the ordinary ornamental slide-rest, the fluting-stop as previously described being used to determine the length of each; these flutes being deeply cut, and the tool of extra size, each one will require a series of cuts to complete it, and in working round a large diameter of this material, it may reasonably be expected that the drill will lose a deal of excellence in its cutting powers, therefore, when cut round, the drill should be taken out and very carefully re-sharpened, and a light cut again taken over each flute ; if from the fact of sharpening the drill a slight deviation of its profile should occur, it will not interfere with the result, as a slightly increased penetration will cause the exact form of the drill to result.   Between each flute, sufficient space is left for a second drill (a round-nosed one) to be inserted.   The original is 4 in. in diameter at this part, and contains twenty-four deeply-cut step grooves or flutes, the smaller drill being inserted between each; at the lower extremity of the flute, a rather larger round-nosed drill is employed to seriate the hollow.

The convex curved lip at the top of this part is now turned, and this affords the first instance of the application of the spherical slide-rest. The curve being approximately reduced to shape, the spherical rest is placed on the bed of the lathe and fixed, the main slide is then adjusted to the precise centre of the lathe-axis; and the slide which carries the worm-wheel so fixed as to place the latter under the centre of the curve to be turned. This will at first be found a somewhat troublesome job, but a little experience will soon obviate any difficulty ; once set, the work is turned in plain form, and, as it is afterwards fluted with a smaller sized step-drill, the drilling instrument is substituted for the fixed tool. Should the point of the drill not traverse round the curve sufficiently, it may be adjusted to do so by turning the tool receptacle in the socket, but on no account whatever must the position of the worm-wheel be disturbed. The difference in the position of the fixed tool and drill, will arise simply from the fact of the plain form being turned with a curved tool, while the drill is central to the stem of the instrument. The distance the drill is allowed to travel is determined by the segment-stop in the worm-wheel. Thus far the body may be considered finished, and the recess in the top of it only remains to be turned out and screwed to receive the foot of the tazza, or upper part.

To proceed, the foot of this part when fitted to the base should be removed, and held in a wood chuck screwed to receive it, and, for further security, a little glue may be placed between the two faces. This is not absolutely necessary, and may be omitted if the fitting is well made, but in the case of any excessive excavation being required, it is always a safeguard against the work moving in the chuck.

The concave curve roughly shaped, the spherical slide-rest is adjusted, and the tool extended beyond the centre to suit the curve, which is then accurately turned ; the vertical cutter

(Fig. 95) is then placed in the tool-box, and, by shifting the tool slide in the socket, the point of the cutter is brought to the desired position to follow the curve.   The vertical cutter alluded to, is the most suitable for application in this slide-rest, from the fact of the spindle extending to one side only, as there is no frame-work to prevent the tool passing round the curve, by coming in contact with any shoulder, or face of the chuck, &c.   The tool thus adjusted, twelve consecutive cuts are made by employing the 96 division arrested at every eighth hole.   At the base of this curve a very small convex curve is seriated, and at the top a circle of small beads; these should be cut with an astragal tool, so that the beads stand well apart.   The intermediate part or stem is carried out in the same way, being first shaped, and afterwards ornamented.

We now arrive at that portion which may be considered the most difficult, and that which, if carefully turned, will complete the design.   The whole of that part forming the tazza is in one piece, and this, perhaps, renders it more difficult to execute.   The rough block of material is held in the universal chuck and the inside turned out, and, in the first instance, a short, slightly taper fitting should be left ; it is then removed from the universal chuck, and re-chucked upon a boxwood plug by the inside fitting; the convex curve forming the bowl is approximately shaped, together with the upper concave curve, the spherical rest is then carefully adjusted to the precise axis of the lathe by the lower slide; while with the second slide, the axis of the worm-wheel is placed under the centre of the hemisphere to be turned.   A straight tool will be found to pass round far enough for this purpose.

The drilling instrument is then substituted and a step-drill employed of smaller dimensions than that used for the base; the segment-stops are arranged so that the drill will pass out at the diameter of the work, and is arrested as it approaches the centre to the desired point.   This part contains forty-eight consecutive incisions, half of which are first cut; the intermediate ones are arrested at half the distance, in order that the form of the curve should not be destroyed by their too close proximity at the centre, and this also allows a series of round-nosed drills of different sizes

R

to be studded seriatim over that part left uncut. It must be mentioned that when cutting the second series of step-flutes, the segment-stop should be re-adjusted to prevent the undue traverse of the drill.

It is found in practice that a deal of the material may be excavated by the partial rotation of the circular movement by hand, but for all finishing cuts the tangent-screw should be placed in gear, and the motion governed by it.

The second slide must now be adjusted to the concave curve; this will require a careful setting. The series of round-nosed drills is again employed to decorate this form; the work is then removed, and again chucked by the convex curve. This will also require considerable care, as it is held by the spaces left uncut by the step-drill; it will, however, hold perfectly tight in the chuck if correctly fitted. The convex curve at the top is then turned, and the spherical rest again set to suit the curve. This is ornamented with a series of ribs or reeds; these were cut with a quarter-hollow drill with an astragal end, which creates a space between each; and as the distance at which the drill was arrested for each cut, did not allow the true form of the hemisphere to result, the reeds are of an elliptic form, which add to, rather than detract from, its appearance.

So far, the whole specimen is complete, with the exception of the cover. Some who have examined this vase, have expressed an opinion that it is improved without the latter; this may at the same time be considered a matter of opinion, and any turner deeming it worthy of reproduction, can omit this part, or not, according to taste.

The manner in which this part is turned, is similar to the details already explained, the vertical cutter being used for the concave curve in the same manner as employed for the foot. The cover, it may be remarked, is not intended to fit closely on the curve, the spaces rendering the vase appropriate as a receptacle for *pot pourri*.

CHAPTER XXXVIII.

ELLIPTIC CASKET.

THE illustration contained in Plate 16 affords an opportunity of explaining the use of the spherical slide-rest, in combination with the ellipse chuck, by which very elegant designs are produced and decorated.

The following instructions will be of service in the reproduction of a similar specimen:—First select a piece of ivory cut from the end of a large hollow, and in doing so let it be of considerable substance, in order that the concave curve may be turned without encroaching too closely to the inside; it must be at least $\frac{3}{4}$ in. thick. Such a piece of ivory is prepared in the following way: First face it over on one side, after which it is fixed to a wood chuck by glue, and placed on the ellipse chuck; when perfectly dry, a rebate is turned out at the opposite end, and the face turned quite true to it.

In setting the sliding-ring of the ellipse chuck to the required eccentricity, it must be arranged to suit the proportions of the material, by which the largest size possible is obtained; the end faced, and the rebate turned, it is removed from the chuck; a second wood plug, driven lightly into a metal chuck, is then mounted on the ellipse chuck, and turned to fit the rebate, accurately, when it is again glued and allowed to dry. The rebate is useful in two ways; first, it forms a means of securely holding the material to the chuck; secondly, it is for the purpose of receiving the false bottom, which is ultimately required. It is absolutely necessary to employ a metal cup chuck, for the reasons explained in Chapter XXIII., on the manufacture of the ellipse chuck; and the eccentricity of the ring, which, for the subject under notice was fixed at $\frac{6}{10}$ in., must remain the same throughout.

To turn the body of the box to the shape, will be the next proceeding. The spherical slide-rest is adjusted by the two lower slides, and as there is a considerable amount of material to remove, a strong tool is necessary, therefore, one with a shaft or stem fitting the tool-box is preferable.

Having roughed out the shape, the tool must be carefully sharpened for a finishing cut, which should be made with the worm-wheel under control of the tangent-screw. At the base a large quarter-hollow tool is employed to form the plain moulding; when turning this, the tool is placed in position by the worm-wheel, and there held while it is inserted by the guide-screw of the top slide; the tool is then changed for one of smaller size, and the corresponding form turned on the top. Before attempting to decorate this part it should be highly polished, as explained in Chapter VIII. relative to that particular branch of the art.

The fixed tool must be replaced by the drilling instrument, with a large round-nosed drill, and the segment-stops adjusted to arrest the partial rotation of the worm-wheel at the desired distance on each side of the centre; the ellipse chuck is then set vertically, and the first cut made at the zero of the 96 circle of holes, the tool is penetrated to the necessary depth, and the stop-screw set. The cut is repeated at every third hole of the division, resulting in thirty-two consecutive cuts. A second drill, smaller in diameter, and with a square end, is then used to cut the recess deeper, the segment-stops being readjusted, so that the same substance is left at each end.

The tool is again changed for a round-nosed drill, about $\frac{2}{100}$ of an inch larger in diameter, it is then set by the tangent-screw to first cut the hollow nearest the base, which is repeated all round. It is then moved by the tangent-screw two-thirds of its diameter, and again inserted, the stop-screw having been fixed to determine the penetration. It only remains to repeat this twelve times to complete that part. It will be seen that the spaces left between the flutes are also cut in a similar way; the drill is replaced by one of larger diameter, and the starting point re-arranged, which will require the aid of the adjusting index, in consequence of the

Plate 16.

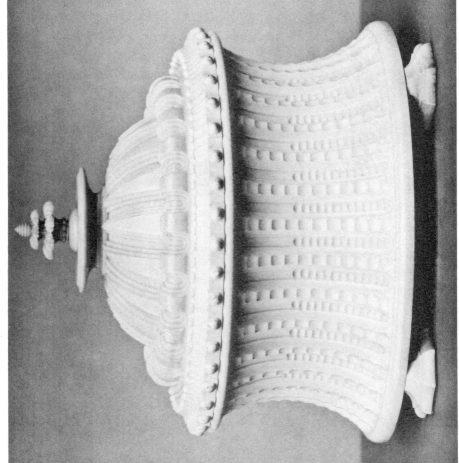

AUTOTYPE

dial-plate being moved three holes for each cut. Having adjusted these points (which have been previously referred to), the drill is inserted to about three parts of the entire curve, and then moved a corresponding distance by the tangent-screw for the second series ; this, repeated twelve times, will carry them throughout the curve. This is a very effective pattern, and if well cut, will not require further treatment in the way of polishing.

The lid or top of the casket must next claim attention ; this, for convenience and economy, is made in five separate pieces. The ring which forms the fitting is the first to turn, and it will be an advantage in every way if it can be cut from the same tusk of ivory. A piece $\frac{5}{8}$ in. thick will be sufficient to allow for chucking, also the part which forms the fitting for the bottom. This should be first held by glue, and the fitting accurately turned ; by this it is again chucked while the top is ornamented.

This part will not require the spherical slide-rest ; which may therefore be removed, and the ornamental rest employed. A hollow is first turned in the face, leaving a rim $\frac{2}{10}$ of an inch wide ; a round-nosed drill is then used, which is passed through the edge at every third hole of the 120 circle of division, resulting in forty incisions ; this process has left practically forty squares, and upon the top of each one it will be seen that a bead is cut. This is done by simply adjusting the tool to the correct centre, and employing a bead-drill with a broad astragal end ; a large round-nosed drill $\frac{40}{100}$ in. wide is then used to seriate the hollow which is incised at every hole of the same division, 120 ; above these, on the top, a row of smaller beads is cut at every second hole, leaving 60 ; the return concave curve towards the centre is also cut with a larger drill in a similar way ; this, however, from the nature of the illustration, is not clearly developed. The following ring it will be seen has required the spherical slide-rest in its decoration : it is first turned true to shape, and to fit a recess in the previous one, which is made to receive it, and then chucked by the inside. The eccentricity of the ring being still the same, the spherical-rest is adjusted to bring the centre of the worm-wheel under that of the ring, and the tool necessarily moved near to the centre of the wheel, to operate on so small a curve; having turned the plain form, it should, like its predecessors be highly polished.

The ellipse chuck is again set vertically, the pulley fixed at the 96 circle, a bold step-drill replaces the fixed tool, and is carried as far round the curve as possible, the segment-stops being again required. There are twenty-four cuts; and it is a pattern that will require considerable attention and patience in its execution, but well repays the time spent upon it.

The dome top will next require to be turned. This is made from a solid piece of ivory, and is carefully fitted at the base to the interior of the ring preceding it. The spherical rest is adjusted in the same way as for turning a hemisphere, which the subject illustrated is similar to, although of an elliptic form. Here again the polishing must claim attention; a still bolder step-drill is then used, and fifteen cuts only are made round it, leaving a broad polished interval, which greatly adds to its appearance; the points of the different steps, all resulting in sharp terminals, are also decorative.

To complete the casket nothing remains to be done but the finial. This, it will be seen from its diminished size, terminates in a long elliptic form, which is left perfectly plain. On the top of this, is an ornament, which is made in three pieces, and cut seriatim at different angles and curves, forming a kind of rosette.

The only parts now to be done are the feet, which, from the fact of their being, so to speak, the foundation, may be considered to be the first part; it is, however, immaterial. Although a somewhat minor portion of the box, they require considerable care to produce them all exactly alike. A brief explanation of the way in which they were made will be of service in their production.

The four pieces of ivory are first turned by hand to the required form, and screwed where they enter the bottom of the box; they are then held by the screw while cut with the vertical cutter, which may be done either with one complete moulding-tool or two separate tools, and being all cut at the same setting they are all precisely the same shape.

CHAPTER XXXIX.

THE GEOMETRIC SLIDE-REST.

THIS slide-rest was invented and patented by Captain R. Pudsey Dawson, and is a most useful and interesting addition to the amateur's lathe; it is applied in combination with the spiral apparatus, as will be seen by reference to the engraving, Fig. 180, and its general construction will be understood from the following details.

A cast iron pedestal is fitted to a cradle in the same way as the ornamental turning slide-rest; in fact, the same cradle can be

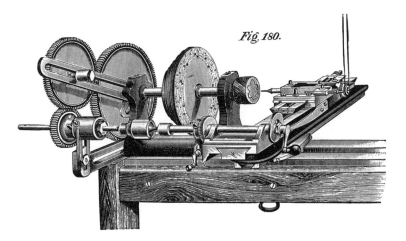

Fig. 180.

appropriated. To this base a metal ring is fitted for the purpose of raising and depressing the height of the tool; a cast-iron slide 12 in. long is then fitted by its stem, in a similar way to Figs. 13 and 14; this slide is set transversely across the lathe-bed when the rest is in use. A metal plate is accurately fitted to slide from end to end, and is actuated by a strong spring, which takes the place of the screw; on the top of the metal plate a second, but shorter slide is attached, and moves with it. This slide is provided with a screw of ten threads to the inch, the tool-box being fitted up in precisely the same way as the ornamental slide-rest.

Across the front end of the lower slide a metal frame is fitted to lay parallel with the lathe-bed; this carries a spindle which extends at both ends, on one of which a cam is fixed, and by this the action of the slide and spring is governed, while the extension at the opposite end is to connect the movement with the spiral apparatus, and as illustrated, it will be seen that on the improved plan, the latter is attached to the back of the lathe-head. To the spindle, close to the metal frame, a worm-wheel is fixed, with a tangent-screw working in a metal frame, the latter being placed in and out of gear by a cam and spring, similar to that on the eccentric chuck.

The action of the slide-rest, when in use, is as follows :—The main slide is set perfectly true, at right angles to the lathe, to turn a flat surface, which is effected by the main screw of the second slide, the depth of cut being decided by the guide and stop-screw of the top slide. The surface of the material must be turned before any connection is made with the spiral apparatus or cam. Having surfaced the work, the necessary train of wheels can be arranged, and the cam adjusted so that sufficient tension is given to the spring to maintain the pressure of it against the small steel roller attached to the curved arm, which is fixed to the first slide as seen in the illustration.

The transverse spindle which carries the cam is then connected to that which passes through the socket of the spiral apparatus by a universal joint, and when the winch-handle is turned, the uneven form of the cam causes the lower slide to oscillate, while, by its combination with the spiral wheels, the work is rotated at the same time.

Many very beautiful patterns may be cut on the surface; a few of the various combinations are illustrated on Plate 16A. For

PLATE 16A.

simple line patterns cut with a fixed tool, the movement of the winch-handle is sufficient, and produces very good work; but the apparatus is by no means confined to this particular class of decoration.

All the revolving instruments may be employed with it, and when these are used, it is necessary to have the tangent-screw in gear with the worm-wheel, and by this the consecutive cuts are spaced out. The worm-wheel having 96 teeth, the distance for each cut is determined by the number of turns of the screw, or the divisions of the micrometer on the same.

When cutting deep patterns, which are very much more effective and useful for decorative purposes, the tool is inserted by the stop-screw; and by the continuous rotating of the tangent-screw by its winch-handle, the cut is carried throughout the work. The variety of designs may be largely increased by the work being placed on the eccentric chuck, or employing the spiral dividing-chuck, especially the latter, in its present convenient position at the back of the lathe-head.

A further variety in line patterns may be obtained by employing a fluting-stop, by which the traverse of the tool is arrested before reaching the limit of the cam, thus leaving part of the pattern a portion of a concentric circle only as in Fig 6, Plate 16A, in a similar way to the corresponding action in the rose cutter, which is explained in a future chapter.

The cams most suitable for the geometric slide-rest, and generally made, are the ellipse, eccentric, and heart-shaped; both the plain eccentric, and ellipse, have their centre apertures elongated, so that each may be made to produce a greater variety of patterns, consequent upon the different positions in which they are fixed upon the spindle.

The examples contained in Plate 16A have all, with two exceptions, been executed with the eccentric cutter, Fig. 5 being cut with the ellipse cutter, while for Fig. 6 a fixed tool only is employed, arrested by the fluting-stop; this style of work may be largely extended by the various combinations of the cam and change wheels; such patterns as this, however, are not suitable for deep cutting. The number of curves may be reduced, and panels, arches, and miniature frames of elegant designs may be produced, moulded and shaped in endless ways by figured drills and cutters. The apparatus altogether forms a most interesting study, and may be made productive of work unattainable by any other means. It may be justly stated that the only reason this slide-rest has not been more largely used is the cost of it, which from the fact of its requiring the spiral apparatus to work in conjunction with it, is a somewhat expensive item; at the same time it is a valuable and interesting addition to a lathe, and by the inventor especially, some very beautiful work has been executed by its aid.

CHAPTER XL.

The Ellipse Cutter.

THIS instrument (Fig. 181), as it is now made, consists of two distinct parts; the means of producing the ellipse, and that also of correcting the angular aberration consequent upon altering the eccentricities. The first part, namely, the means of cutting an ellipse, was invented by the late Major James Ash, but from the inability to correct the position of the figure, or to compensate the movements, it was not considered, nor was it, a perfect instrument.

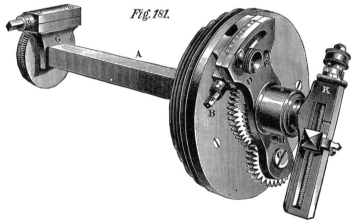

Fig. 181.

The second part, which consists of a worm-wheel and tangent-screw movement at the back, was afterwards invented by Mr. H. Perigal, F.R.A.S., and this, it will be seen from the following details, has overcome the difficulty and rendered it a complete and perfect tool. It produces also looped figures of many proportions, which may be cut in a variety of positions, and grouped to form a very large number of different patterns; its manipulation will be materially assisted by the details of its manufacture, of which the following is a brief outline; the same will also be of service to scientific amateurs in making one of the kind.

A square stem, A, is fitted to the tool receptacle of the usual size; at the front end a flange is forged, with a plain pin about $\frac{7}{8}$ in. in diameter projecting from it; a long spindle passes entirely through the length of the stem, and has a wheel of 48 teeth fixed to it. The metal plate, B, which has a deep boss on the back, is then bored out, and a hardened steel collar driven tightly into it; it is then ground out and accurately fitted to the front part of the stem, and revolves between the face of the flange and that of the spindle to which the forty-eight wheel is attached, a portion of the latter being turned away to relieve the friction; a hard-wood pulley is then fixed to the plate by two screws, for the purpose of driving the instrument by the overhead motion. When thus driven it will be seen that the metal plate, in its revolution, carries every part attached to it, and moves round the forty-eight wheel on the spindle.

On the front of the plate a steel stud is fixed, being under the screw, C; and at the opposite side a metal block is securely attached by two screws at the back, and is turned to a true curve from the centre of the axis of the stud. A metal flange, D, is then fitted (as seen in the engraving Fig. 181), one end being made to fit over the end of the stud, while the opposite extremity is turned from that centre, to fit the curve which has been previously turned from the same point (great accuracy is necessary in these parts, as the flange rests and moves upon them); a curved mortise is then made in the wide end, through which a milled head screw passes and holds the flange tightly to the block. A short piece of metal is then fitted through the plate, B, and held to it by a screw at the back, but with a freedom of movement; through this a screw of ten threads to the inch is fitted, having a flange in front and a small metal collar pinned to the opposite side to retain it in its place; the screw is equal to ten threads to the inch, and works in a nut which fits in a round hole in the flange, marked E, the end of the screw, F, being made square, so that the ordinary key

will move it when required. The socket that holds the screw is
made to turn, to admit of its moving the flange from one point to
another to adjust the various eccentricities required. The top edge
of the flange is divided to an accurate scale from 0 to 40, and read
by a line marked on the block to which it is attached. On the
end of the spindle, which extends through the opposite extremity
of the stem, a worm-wheel of 150 teeth is fixed, a chamfer being
turned on the face, which, for convenience in reading, is divided
into seventy-five equal parts, and figured 0, 5, 10, 15, 20, and so
on; a metal upright is firmly attached to the end of the square
stem by two steel screws, to which is fitted the frame holding the
tangent-screw that actuates the worm-wheel, the head of the screw
being divided into four equal parts.

Having this part so far finished, the instrument should be put
together and mounted in a slide-rest, or on a block, so that the
hole in the front flange that receives the eccentric cutter, may
be turned out perfectly true, while revolving on the stem;
before the flange is moved, after the above process, the zero-
line of the division should be marked, as this point will denote
the accurate centrality of the instrument. The hole thus turned
out, is provided with a steel collar accurately fitted. The front
eccentric cutter, which is precisely the same as Fig. 62, as far as
it goes, is then fitted, having a short stem which projects through
the flange, and to which is fixed a wheel of 36 teeth; two wheels
24 and 36 teeth fixed together, are then fitted to revolve upon the
stud, and by these, the 48 on the spindle and 36 on the eccentric
cutter are connected; and upon rotating the pulley and flange
one complete circle, the eccentric cutter revolves twice in the
opposite direction, thus causing the tool to cut an ellipse.

The screw and division of the flange, D, are of the same value as
that on the micrometer of the screw in the eccentric cutter, K, which
agrees with all screws of a similar description, one turn moving
the tool to a radius of $\frac{1}{10}$ of an inch, while a corresponding movement of the screw, F, results in the same amount of eccentricity to
the flange, D, and in this way the two movements are adjusted, in
the proportions required for ellipses of various degrees.

When the instrument is adjusted for use, the eccentric cutter, K, should stand across the face of the flange at a right angle, and to facilitate this adjustment, a hole marked H is made through the face of the flange, D, over the teeth of the wheels, the tooth and space of the latter being marked with a small dot, seen through the hole, thus ensuring the correct readjustment of the wheels when the instrument has been taken apart.

When the flange, D, and the eccentric cutter, K, are both set to their respective zeros, the tool simply cuts a minute dot, and this may be described as one test of its accuracy, and if the instrument will not perform this, good work cannot be executed. If eccentricity be given to either the flange, D, or eccentric cutter, K, the tool will describe a circle equal to the same eccentricity, while if the eccentric cutter, K, be set to a corresponding eccentricity to the flange, the tool will cut a straight line twice the length of the combined eccentricities, and if the eccentricity of either be increased, the tool will cut an ellipse.

The exact proportions of the ellipse produced are decided by the eccentricities of the flange, D, and the cutter, K, the longer or transverse axis being always twice the amount, while the short diameter or conjugate axis equals twice the difference; therefore, any variation may be given to the curve, by the adjustment of the eccentricities, to produce an ellipse of an elongated form, or the same may be reduced to a circle if necessary.

When cutting a series of ellipses, it will be necessary to employ the worm-wheel or tangent-screw at the back, in order to compensate each row, otherwise they will not stand vertically or coincide in any way. The necessity for this compensation arises from the fact that the course traversed by the revolution of the eccentric cutter, K, with each separate movement of the flange, D, will cause each succeeding series of ellipses to be more or less at an angle, their direction being to the left if the eccentricity is decreased, and to the right when the same is extended. As before mentioned, the worm-wheel has 150 teeth, with a division of 75 equal parts on the face, the micrometer being divided into four equal parts and figured 0, 1, 2, 3. It will be obvious that one turn of the screw will move the wheel through the space of one tooth, by which the forty-eight wheel, attached to the same spindle, is moved a corresponding distance.

One quarter of a turn, or one division of the micrometer, precisely compensates the angularity occasioned by the flange, D, being moved one division of the scale, and as the movement of the flange is increased, the worm-wheel is correspondingly moved in the required proportion, while if the ellipses are cut with the eccentricity of the flange reduced, the worm-wheel must be moved in the same equal proportion, but in the reverse direction. In most instances the worm-wheel is employed to compensate every individual movement of the flange, but it is also used in placing the various patterns in different positions on the work, and is at times used entirely for this purpose, the work being held stationary by the index point in the dial-plate of the lathe-pulley.

To use the words of the inventor, Major Ash, with whom the author worked at many points of the instrument for hours together : it should in the first place be set all at centre, that is, the worm-wheel, flange, and eccentric cutter are all adjusted to their respective zeros, and when thus set, if the instrument is accurate, the tool will cut a small dot. The height of centre must also be studied, and the tool adjusted precisely to it by the elevating ring of the slide-rest, it must also be set to the same point laterally ; by these adjustments the ellipse cut is precisely in the centre of the material to be decorated.

As an example of simple patterns and adjustments ; to place a series of ellipses of equal proportion, or in other words concentric, the eccentric cutter may be moved, say, eight divisions of its micrometer, while the flange is moved four divisions of its scale, and to place the separate cuts in equal proportion, the movements of each must coincide.

To produce a pattern in which the ellipses all lay parallel, the eccentricity of the flange remains stationary, while that of the eccentric cutter is reduced in equal ratio for each cut. Another effective pattern is one in which the straight line is first cut and the proportions gradually reduced until a circle is the result. To effect this, the eccentric cutter, K, and the flange, D, are both equally extended, as to eccentricity, to cut the straight line; the cutter, K, then remains unaltered, while the flange, D, is reduced for each consecutive cut until the zero coincides with the reading line, when the tool will again cut a circle equal to its eccentricity.

The three foregoing examples explain how the instrument is to be employed for simple ellipses, but as the more complex patterns are approached, it will be found necessary to employ the worm-wheel and tangent-screw, to adjust the various cuts to the required positions. The worm-wheel having 150 teeth, the micrometer on the screw being divided into four, and one turn moving it through the space of one tooth, it will require $37\frac{1}{2}$ turns to place two ellipses at right angles, but that number of turns must be calculated from the division at which the wheel may stand when it has been moved to compensate for any extension of the flange, D, for the first cut. To place three ellipses equidistantly, it will require twenty-five turns of the screw for each, and, by calculation, any number of ellipses may be thus placed equally round the work.

So far, the instrument has only been regarded as to its powers of cutting ellipses of any proportion between the straight line and circle; its powers, however, are largely extended by the introduction of extra wheels of 24 and 48 teeth. These two wheels replace the 24 and 36 on the stud, and that on the stem of the eccentric cutter has substituted for it, one of 24 teeth in place of that having 36. To make this alteration, the screw, C, is removed from the stud, and the milled head screw taken out, the flange is then withdrawn from the face, the 24 wheel is fixed to the eccentric cutter, the 24 and 48 placed on the stud, and the flange replaced; the wheel of 48 teeth attached to the spindle running through the stem, is not changed. The screw, F, need not be removed from the nut, as the fitting by which it is held to the flange, being circular, it can be drawn off the nut without the least difficulty. This train of wheels is thus 48 —24, which causes the eccentric cutter to revolve four times, to one rotation of the pulley, thus creating a four-looped figure. The various ratios between the two points, that is, the flange and tool, with regard

s

to these eccentricities, of course alter the character of the figure to a large or small degree, according to the movement of either, or both.

As an example of the difference to be obtained, we will once more set the instrument all at centre, and, if from this point, the flange and eccentric cutter are extended a like distance, the loops will touch at the centre, and the result will be that the four will each resemble an egg in shape, the curves decreasing in width towards the centre. If the eccentricity of the flange alone be increased, it will be seen at once that the figure is entirely different, resulting in an open cusped figure with looped extremities; the amount of open space in each loop depending upon the variation in the eccentricity given to the flange, which may be made to eventually result in a square; the radius of the tool also varies the shape of the figure.

The above explains the result of extended eccentricity to the flange only; now to affect another variation, if the movement of the tool as to eccentricity be increased beyond that of the flange, the course of the loops will be round the centre, leaving a figured space at that part, the amount of curve left in the centre of the different figures, resulting from the ratios of the two settings.

It will be found necessary to resort to the worm-wheel and tangent screw at the back, to correct the angularity of the figures, that is, where each successive cut requires an increase of eccentricity to the flange, and supposing that a series of loops is to be placed on the work, eccentric to the axis, the instrument receives lateral adjustment from the main screw of the slide-rest, by which means the figures may be placed any distance from the centre.

The figure itself may be multiplied by varying the position of the tool with the worm-wheel; if, for instance it is desired to have two four-looped figures so placed as to represent eight loops all equidistantly apart; the first cut having been made, the worm-wheel at the back must be moved by $18\frac{3}{4}$ turns of the tangent-screw, the same proportionate movement of the screw being necessary for increased numbers, the adjustment as in the previous instance, being calculated from the point at which the wheel stands after the figure has been adjusted to the vertical position. A still further improvement is made to this instrument by the addition of a second radial arm, which is fitted over the circular boss of the flange, and has a curved slot concentric to it, through which a screw fixes it to the face of the flange. This again carries two wheels attached to it, revolving on pivots, so that either or both may be employed to produce the figures in either direction, that is inwards or outwards. To engage with this arrangement, a small wheel of 18 teeth is placed upon the end of the eccentric cutter, the forty-eight wheel on the centre spindle still remaining unchanged.

CHAPTER XLI.

The Epicycloidal Cutter.

This instrument (Fig. 182) may be considered an extension of the ellipse cutter, with additions that render it capable of producing a very large number of different patterns   It represents, in point of fact, the first part of a small geometric chuck, mounted on the slide-rest instead of on the mandrel nose, and although very similar to Fig. 181, its construction in many respects differs. The diameter of

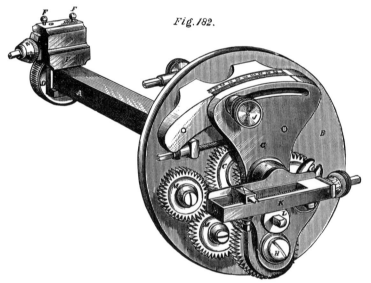

Fig. 182.

the driving-pulley, the groove of which is turned on the edge of the plate B, is $5\frac{3}{4}$ in. in diameter, the increase in size admitting of a larger number of change wheels being employed. A considerable advantage is found in all the necessary changes of the trains of wheels being confined to one arbor only, which is easily removed, and does not necessitate the partial taking apart of the instrument each time different wheels are required. The ability to introduce a greater number of wheels, and consequent variations in ratios, gives a largely increased range of loops, both consecutive and circulating, the former ranging from 2 to 6, that is, 2, 3, 4, 5, 6, emanating, from the number of revolutions of the eccentric cutter in proportion to the rotation of the pulley, while the latter are to be obtained from 5 to 90 by delaying the rotation of the eccentric cutter, and introducing to the train of wheels a fractional value. With this instrument all figures may have their loops turned inwards or outwards, but require compensating, which is effected by the worm-wheel and tangent-screw at the back, the same as in the ellipse cutter, with the exception that the wheel has 96 instead of 150 teeth. The amount of compensation required will depend entirely upon the relative movements and ratios of the eccentric cutter and flange. The details which follow will render the manipulation of this instrument comparatively easy.

CONSTRUCTION OF THE INSTRUMENT.

The square stem, A, is fitted to the tool-box of the slide-rest, and has a round end upon which the driving-pulley, B, revolves, the metal being bushed with a hardened steel collar; through the square stem a spindle is fitted, having fixed to the front end, a wheel, C, of 64 teeth; on the opposite extremity, the worm-wheel, D, of 96 teeth is attached by a hexagonal hole and a screw in the end, a metal upright, E, is also fixed to the square stem, to hold the frame in which the tangent-screw works; on the top of the frame two set screws, F F, are fitted, to more accurately adjust the movement; the micrometer of the screw is then divided into fifty equal parts, and figured at every ten, by which the wheel may be subdivided into the numbers required.

On the face of the plate, B, a stud is fixed at the lower extremity as the instrument stands vertically in the tool-box, at the opposite side a block of metal is attached to the same plate; a metal flange, G, is then fitted, one end to the upper part of the stud, the opposite, resting upon the block of metal before referred to; this is fixed by a screw in the stud, H, and a milled head screw, J,

passing through a curved slot in the flange; when this is so far
fitted the instrument should be mounted on a block, as recommended for Fig. 181, and the centre of the flange turned out
perfectly true to receive a steel collar. In this the stem of the
eccentric cutter, K, is fitted, and on the end that passes through
the flange, a wheel of 40 teeth is securely attached by a screw and
steady-pin; this wheel, unlike that fixed in a similar way to the
stem of the ellipse-cutter, never requires to be moved, but
remains constant.

To the stud under the screw, H, two wheels are fitted to revolve
on a socket, in which is a steel collar. These have 60 and 32 teeth
respectively, the latter being on the lower end near the face of the
plate B, and in the same plane as the sixty-four wheel attached
to the spindle in the centre of the stem A; the two wheels are fixed
together, and of course revolve simultaneously. Above the surface
of the flange, G, and fitting over the end of the stud, H, a steel
radial arm with a mortise (open at the end) is attached, and
partially rotates, being fixed when required by a screw, L, which
passes through a short semi-circular slot, allowing sufficient movement to admit of any of the changes of wheels passing into gear.

To the radial mortise in this arm a removable arbor is fitted,
to slide throughout its length, and in this again a spindle revolves
to carry the change wheels, two of which are always attached to it
by a circular milled head nut. This arbor is so arranged that the
upper wheel gears with the forty on the end of the eccentric cutter,
while the lower one performs the same office with the upper wheel of
the two on the stud, H, which has 60 teeth, and until the removable
arbor is interposed, there is no connection between the wheel on
the stud and that on the eccentric cutter; and provided two wheels
of the same number are employed to make the connection, the value
of the train remains the same, and will produce a three-looped figure,
the tool in the eccentric cutter rotating three times for one complete
revolution of the plate or pulley, and the various wheels employed
on the removable arbor, multiply or divide the initial value of the
permanent train of wheels, which is: $\frac{64-60}{32-40}$

To alter the wheels on the arbor, the screw is loosened by the key and the arbor withdrawn, the screw that binds the arm to the flange is also slackened, and when the wheels are changed, the arbor is returned and the wheels geared by the lateral adjustment in the radial slot, and the semi-rotation of the arm, both screws being then re-tightened. The sixty-four wheel on the spindle through the stem, and the thirty-two on the lower portion of the socket that revolves upon the stud, are connected by two carrier wheels, M M, which are attached to the plate, B, by screws from the back; the plain part which goes through the plate, moving freely in a hole larger than itself, so that each one may be thrown in or out of gear as required. Under the screw-head a washer is placed to cover the hole, and to more readily clamp the stud upon which the wheels revolve.

The object of these two wheels is to change the direction of the figures; for instance, if both are employed at the same time, we have an even number of axes at work, which causes the loops of the figure to turn inwards, while if one only is geared, the result is that the loops turn outwards; the carrier wheels do not alter the value of the train in any way, but simply afford the means of changing the direction in which the tool traverses.

The eccentric cutter is fitted up in precisely the same way as for Fig. 181; the edge of the block is divided to a scale of 100 divisions, read by a line marked on the flange, G; and the means of adjusting the flange by a screw of ten threads to the inch is also fitted in the same way as that on the ellipse cutter, so that equal movements of the tool and flange, result in corresponding eccentricities to both. The worm-wheel and tangent-screw for the compensation of the angular aberration of the figures is in all respects the same as in Fig. 181, with the exception, as before mentioned, that the wheel has 96 teeth in place of 150.

In order that the figures to be produced may be in a vertical position, it is necessary that the flange should stand horizontally when the wheel on the removable arbor is geared with that fixed to the eccentric cutter, the latter being then in the vertical position, and the division on the flange being set also at its zero. To regain this position two lines are marked, one on the cylinder boss at the back of the pulley, the other, which represents the reading line, upon the edge of the circular flange of the stem, against which the fitting of the pulley revolves.   When these two lines are coincident the above adjustments are made.

The epicycloidal cutter as already described, produces many very beautiful figures of a fine line description, the beauty of which is really more advantageously seen when printed, and although the variety of patterns to be produced is practically endless, the

Fig. 184.   Fig 183

particular description of work to which it is confined, greatly detracts from its value, and it was after a long series of experiments with the instrument, that the author arrived at the conclusion that its merits would be very much enhanced by the introduction of a means of cutting the patterns deeply into the surface of the work, and removing the superfluous material; thus leaving the figure in relief upon the surface.

To effect the above result, it is of course necessary that the combined motions of the instrument travel precisely the same course, but at a very slow speed.   This is provided by the addition of the worm-wheel, A, Fig. 183, which is fixed to the short cylinder body, at the back of the Plate, B. This wheel has 140 teeth cut on its periphery, the edge of it being divided, to note its partial rotation. A plate of steel, C, is then fitted to the square stem and attached to the face of its flange, also by two screws. This plate, it will be seen, extends upwards, high enough to admit of the frame, D, which carries the tangent-screw, E, being held to it by a screw, F, which forms the axis upon which it moves; a milled head thumb-screw, G, passes through a short curved mortise in the steel plate, described from the axis of the screw, F, and is tapped into the frame, D, which is cut away in the centre to receive the tangent screw, E; the latter is supported at the opposite end by a centre screw, H, and shouldered in at the front end, the face being chamfered to receive the divisions to act as a micrometer, the end being squared to receive a winch handle, and the division read by a line on the frame, D; the micrometer is divided into four equal parts, figured 0, 1, 2, 3.

With this arrangement it will be seen that the motion of the two parallel movements is not in any way influenced with regard to their value one to the other, but the speed at which they move is placed entirely under the control of the operator by the winch-handle, J, so that a slow continuous traverse, or a series of partial rotations may be made to suit the work to be decorated. So far we have the means of controlling the revolution of the instrument, and by reference to the following description of the small drilling instrument, Fig. 184, it will be seen that the power of deep cutting is also supplied.

This little instrument which is fitted to the tool-box of the eccentric cutter, K (Fig. 182), is made so that its axis agrees with that of the instrument, when set all at centre; on the front of the stem a short cylinder with a cone at the back, is turned perfectly true, and hardened; this is necessary from the high speed at which it revolves; to this is fitted a steel pulley, retained in its place by a screw countersunk into the stem; to the front of the pulley a steel nozzle is fitted, so that it can be detached, and in this a small taper-hole is bored to receive the drills, which may be made of many patterns, similar to those used in the ordinary drill-spindle, the drills should all be turned in their place to ensure accuracy, which is a most important point.

When used, the drill is driven from the overhead motion at a high speed, which is easily obtained, in consequence of the minute diameter of its pulley, the penetration of the tool is decided in the same way as for other works, by the depth and stop-screws, and the movement of the instrument for the looped figure governed by the winch-handle.

One of the difficulties that at first stood in the way of the progress of this introduction, was the inability with the old style of overhead motion, Fig. 10, to follow the course of the instrument as it carries the drill from point to point through a looped figure, its position being continually altered, as more or less eccentricity

Fig. 185

is given to either the flange or the eccentric cutter, and the same objection applied to it as when used in the rose cutter, which will be explained in a following chapter. This was overcome in a great measure by employing a flexible band, but this, although it was found to answer fairly well, had its disadvantages.

Many leading amateurs at once decided to have the improved overhead motion (Fig. 11) fitted to their lathes, by which the drill under notice, and all other instruments (that do not require a rise and fall), are more evenly and smoothly rotated, without the continued changing of the band.

A further addition, emanating from the same source, will be readily seen by reference to Fig. 185. This is a miniature eccentric cutter, fitted at the stem in precisely the same way as the drill (Fig. 184); attached to the front of the pulley is the slide by which the eccentricity is obtained, its axis being also coincident with the instrument. By the use of this addition the variety of patterns may be largely increased, as it affords the opportunity of cutting a second figure over the course already traced by the action of the instrument. For a variety of figures composed of consecutive cuts, the worm-wheel, A (Fig. 183), forms the means of dividing the work, as it is by this, in conjunction with the tangent-screw and micrometer, that it is equally spaced out ; the drill may be usefully employed to place a series of beads or pearls throughout the looped figure ; such patterns, however, may be said to apply to figures of consecutive loops only, for the reason, that when the higher numbers of circulating loops are approached, the pattern becomes mixed up and the effect marred.

CHAPTER XLII.

THE ROSE CUTTER.

THIS instrument, as illustrated by Fig. 186, produces on a limited scale, similar patterns to those emanating from the rose engine, and the latter may now be said to be quite out of fashion, being very seldom made, except for trade purposes, and then in a plain form only. It will be seen that the instrument under notice receives a rotary and oscillating motion at the same time, while the work is held stationary by the index, the various adjustments being made, in the radius of the tool, the lateral traverse of the slide-rest, and the movement of the worm-wheel, D, attached to the disc, upon which the rosette is fixed. With the rose engine the same movements occur to the apparatus fitted to the mandrel and head-stock, which rocks on centres, while the tool is stationary in the slide-rest. The number of patterns to be cut on the face are practically endless, and, by various combinations, may be made very beautiful indeed. Those illustrated, however, are only for the purpose of more fully explaining the movements of the instrument, which, like its predecessors, will be more easily understood by the details of its manufacture.

The square stem, A, is made to fit the tool receptacle of the slide-rest; and is provided with a plain circular fitting with a flange. Through the entire length a steel spindle passes, fitting a slightly taper hole in the stem, A; on the rear end of this spindle a worm-wheel, B, is fixed, actuated by a tangent-screw working in a metal frame fixed to the support, C, on the end of the stem. A pulley is fitted to the tangent-screw for the purpose of driving it from the overhead motion, whereby the instrument is set in motion. On the front, or opposite extremity of the stem, a circular disc is fitted, to which the rosette is fixed by a circular ring or nut, with lever holes in the edge. In order that the necessary changes may be

made, the centre aperture in the rosette is made just large enough
to pass over the frame and pulley at the other end. To this disc
is attached a worm-wheel, D, of 96 teeth, and a tangent-screw to
move it in both directions, so that the undulations in the figure
may be placed as desired; the disc revolves between the face of
the flange on the stem, and that of the collar, E, which is part of the
spindle that passes through the stem, and to which the worm-wheel

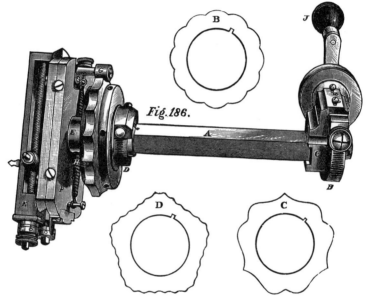

Fig.186.

and tangent-screw at the back are fixed. To the face of this collar
a gun-metal oblong plate, F, is securely fixed by a strong screw and
steady-pin; to this plate is fitted a steel slide, K, to work at right
angles to the stem, between two chamfered side bars; this slide
carries a steel tool-box similar to that in the eccentric cutter, and
is actuated by a main screw of ten threads to the inch to correspond
with all others of a like nature, the micrometer being divided also
in the same way. The slide, it will be seen, is made the entire
length of the plate, and the tool by this means can be placed on
either side of the axis of the stem, in the same diametrical line. To
obtain the oscillating motion necessary to the slide, the end of the
plate, F, has a slot cut in it, and to the slide a steel post is fixed,

upon which a small steel roller revolves. This, when in use, is kept in contact with the rosette by a strong spring, H, attached to a screw in the metal plate, F, at one end, and through the pillar that carries the roller at the other, a small milled nut is fitted on the end of the spring, by which the tension is altered; the spring passes freely through a hole in the centre of the collar, E. By this it will be seen that as the roller passes round the rosette it is always in contact with it, and the tool traces the figure on the work.

At the end of the plate, F, opposite to that on which the pillar holding the roller is fixed, a steel stop-screw is fitted to a projection, also fixed to the same plate; this is used to prevent the roller from following the full depth of the figure contained in the rosette. It is also employed to keep the roller from coming into contact with the rosette in any way, in which case the tool describes a circle only, the diameter being determined by the radius given to the tool.

This instrument, like the epicycloidal cutter, also receives the small drilling instrument (Fig. 184), and when this is employed, the movement of the roller round the rosette is controlled by the winch-handle on the tangent-screw of the worm-wheel. The miniature eccentric cutter (Fig. 185) is also applicable, and renders some very beautiful work, as the patterns emanating from its introduction may be carried out entirely through the form of the rosette employed, which adds so much to the effect of this style of decoration.

The manipulation of the rose cutter is by no means a difficult process, as will be seen by the following examples. Fig. 187 is the result of employing the rosette, B. The roller is first moved by the stop-screw, so that a circle only is described by its revolution, and the slide-rest adjusted laterally till the axis of the instrument is perfectly true to that of the work on which the pattern is to be cut; the stop-screw is then withdrawn, in order that the roller may take effect on the undulations of the rosette; the tool is then set to a radius of $\frac{11}{10}$, that is, eleven turns of the main screw of the right-angle slide, by which the tool is carried towards the micrometer of the slide; the penetration is then adjusted by the stop-screw of the top slide, to cut a fine line, the tool being a double angle of 45° ; the instrument is then

Fig. 187

set in motion by the pulley on the tangent-screw at the rear end, a slow speed being in most cases necessary. The result of this rosette, is as seen throughout the different patterns cut on Fig. 187,

Fig. 188.

the simple waved line nearest the margin being produced by the adjustment referred to.

The eccentricity of the tool is reduced by one turn, and the same form again traced. The result of the two lines seen in the second pattern is for the purpose of explaining the use of the worm-wheel, D, attached to the disc on which the rosette is fixed. Having cut the first line, the rosette is moved by the tangent-screw, so that the second line crosses the centre of the first, and this may be divided into many parts for various patterns. This will be referred to again ; at present, the two lines are quite a primary example of the manner in which it is used.

By reducing the radius of the tool one turn more, the same figure is again cut, while by a further reduction of one half turn, or $\frac{5}{100}$ in., for each consecutive cut, the six following are equidistantly placed, gradually decreasing in diameter and width of wave. From this point, a different movement is added to the adjustments, by which the pattern is carried out in the same way, as for similar results in plain circles, cut by the eccentric cutter. The tool is again reduced in radius by one half turn, and moved laterally by the main screw of the slide-rest a corresponding distance—namely, one half turn ; by repeating these movements nine times, a shell composed of waved lines is the result. It will be seen, that as each cut nears the centre, the figure becomes more pointed. This is not from any additional movement, but simply from the gradual diminution in the diameter.

Fig. 188 is produced by employing what may be termed the opposite rosette to that used for the previous example, inasmuch as the curves cut are all convex instead of concave, the instrument is adjusted as before to agree with the periphery of the work, the tool set out to a radius of $\frac{12}{10}$, and the first cut made. This gives simply the result of the combined motions round this particular description of rosette. For the two next cuts the tool is reduced in radius by one turn of the screw, and the same penetration inserted, the rosette is then moved by two turns of the tangent-screw of worm-wheel, D, attached to the disc, and the second cut made. By this it will be seen that the pattern crosses in the same way as the second series in Fig. 187.

The inner pattern illustrates an additional movement, by which
the pattern is twisted.   To produce this, the following adjustments

Fig. 189.

are necessary: For the first cut the radius of the tool is again
reduced by one turn, for the second the radius is further reduced
by one half turn of the screw, and one and a half turns of
the tangent-screw of the worm-wheel, D, these movements being

Fig. 190.

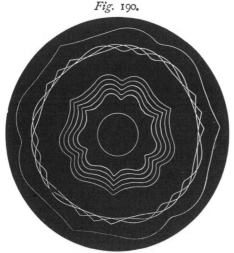

precisely the same for each succeeding cut.   The patterns may be
reversed by moving the tangent-screw in the opposite direction.

T

Fig. 189. This example is produced by employing the same rosette; as the line nearest the margin will show. The succeeding out, however, illustrates the use of the stop-screw. Having reduced the radius of the tool by one turn of the main screw, the stop-screw is brought to bear lightly upon the slide, and then moved forward one turn. The effect of this is to prevent the roller reaching the lowest part of the undulation in the rosette, by which the true form of the latter is destroyed, and a portion of the figure becomes a part of a concentric circle only, the curves resulting from that part of the rosette which touches the roller in its rotation. This process is repeated throughout the rest of the pattern, and it will be seen that, as the centre is approached the figure gradually decreases in proportion.

Fig. 190 portrays the form of the rosette, c; the adjustment of the instrument as to centre is the same, the marginal line being simply the result of the figure; the second series is produced by the reduction of the radius of the tool for the first cut; for the second the worm-wheel, D, is moved by two turns of the tangent-screw, while for the third the same amount is necessary; by this the pattern is crossed. The inner pattern is produced from the same rosette, each consecutive cut being made one half turn of the screw nearer the centre; the concentric circle is cut perfectly true to the figure by reducing the radius to the diameter required, and by the stop-screw being moved forward so that the roller will not touch the rosette.

Fig. 191 illustrates the application of the rosette, D, the movements of the tool being similar to those for the preceding figures.

Fig. 192. By this example we arrive at the means of placing the various figures to be obtained by the rose cutter, eccentric to the axis of the work. These may be varied to a very large extent, and by employing either of the ornamental chucks, may be placed in almost any position that can be desired as to distance from the axis of the work; the pulley is then held stationary at the four quadrants of the circle. The four patterns are all produced from different rosettes, the radius of the tool being adjusted to the diameter required, and the instrument moved by the slide-rest screw, so that each pattern may be contained within the space.

Fig. 191.

The author wishes it to be clearly understood that the foregoing examples are not illustrated as figures of beauty, but simply to show clearly the manner in which the instrument is

Fig. 192.

manipulated, and for such purposes the least complicated are most appreciable.

CHAPTER XLIII.

Circular Miniature Frame.

Plate 17 illustrates a specimen of work which necessitates the use of various instruments, and may be considered one, the details of which will be both instructive and useful in its reproduction, should it be deemed worthy of such. It will be seen that it is made from an exceptionally large piece of ivory, which in the rough was 6¾ in. in diameter, and although it was the author's original intention to cut the thirty-two projecting beads out of the solid material, it was found that it would so reduce the finished size of the inner parts, that the idea was abandoned, and it was then decided to make them separately, and attach them, as seen.

The ivory was cut from a very fine tusk, and one great feature in it was, that it represented as near a true circle as possible, requiring so little reduction to bring it to absolute truth, that its original diameter was almost maintained; when cut from the tusk it was ⅝ in. thick, one side was then roughly surfaced and attached to a large wood chuck by strong glue; the rebate at the back was then turned out to receive the internal fittings, the face carefully finished, and by this and the rebate it was re-chucked in the same way.

The front must now be turned to the shape required, which consists of two hollows, with a projection in the front, which is afterwards cut with a moulding drill; having turned the form to the necessary outline, it should be highly polished.

The slide-rest is then set parallel with the lathe-bed, and the universal or vertical cutter placed in the tool-box (the former was employed for the example under notice, having greater power,

Plate 17.

and as a deal of material had to be removed, it was more easily done with it).

The cutter was adjusted to a radius of $\frac{6}{10}$ of an inch, and penetrated so that the terminal points of the concave curves were just brought up sharp, without reducing the diameter of the material, the 96 division was then arrested at every third hole; the tool must be carefully sharpened, and with a slow lateral traverse, it is carried across the width of the part to be cut; by exercising care the surface may be brought to a brilliant polish, which adds considerably to the beauty of the work. Thirty-two cuts having been finished, the universal cutter is replaced by the drill-spindle, and a small hole about $\frac{1}{20}$ in diameter then drilled in the centre of each segment, for the purpose of holding the pearls securely.

The slide-rest must now be set to an angle, and a round-nosed drill (Fig. 127), $\frac{16}{100}$ in. wide, is then inserted to about two-thirds of the curve contained in its form ; for this the 120 circle of division was used, arrested at every hole ; the rest is then moved to an increased angle, and a second row of incisions of a like character made, but nearer to the front of the curve.

A moulding-drill is then used to cut seriatim, on both sides of the projecting rim on the front of the frame, for which purpose the slide-rest is fixed at right angles to the lathe-bed (the figure of the drill is a plain ogee with a fillet and astragal end); the 120 circle again employed, but arrested at every alternate hole, by which sixty consecutive cuts only are made. The depth of the cut should be decided by the stop-screw of the top slide, and, from preference, the drill should be moved into cut by the lateral traverse of the slide ; the termination of each cut is decided by the fluting-stop.

Having cut the mouldings on the outer edge, the drill is moved to the opposite side to cut the inner circle, the stop on that side forming the means of arresting its progress. The division must be moved one hole, and a small drill inserted in the centre of the two mouldings at every second hole; this, it will be seen, is for the purpose of attaching the second circle of smaller pearls, which are also made separately, and fixed afterwards; a large round-nosed drill is then used to seriate the inner concave curve; it is adjusted by the slide-rest to suit the form, and penetrated at every hole of the division, with the result seen in the illustration.

To turn the beads will form the next proceeding, and the thirty-two large ones should be first made. The best way to set about a job of this kind, which, to say the least of it, becomes monotonous before the last one is finished, is to select the ivory from the smallest and most suitable at hand, it should then be cut up and rounded down with a file or rasp, and then held in the die chuck, the most suitable for the purpose being that illustrated by Fig. 1, and described in Chapter I. The balls should be finished with a suitable sized bead-tool, and the smaller stem which fits into the hole completed afterwards; after this is done it may be cut off. The ball should be highly polished before the pin is too much reduced in size, or the pressure required will detach it before it is finished.

The smaller pearls must now claim attention, and as there are sixty of them, it is somewhat of an undertaking, and will require a due exercise of patience; great care should be taken to make them all the same size; they are then fixed with diamond cement. Like those on the outer diameter, these might have been cut from the solid, but economy in material of such dimensions is not to be ignored, even at the expense of a little extra labour.

We now come to the inner portion of the frame. This again requires a piece of ivory of large diameter, namely, 5 in. by about $\frac{3}{16}$ in. thick, and as the width of the face when finished is 1 in., sufficient material must be left. It was first surfaced on one side, being held for this purpose by its periphery, in a wood chuck, and afterwards held by the face to another of the same description, mounted upon the eccentric chuck, and as a deal of work has to be executed upon it, it must be fixed by glue. It will require to be very carefully chucked, in order that the whole face of the ivory may be kept in close contact with the surface of the wood, and the most effective way of doing this is to remove the chuck from the nose of the mandrel and place it on a flat surface, and after the two surfaces are glued, place a heavy weight on the ivory, until the glue is quite dry. If the lathe is not likely to be required for immediate use, the ivory may be forced against the chuck by the popit-head cylinder and left to dry. In the latter case a flat surface must be placed in front of the popit cylinder.

When properly treated in this way, a vast quantity of work may be safely executed without risk of damage. The face is first carefully turned and polished, the slide of the eccentric chuck is then moved out to 1 in. by ten turns of the main screw, the drilling instrument is placed in the slide-rest, having in it a drill about $\frac{10}{100}$ in. wide made to cut on the sides as well as the front. The drill is moved laterally by the screw of the slide-rest to the necessary radius; it is then inserted to a moderate depth, and the work slowly rotated by the worm-wheel of the segment apparatus. By this means the first segment is removed, and the dividing-wheel being turned to 24, 48, and 72 respectively, and the cuts repeated, the figure is completed, as seen in the illustration.

Having cut out the first four segments, a fixed bead tool is placed in the tool-box, and the continuous plain bead cut. This, it will be seen, cuts out at each point, the crossing of the cuts producing a small square. The drilling instrument is again employed, and has in it a broad square-end drill of $\frac{27}{100}$ in diameter. It must be moved by the slide-rest screw to the required distance and penetrated to the depth of the bead previously cut. To arrest the drill at the necessary distance, by which it is prevented from approaching too close to the previous bead, and so damaging it, the segment apparatus must be employed and the stop adjusted. Considerable care is required in the penetration, so that each cut is made exactly the same depth, otherwise an unsightly mark will be left where the drill meets at each point. The four segments having been thus cut, the drill is replaced by one of $\frac{15}{100}$ in., which is adjusted to cut right through the ivory, in the centre of the flat cut by the larger one. The drill is again exchanged for one of $\frac{20}{100}$ in., which is simply inserted at the terminal point of each segment.

The dividing wheel is now moved to 12, which will bring the centre of the segment opposite the centre of the tool; at this point it will be seen the curve is separated ; to do this, the eccentric cutter was used, with a narrow parting-tool set to a radius of $\frac{5}{20}$ of an inch, and then very carefully passed through into the wood. Having cut all four in the same way, a side tool is fixed in the tool-box, and moved towards the margin where, by careful semi-rotation of the mandrel, a second curve is cut; beyond this, close to the edge where it fits the frame, a circle of penetrations is made by a round-nosed fluting drill $\frac{8}{100}$ in. wide.

The eccentric cutter is then employed to cut the final pattern at the centre of the plain part left from the previous operations ; these are simply barleycorn figures, and may be cut to suit the taste, the coarser patterns being the most effective.

We now come to the centre which holds the medallion, the outer form being cut with the vertical cutter, a round-nosed tool being employed, the drilling instrument again used to produce a circle of cuts similar to those on the margin of the outer frame; the drill is exchanged for a bead-drill of corresponding size, and a row of beads cut, between each of which the round-nosed drill is again inserted, the centre being pierced with a drill $\frac{18}{100}$ in. wide at the centre of the marginal line ; the ivory for this was first turned out to receive the medallion, and chucked by that part.

The medallion of Her Gracious Majesty the Queen was cut from the gold medal awarded to the author at the Inventions Exhibition, in 1885.   This, however, requires a special machine, and although an interesting study, the fact of its inability to produce anything but a true copy, deters many amateurs from studying it; it may at the same time be employed with excellent results, and very beautiful and intricate medals reproduced.

The ring at the top and the eye through which it passes will not require detailing, as it will be clearly seen from the photo how they are produced.

CHAPTER LXIV.

ELECTROTYPING.

THE beauty of many surface patterns, especially those produced by double counting, is very much enhanced, and they are capable of being developed in a somewhat novel direction, by the electrotype process, that is by transferring them from intaglio to relievo. In many cases effects differing from any obtained direct in the lathe can be produced.

Using the eccentric cutter, the result does not differ much from ordinary surface work, nor is it particularly pleasing, but the greater depth of cut obtainable by the horizontal or vertical cutter, and the variation in depth caused by the sweep of the tool, makes the pattern stand out boldly from the face of the work, and it affords even a greater play of light than that which is obtained by mere scratching of the surface. Again, by using the half-round or other drill, beads are formed equal in effect to those produced in the ordinary way, with this peculiarity, that they may be made to form part of a device, under or over which they may appear to stand. There is also this advantage, that a pattern—the result, it may be, of much patient work in accurate setting of the tool to height of centre, and of chuck for horizontality, both of which are so essential in double counting, to say nothing of the labour of cutting—may, if it is so desired, be multiplied almost indefinitely ; and lastly, with very little additional trouble, great additional beauty and effect may be obtained by depositing silver on the pattern, and copper on the ground, making the pattern show up bright on a bronze ground, or *vice versa*.

The simplest way of producing these electrotypes is to employ type metal which requires no conducting material to be applied to it, as would be the case with wood, and gives sharper impressions for this reason : discs of this are cast, surfaced, and either polished or grailled. The tool used in this, and the subsequent cutting of the pattern must have a cutting edge nearly approaching that required for soft wood, and to produce in the metal a perfectly clean edge, where one cut crosses or merges into another, it must be made very keen and burnished. The mould then leaves the lathe with a surface like polished silver.

The ordinary electrotyping process is that which is employed, but it may be mentioned that if the mould is incautiously handled, finger-marks will be reproduced in the most perfect, or rather provoking, manner on the surface of the copper, and it is the best plan not even to touch the surface of the mould with an oiled camel's-hair brush, as recommended with ordinary moulds, to prevent adhesion of the deposited metal, but carefully to pour on and off a little benzine, in which the minutest quantity of wax has been dissolved.

To produce a pattern in one metal on a ground in another, the disc when ready for the pattern is covered with a thin non-conducting material, such as the resist in parcel-gilding, and in the fresh cut lines either silver or copper is deposited, the resist is then cleared off, and the whole mould receives a deposit. The Rev. A. B. Cotton, to whom the author is indebted for these remarks, has made this particular branch of turning a careful study, and is possessed of a collection of some of the most beautiful specimens of its production, which are most decorative when mounted in ivory or black wood.